The Battle of Pharsalus (48 BC)

The Battle of Pharsalus (48 BC)

Caesar, Pompey and their Final Clash in the Third Roman Civil War

Gareth C. Sampson

Pen & Sword
MILITARY

First published in Great Britain in 2023 by
Pen & Sword Military
An imprint of Pen & Sword Books Limited
Yorkshire – Philadelphia

Copyright © Gareth C. Sampson 2023

ISBN 978 1 52679 362 1

The right of Gareth C. Sampson to be identified as
Author of this Work has been asserted by him in accordance
with the Copyright, Designs and Patents Act 1988.

A CIP catalogue record for this book is
available from the British Library

All rights reserved. No part of this book may be reproduced or
transmitted in any form or by any means, electronic or mechanical
including photocopying, recording or by any information storage and
retrieval system, without permission from the Publisher in writing.

Typeset by Mac Style
Printed in the UK by CPI Group (UK) Ltd, Croydon, CR0 4YY.

Pen & Sword Books Limited incorporates the imprints of After
the Battle, Atlas, Archaeology, Aviation, Discovery, Family History,
Fiction, History, Maritime, Military, Military Classics, Politics,
Select, Transport, True Crime, Air World, Frontline Publishing, Leo
Cooper, Remember When, Seaforth Publishing, The Praetorian Press,
Wharncliffe Local History, Wharncliffe Transport, Wharncliffe True
Crime and White Owl.

For a complete list of Pen & Sword titles please contact

PEN & SWORD BOOKS LIMITED
47 Church Street, Barnsley, South Yorkshire, S70 2AS, England
E-mail: enquiries@pen-and-sword.co.uk
Website: www.pen-and-sword.co.uk
or
PEN AND SWORD BOOKS
1950 Lawrence Rd, Havertown, PA 19083, USA
E-mail: Uspen-and-sword@casematepublishers.com
Website: www.penandswordbooks.com

Dedication

In loving memory of Geoff Sampson (1947–2019)

Contents

Acknowledgements   viii
List of Illustrations   ix
Maps & Diagrams   x
Introduction: The Battle of Pharsalus: Winners, Losers and the Judgment of History   xvi
Timeline: Pre-Third Civil War (70–49 BC)   xix
Notes on Roman Names   xxiii

Section I: The Early Campaigns of the Third Civil War (49–48 BC)   1

Chapter 1   The Third Civil War & The Western Republic (49 BC)   3

Chapter 2   Pompeius Victorious – The Battle of Dyrrhachium (48 BC)   25

Section II: The Pharsalan Campaign (48 BC)   51

Chapter 3   From Dyrrhachium to Pharsalus   53

Chapter 4   The Battle of Pharsalus (Palaepharsalus) (48 BC)   74

Section III: Aftermath & Consequences (48 BC)   101

Chapter 5   The Impact of Pharsalus on the other Campaigns   103

Chapter 6   Responding to Victory, Recovering from Defeat   111

Chapter 7   The Civil War Without its Architect   139

Appendix I: Who's Who in the Third Roman Civil War (48 BC)   164
Appendix II: How Many Civil Wars?   177
Notes   184
Bibliography   192
Index   198

Acknowledgements

As always, the first and greatest acknowledgement must go to my wonderful wife, Alex, without whose support and understanding none of this would be possible. Next must come Thomas and Caitlin, who are a constant source of joy and anxiety.

Special thanks go to my parents, who always encouraged a love of books and learning (even if they did regret the house being filled with books). My father, Geoff, is no longer with us, and his loss is still felt by us all.

There are a number of individuals who, through the years, have inspired in me the love of Roman history and mentored me along the way: Michael Gracey at William Hulme, David Shotter at Lancaster and Tim Cornell at Manchester. My heartfelt thanks go to them all.

A shout goes out to the remaining members of the Manchester diaspora: Gary, Ian, Jason and Sam. Those were good days; we will not see their like again.

As always, my thanks go to my editor, Phil Sidnell, for his patience and understanding.

It must also be said that as an independent academic, the job of researching these works is being made easier by the internet, so alumnus access to JSTOR (Manchester and Lancaster) and Academia.edu must get a round of thanks too.

List of Illustrations

1. Possible bust of C. Marius.
2. Bust of L. Cornelius Sulla.
3. Bust of Cn. Pompeius Magnus.
4. Possible bust of M. Licinius Crassus.
5. Bust of C. Iulius Caesar.
6. Bust of M. Tullius Cicero.
7. Bust of M. Antonius.
8. Bust of M. Porcius Cato.
9. Bust of Sex. Pompeius.
10. Coin of Q. Caecilius Metellus Scipio.
11. Bust of Juba I of Numidia.
12. Coin of Bocchus II of the Mauri.
13. Coin of Deiotus of Galatia.
14. Coin of Pharnaces II of Pontus.
15. Plain of Pharsalus.
16. River Enipeus. (*Robin Rönnlund via Wiki Commons*)

Maps & Diagrams

Map 1: The Mediterranean World in early 48 BC
Map 2: The Epirote/Illyrian Campaigns (48 BC)
Map 3: The Greek & Macedonian Campaigns (48 BC)
Map 4: The Dyrrhachium Campaign (48 BC)
Map 5: The Mediterranean World in late 48 BC

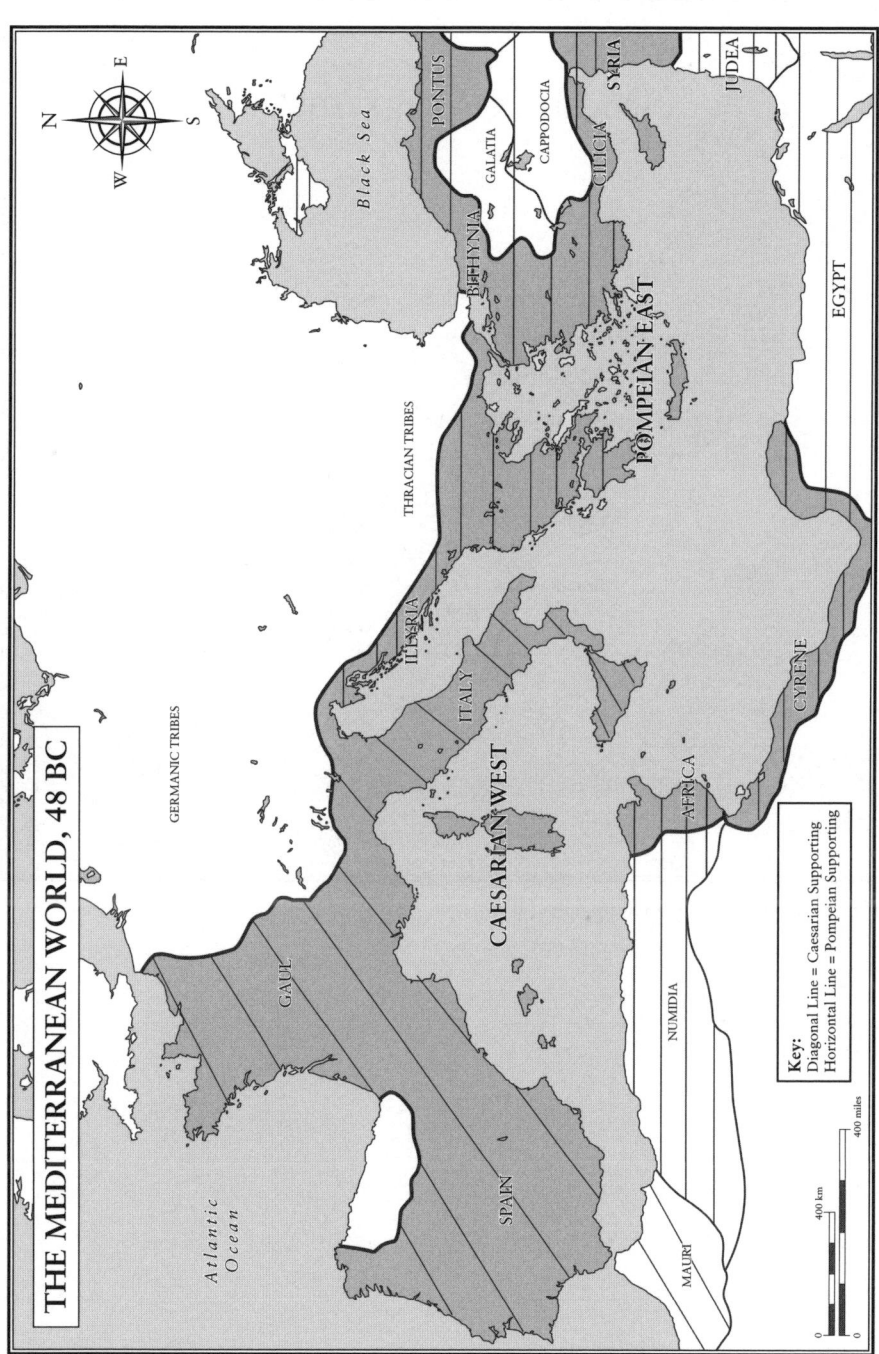

Map 1: The Mediterranean World in early 48 BC

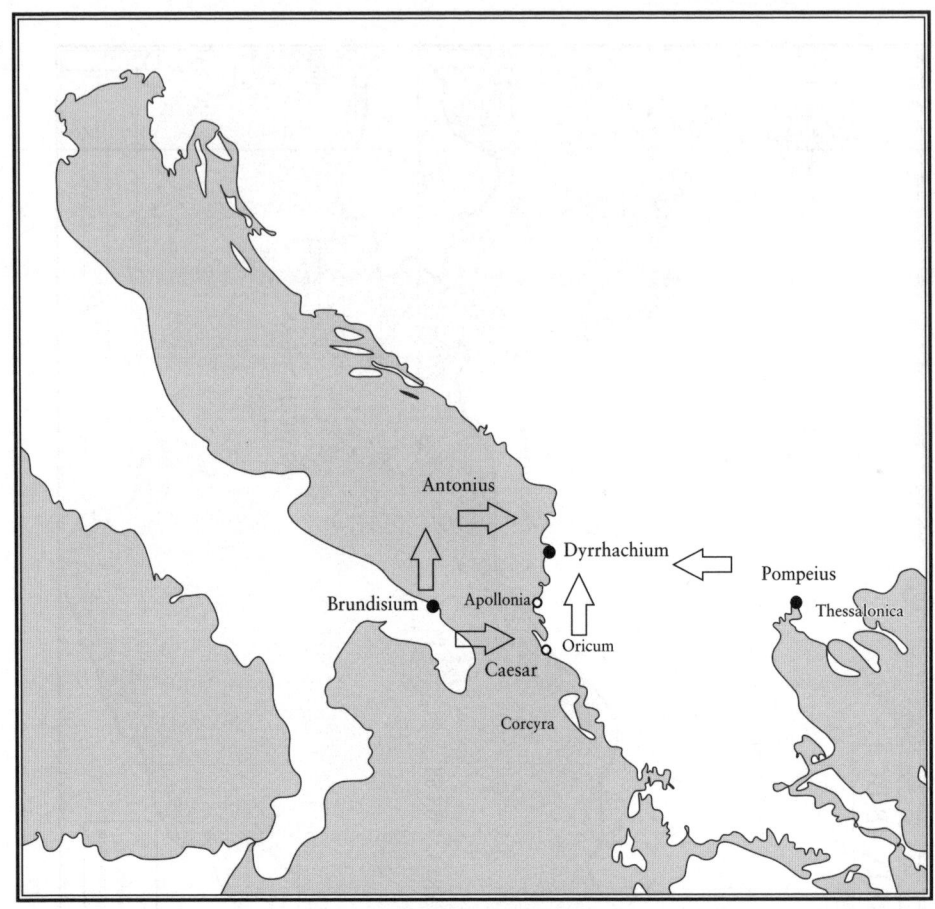

Map 2: The Epirote/Illyrian Campaigns (48 BC).

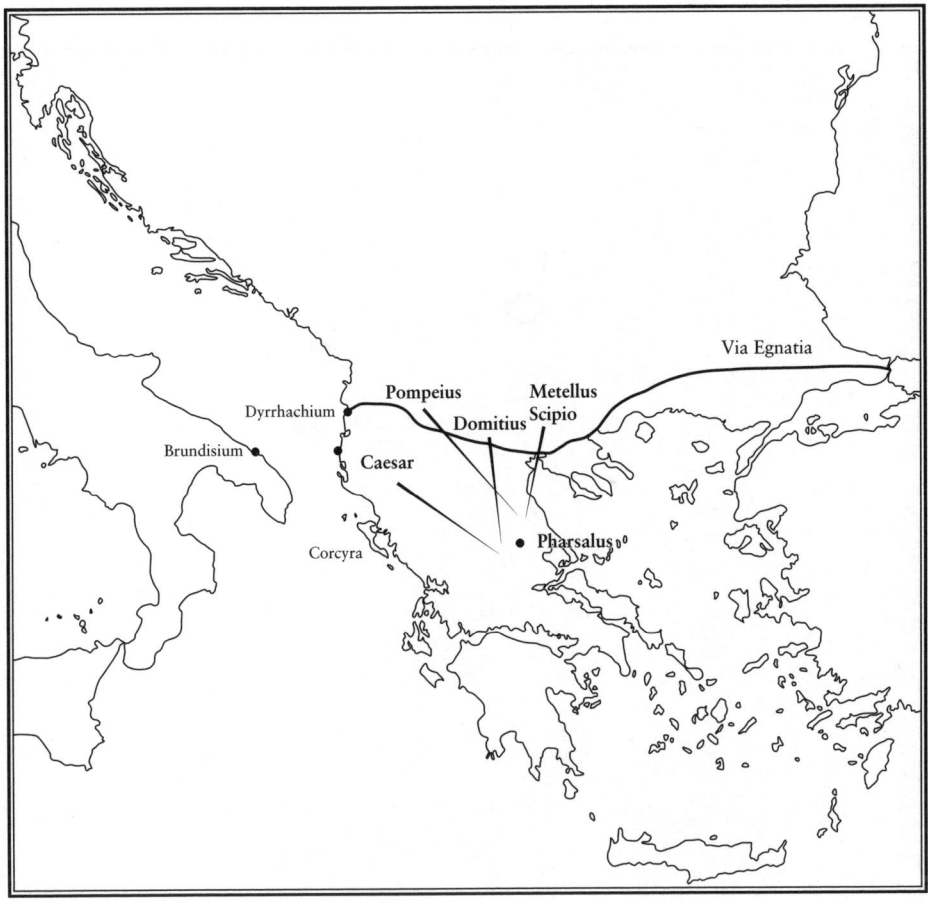

Map 3: The Greek & Macedonian Campaigns (48 BC).

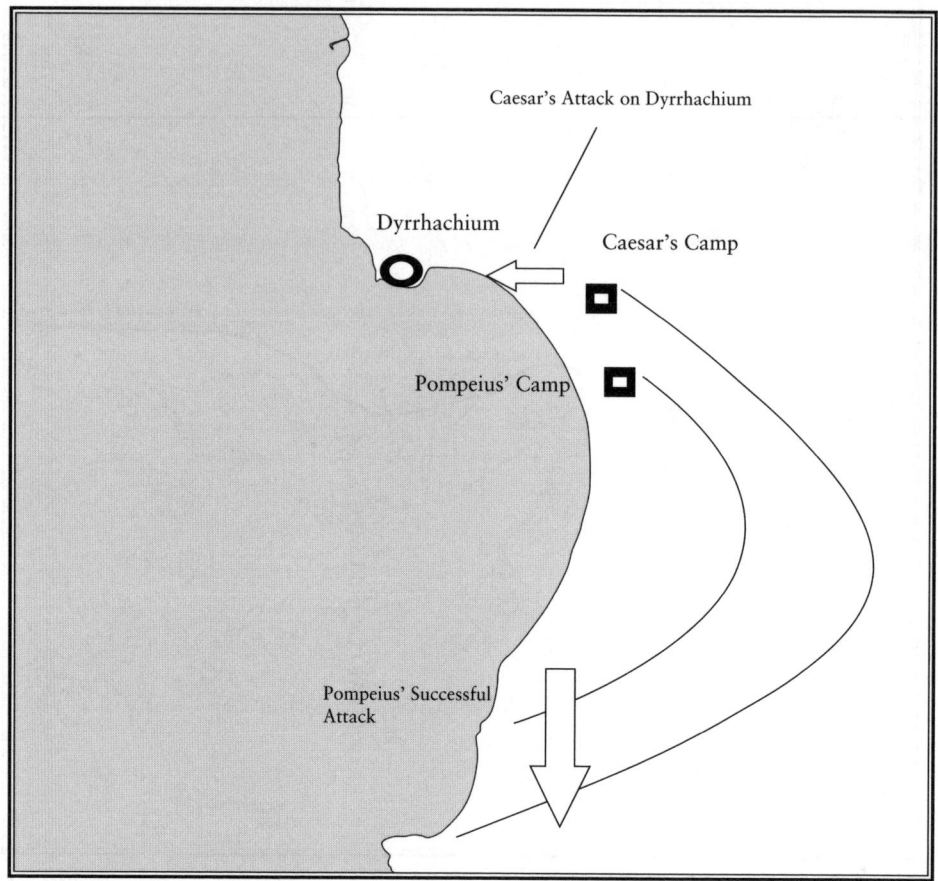

Map 4: The Dyrrhachium Campaign (48 BC).

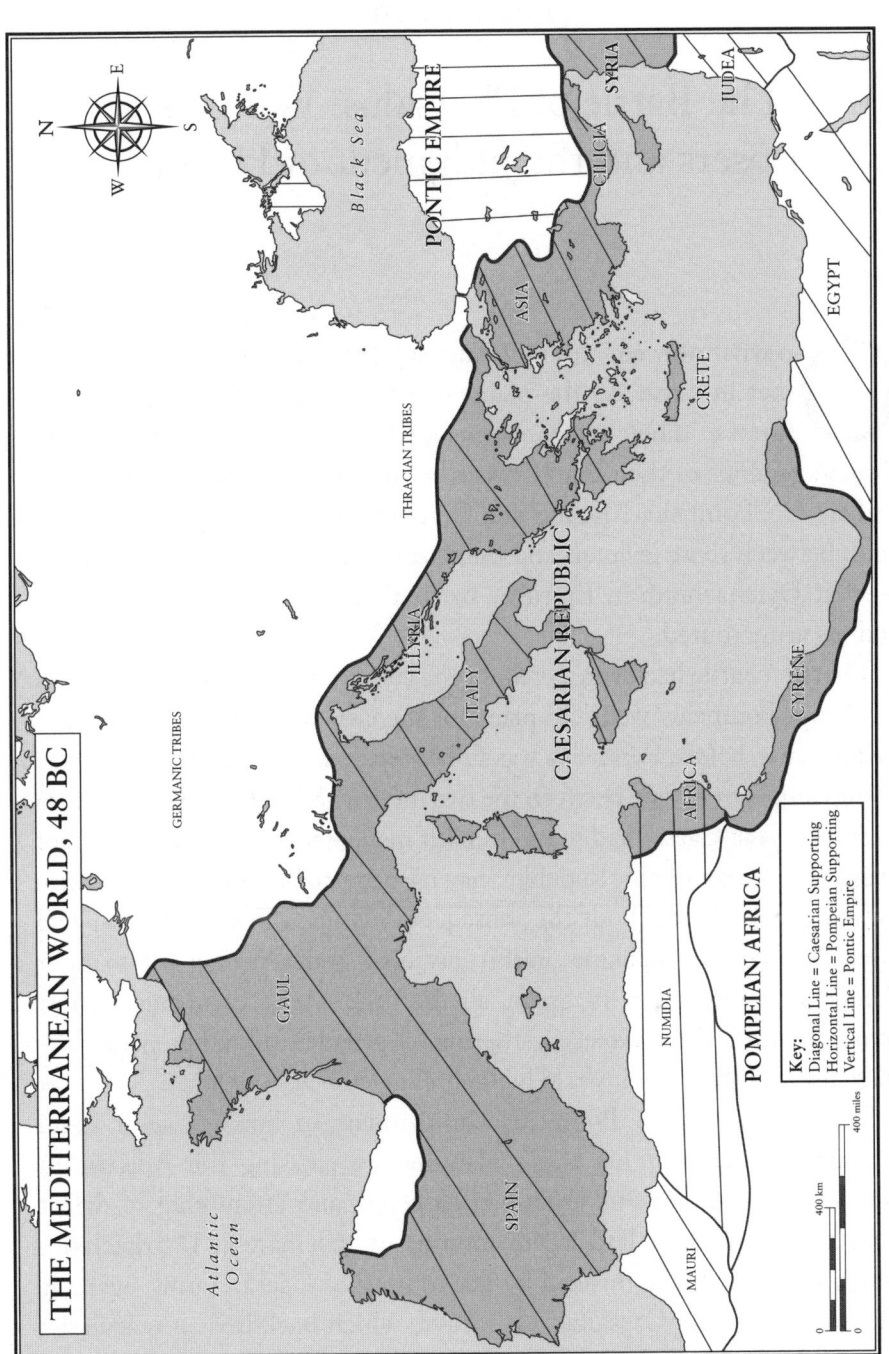

Map 5: The Mediterranean World in late 48 BC.

Introduction

The Battle of Pharsalus: Winners, Losers and the Judgment of History

On what now equates to 9 August 48 BC, two great Roman armies met in battle on the plains of Pharsalus in Thessaly, northern Greece. They were commanded by the two greatest living Roman generals of their day (Crassus having been killed some five years earlier), Cn. Pompeius Magnus and C. Iulius Caesar. This was the second clash between these generals and their armies in a month, the first having been at Dyrrhachium in Epirus, a battle that had seen Caesar defeated and his army routed.

That first battle had been a prelude, the culmination of Caesar's attempts to disrupt Pompeius' well-laid plans for the civil war between the two by striking first, before Pompeius was fully prepared. This had been the tone of the campaign to date between the two men, with their civil war now into its second year. Caesar had found himself manoeuvred into the position of being the enemy of the Republic, having been forced by Pompeius into invading Italy. Throughout the subsequent eighteen months, Caesar had been the manic campaigner, rashly invading Italy, rushing off to fight Pompeius' commanders in Spain, all the time whilst Pompeius sat just across the Adriatic, in Greece, gathering his grand army and preparing the stage for what he hoped would be their climactic clash of arms.

Having disposed of Pompeius' commanders in Spain, Caesar again attempted to disrupt his rival's planning by crossing the Adriatic in January, before Pompeius' army had gathered, and attempting to defeat him. This bold move had led to months of stalemate at Dyrrhachium which was only finally broken by the routing of Caesar's army, again as the result of a bold Caesarian manoeuvre which backfired spectacularly; an analogy for Caesar's whole campaign of 48 BC to date.

Having regrouped from the disaster at Dyrrhachium, Caesar regrouped and again doubled down, heading further into Pompeian-held Greece in a final push to prevent Pompeius' two armies from meeting. Having failed to accomplish that, Caesar rolled the dice once more and faced the might of Pompeius' army, which nearly outnumbered his own by two to one, on the plains of Pharsalus.

At this point, on the eve of battle, the outcome seemed a certainty: the destruction of Caesar's army and the death of the renegade Roman general, which would prove to be the final stepping stone for the ascent of Pompeius Magnus to become the undisputed Princeps of the Republic, thereby relegating Caesar to a footnote in the Republic's history.

Within a few hours of battle at Pharsalus, however, history was turned on its head and Caesar emerged victorious, thanks to one innovative tactic. It can truly be said that the impact of the battle far outweighed the immediate military consequences. Pompeian casualties were between 6,000 and 15,000, but Pompeius and virtually all his key commanders survived and escaped.

Yet the battle changed the tide of the civil war, instantly transforming Caesar from rebel and enemy of the state to the master (albeit temporarily) of the Republic and its empire. Furthermore, the myth of Pompeius' invincibility, carefully cultivated over nearly forty years of warfare (however far from reality it was), was shattered in those few hours at Pharsalus. It was the destruction of this myth that ultimately led to Pompeius' demise soon afterwards, an act that rivalled Caesar's victory on the battlefield.

Yet for all that, we must acknowledge that Pharsalus was a turning point, not an end point. Throughout the centuries of modern scholarship on Rome, historians have been searching for the elusive date that the Republic ended, and for a while many settled on Pharsalus. Yet we must be clear that whilst Caesar's victory at Pharsalus changed the dynamic of this Third Roman Civil War, it did not end it. If anything, the nature of Caesar's victory, considered by many to be a fluke, and the anger over Pompeius' subsequent treacherous murder merely added fuel to the desire of his opponents to fight on.

Furthermore, just as Pompeius failed to build on the victory at Dyrrhachium to finish the Caesarian faction as a military force, so Caesar equally failed to complete his victory at Pharsalus by finishing off his opponents. Indeed, he actually contributed to their recovery by his subsequent decisions, which saw him end the year entangled in a Ptolemaic civil war in Egypt.

In point of fact, this first stage of the Third Civil War was to continue for another three years and another two great battles (Thapsus in 46 BC and Munda in 45 BC). Although Caesar emerged victorious time and again on the battlefield, the anger that his victories engendered amongst the Senatorial oligarchy led to his own murder, less than year after his final victory (on the now-infamous Ides of March 44 BC).

The civil war that Caesar and Pompeius started outlasted both men by nearly two decades, leaving it for their sons and lieutenants to fight out, and only ending in 27 BC when Caesar's adopted son (having murdered Caesar's natural son) created a new version of the Republic and restored peace and stability to the Roman world.

The subsequent work is split into four sections, starting with an analysis of the reasons for the collapse into Civil War, an examination of the first eighteen months of the war and the build-up to the battle, which saw Caesar struggling to overturn Pompeius' masterplan for the conflict. It will then analyse the Caesarian disaster at Dyrrhachium and the buildup to Pharsalus, which saw Caesar as the underdog, outnumbered and on the run, facing seemingly inevitable defeat.

The third section will look at the battle itself, in particular how Caesar's innovative tactic turned defeat into victory, asking whether it was a fluke, good generalship, Pompeian incompetence or a mixture of all three. The final section will examine the aftermath of the battle, which saw Caesar fail to build on his victory and allow his opponent to regroup and continue the war. By the conclusion, this work will have placed the Battle of Pharsalus in its proper context in the history of the Republic and the Third Roman Civil War.

Timeline: Pre-Third Civil War (70–49 BC)

91–70 **First Roman Civil War.**
72   Pompeius victorious in Spain against Perperna.
71   Crassus victorious in Italy against Spartacus.
         Formation of the Duumvirate between Pompeius and Crassus.
70   Consulship of Pompeius and Crassus – constitutional reforms enacted.
68   Pompeius is appointed to command the war against the Mediterranean pirates.
67   Pompeius is appointed to command the Eastern War against Armenia and Pontus.
65   Crassus as censor tries to annex Egypt.
64   Pompeius annexes the remnants of the Seleucid Empire.
63–62 **Second Civil War.**
62   Pompeius returns to Italy.
60   Reformation of the Duumvirate between Pompeius and Crassus.
59   Consulship of Caesar – passes Duumvirates' legislation.
         Marriage of Pompeius to Caesar's daughter.
58   Tribunate of Clodius – street violence in Rome.
         Caesar launches the Romano-Gallic War.
57   Tribunate of Milo – street violence escalates.
56   Pompeius is appointed to take charge of Rome's grain supply.
         Conference at Luca – formation of the Triumvirate.
55   Consulships of Pompeius and Crassus.
54   Crassus takes command in the First Romano-Parthian War.
53   Battle of Carrhae – Crassus defeated by the Parthian Surenas; killed in the retreat.
         Violence in Rome prevents Curule elections.
52   Murder of Clodius; burning of the Senate House.
         Pompeius appointed sole consul, conducts judicial purge.

xx   The Battle of Pharsalus (48 BC)

50   Breakdown of the relationship between Pompeius and Caesar.
49   The Senate pass the *senatus consultum ultimum* against Caesar. Caesar commits treason by invading Italy across the River Rubicon.

The Early Years of the Third Roman Civil War (49 BC)

Italian Campaign:
Caesar invades Italy.
Battle of Corfinium.
Pompeius withdraws to Brundisium.
Battle of Brundisium.
Pompeius withdraws across the Adriatic to Dyrrhachium.
Caesar seizes Rome.

Gallic Campaign:
Caesarian forces lay siege of Massilia.
Pompeian-Massilian fleet defeated twice off Massilia.
Massilia surrenders to Caesar after the fall of Spain.

Spanish Campaign:
Caesarian forces cross Pyrenees and invade Pompeian Spain.
Battles of Ilerda – Caesar trapped in a deteriorating position.
Caesar convinces more Spanish tribes to back him.
Pompeian forces decide to retreat and are routed by Caesar.
Caesar wins over the Pompeian army and allies in southern Spain.

Western Mediterranean Campaigns:
Pompeian forces evacuate Sardinia after a local revolt; Caesarian forces occupy island.
Caesarian forces invade Sicily; Cato withdraws without a fight.
Caesarian forces invade Roman Africa.
Siege of Pompeian-held Utica.
Caesarian victory at the Battle of Utica.
Caesarian army destroyed at the Battle of Bagradas River by Numidian forces.
Africa held by the Pompeians.

Adriatic & Illyrian Campaign:
Pompeian fleet defeat Caesarian fleet and ensure control of the Adriatic.
Caesarian army starved into surrender; Illyria conquered by Pompeians.

The Early Years of the Third Roman Civil War (48 BC)
Epirote/Illyrian Campaign:
Caesar crosses the Adriatic and lands in Epirus; Pompeius moves to intercept.
Pompeian fleet cuts Caesar off; skirmishes between Pompeius and Caesar.
Pompeian attack on Brundisium.
Political disorder in Italy.
Antonius crosses the Adriatic with Caesarian reinforcements.
Caesar marches on the city of Dyrrhachium; Pompeius follows.
Caesar lays siege to Pompeius' army in the Bay of Dyrrhachium.
Failed Caesarian attack on the city of Dyrrhachium.
Failed Pompeian attack on Caesar's siege lines.
Pompeius breaks through Caesar's sieges lines to the south of the bay.
Caesar launches a counterattack on the Pompeian bridgehead.
Pompeius launches a counterattack on Caesar.
Caesarian army is routed, with thousands of casualties.
Caesar regroups his army, breaks off the siege and marches inland to Macedonia, to join up with his other forces and face Metellus Scipio.
Pompeius harasses Caesar's army south and then break off and marches inland.

Greek/Macedonian/Thessalian Campaigns:
Metellus Scipio crosses into Thessaly from Asia Minor.
Caesarian forces spread into Greece, Thessaly and Macedonia.
Metellus Scipio defeats Caesarian forces in Thessaly, but is slowed down.
Caesarian forces defeated in Macedonia by Faustus Sulla.
Caesarian forces secure Aetolia and Acarnania.
Pompeian forces fall back to the Isthmus of Corinth.
Two Pompeian and two Caesarian armies converge on each other.
Domitius' army avoids marching into Pompeian trap and turns southward.
The two Caesarian armies unite.
Metellus Scipio's army marches to Larissa and is joined by Pompeius.

xxii The Battle of Pharsalus (48 BC)

The two Pompeian armies unite.

Caesar marches towards Pompeius and offers battle on the plain of Pharsalus.

Battle of Pharsalus – Pompeius is defeated.

Pompeius retreats eastwards by ship, followed by Caesar on land.

The bulk of the Pompeians retreat to Dyrrhachium and Corcyra and then try to hold the Peloponnese before retreating across the Mediterranean to Cyrene.

Cassius and his fleet fail to attack Caesar at the Bosphorus and defect, giving Caesar the ability to chase Pompeius effectively.

Pompeius chooses to land in Ptolemaic Egypt and is murdered on the beach.

Caesar becomes entangled in a Ptolemaic Civil War.

The Pompeians retreat to Roman Africa to regroup.

Pharnaces II invades Roman Asia Minor.

Notes on Roman Names

All Roman names in the following text will be given in their traditional form, including the abbreviated first name. Below is a list of the Roman first names referred to in the text and their abbreviations.

A.	Aulus
Ap.	Appius
C.	Caius
Cn.	Cnaeus
D.	Decimus
F.	Faustus
K.	Kaeso
L.	Lucius
M.	Marcus
Mam.	Mamercus
P.	Publius
Q.	Quintus
Ser.	Servius
Sex.	Sextus
Sp.	Spurius
T.	Titus
Ti.	Tiberius

Section I

The Early Campaigns of the Third Civil War (49–48 BC)

Chapter One

The Third Civil War & The Western Republic (49 BC)

The Architects of the Third Roman Civil War

In what now equates to January 49 BC, the Roman Republic collapsed into civil war; its third in forty years. No civil war is inevitable, requiring both the necessary background factors and the determination of key people involved, and Rome in 49 BC was no different. This Third Civil War started because of the actions of two particular men, who were to dominate the first two years of the war and who were both ultimately consumed by it. The war itself outlived its two originators and, as is often the case, developed a momentum of its own, one which ultimately transformed the Roman Republic over a near two-decade period of fighting. The two men in question were of course Cn. Pompeius 'Magnus' and C. Iulius Caesar.

Though similar in age, the two men represented different generations of Roman oligarch; Pompeius had been a key player in the First Roman Civil War (91–70 BC) and one of the two architects of the resulting New Roman Republic (70–50 BC), whilst Caesar only rose to prominence as an agent of Pompeius and his long-time ally/rival, M. Licinius Crassus. In 56/55 BC, the three men combined their forces to (briefly) seize control of the New Republic and 'save' it from an anarchy that they had greatly helped to foster. Crassus' death in the aftermath of the Battle of Carrhae in 53 BC destroyed this brief alliance and left the two remaining men in an uneasy standoff: Pompeius dominating Rome and Roman politics, with Caesar heading Rome's largest military campaign, the conquest of Gaul.

In many way, the origins of the Third Civil War can be dated back to 53 BC and the disastrous (for the Romans anyway) defeat on the plains of Carrhae in the Parthian Empire. Despite having survived the defeat itself, Crassus, then one of Rome's two leading oligarchs, was murdered in the retreat. Though the effects on Roman foreign policy were severe,

4 The Battle of Pharsalus (48 BC)

the effects on Roman domestic policy were ultimately more disastrous. Crassus had been one of Rome's two leading men for a generation, and his on–off partnership/rivalry with Pompeius had been the defining aspect of the New Republic, which the two men had co-founded in 70 BC.

With Crassus dead, there was only ever going to be one beneficiary: Pompeius, who swiftly moved to marry the widow of Crassus' eldest son (Publius, also killed at Carrhae) and thus sweep up the Crassan faction clients. With no ally/rival to hold him back (and Caesar in Gaul), Pompeius immediately ratcheted up his campaign to destabilize the running of the Republic (via agents) and was duly awarded with the Senate elevating him to a sole Consulship in 52 BC (the Dictatorship in all but name). However, the elevation proved to be temporary, as Pompeius had to deliver on his promises to save the Republic, which he duly accomplished. Permanent elevation to sole power (albeit a subtly utilized power) would require a crisis of a far greater magnitude, of the level that only Rome itself could provide.

Even with the Eastern Republic menaced by an invading Parthian Empire, Pompeius required a far more immediate threat to Rome – and in particular to the ruling oligarchy – if he was to use the crisis to rise to sole power. This was where Caesar entered the picture. It is important to understand that Caesar was not Pompeius' equal in this period, and the Triumvirate was not one of equals; it was a Duumvirate (of Pompeius and Crassus), with Caesar as an effective agent of the two men, albeit by 55 BC one who held the bulk of the Western Republic's military under his command.

Caesar's political career had been determined by his inheriting the mantle of the Marian faction, which had been mostly wiped out during the First Civil War, and his patronage by Pompeius and Crassus, who elevated him to the consulship in 59 BC; his political career to date having been mediocre at best. His reward had been the Duumvirate's sponsorship of his seemingly fanciful idea of conquering Gaul (something no Roman had even attempted before). It was also his punishment, as it exiled him from Roman politics for nearly a decade and got him out of Pompeius' and Crassus' way.

Thus, when Pompeius was pondering the best way to engineer a crisis in 51–50 BC which would frighten the Roman oligarchy to the extent that they would turn to him on a longer-term basis, his thoughts turned to his junior partner, Caesar, who against all odds had actually succeeded in conquering Gaul and now had a military reputation which was beginning to rival his own, albeit remaining a political novice. In Caesar, Pompeius clearly believed he could forge a new and deadly enemy of the Republic – the rogue general, whose armies stood on the brink of Italy. The problem he faced was in politically outmanoeuvring Caesar into playing this role.

Caesar however, despite his military success, had a clear weakness, and one which could be exploited. His success in Gaul was based on two aspects: clearly his own brilliant generalship, but also the political backing of the Duumvirs, who ensured that he had the time needed to complete such a conquest, with two extraordinary commands in the Gallic provinces, each of five years. This ensured that he was not replaced as Gallic commander by his jealous rivals within the oligarchy. Unfortunately for Caesar, he was facing the twin pressures of the conquest not being completed (as seen by the revolt of 52 BC) and his latest five-year command running out. Any extension would need either the goodwill of the rest of the oligarchy (which was unlikely) or the overwhelming support of Rome's remaining Duumvir.

Thus Caesar opened negotiations with Pompeius, for not only an extension to the Gallic command but a supportive welcome when he returned to Rome, with backing for further commands to follow. One clearly gets the impression that Caesar had no wish to retire to the Senate and play the political game, for which he clearly had not the patience, but wanted a fresh consulship and then an Eastern command. Within the Roman oligarchy there was only so much kudos one could claim for a campaign against 'barbarians', and even if he had conquered Gaul and thereby forever ended the Gallic menace, the cachet always lay with a command in the then Near and Middle East, following in the footsteps of Alexander.

It was Pompeius himself who had gained the Roman reputation of being the 'new Alexander' by his actions in Rome's Great Eastern War (74–62 BC), when he had defeated and annexed the Pontic, Armenian and Seleucid Empires and made Rome the pre-eminent power in the region.[1] We can well believe that Caesar, despite being the conqueror of Gaul, had ambitions for an Eastern campaign against Rome's one remaining foe, the Parthians, whose own reputation had been enhanced by their victory at Carrhae.[2]

6 The Battle of Pharsalus (48 BC)

On the one hand, there were clearly grounds for a renewal of the Duumvirate, with Caesar replacing Crassus. Pompeius would remain in Rome and attempt to dominate Roman politics, whilst maintaining his command of the Spanish legions, meanwhile packing Caesar off to the Middle East, but with control of the armies of the Eastern Republic. Thus the two men would dominate the New Republic, controlling the bulk of its armed forces once more (as the Triumvirs had briefly done from 55–53 BC).

Yet such an outcome would have been the last thing that Pompeius wanted. Even whilst planning to elevate his own position via a crisis, he did not judge Caesar as his equal nor would he want him to succeed in the Middle East and eclipse his own accomplishments. Whilst there must have been a temptation to pack Caesar off to the Middle East and trust that his fate matched that of Crassus (himself an excellent general), Caesar's record in Gaul (a long-time graveyard of careers) had shown that he may very well have succeeded and conquered the Parthians, with who knows what subsequent campaigns – perhaps India, following in Alexander's footsteps?

In all fairness, Caser was not admitted into the Triumvirate for his political acumen, but for the fact that in 56 BC he controlled the bulk of the Western Republic's military forces (in Gaul), an imbalance that both Pompeius and Crassus quickly rectified.³ Pompeius gained for himself another extraordinary command (under the Lex Trebonia of 55 BC), not in terms of its size (Africa and the two Spanish provinces), but in the fact he was granted the right to rule through legates. This meant that he had both command of legions but could also remain in Rome (a dangerous combination). Furthermore, with the Gallic War ended and Caesar's armies disbanded, and a rump garrison controlled by someone other than Caesar (likely to have been a Pompeian supporter), Pompeius would have complete control of the armed forces of the Western Republic.

Consequently, Pompeius had no need of Caesar and thus had every reason not to help him. However, there was a great difference between ensuring Caesar received no further commands and became a private citizen (as Pompeius himself had done in 62 BC) and antagonizing him so much that he was forced to commit treason and march his army from his province into Italy. Based on the surviving evidence, there are two clear options for our interpretation of events, both based on Pompeius' intentions. The first option is that Pompeius blundered and deliberately set out not only to disarm his rival but to humiliate him, and was not expecting Caesar to turn to an armed response. The second option is the exact opposite; namely that Pompeius was trying to instigate an armed response and was cynically exploiting the tense situation to provoke a civil war.

In an ordinary political situation, we can rightly ask why a member of the ruling elite would provoke his opponent into military action, especially when he had armies poised on the borders of Italy. The short answer is that this was not an ordinary political situation. Pompeius' career was forged by the First Civil War, which elevated him from being the son of a Consul from an Italian family to being one of the key lieutenants in the ruling faction that conquered Rome (and son-in-law of the Dictator).[4] Thus, Pompeius learnt all his political lessons from that civil war, which ones to use (the threat of force) and which ones to avoid (the Dictatorship and Proscriptions). We will never know for certain what Pompeius' remaining ambitions were; he was already the greatest general in Rome (the 'new Alexander') and dominated the Republic. Nevertheless, it can be argued (and rightly in the view of this author) that for Pompeius this was not enough and that his ambition was to become the new guardian or overseer of the Republic, its Princeps.

This goal may well have not been purely down to personal ambition, but the realization of a man who had grown up watching the Republic collapse and the bloody civil wars that followed. We will never know what Sulla's (Pompeius' mentor) thoughts on the matter were, but though he retired from holding formal office, after having rebuilt the Republic (in 82–80 BC), subsequent events showed him intervening in its political life. It is entirely possible that Sulla saw himself taking the role of a Princeps in the New Republic, ensuring its peaceful running from the background, supported by tens of thousands of veterans throughout Italy.

Pompeius too could well have believed that for the Republic to survive, it needed a permanent guardian in the background. It is always necessary to point out the rank hypocrisy of such a view, given how much he himself had undermined the running of the Republic, but then we are dealing with a Roman oligarch. In both 70–68 BC and 52 BC, he had briefly held such a role, but could not hold onto it in a constitutional sense.

Sulla had won such a role through civil war and bloodshed, yet throughout his career Pompeius had always shied away from such overt methods, clearly understanding that no matter how much blood was spilt, the Roman oligarchy would never accept a 'tyrant' who imposed himself on them. However, as 52 BC had shown (with his sole consulship), under certain circumstances the Roman oligarchy would accept a 'guardian' to restore order. Thus, 52 BC had given Pompeius a taste of the power and control he wanted, and probably felt was needed. What remained was a calculation: if a political crisis in Rome could result in one year's domination, what would be needed for a longer rule? The answer, clearly, was a far larger crisis.

So it is entirely possible (and to this mind probable) that Pompeius did not stumble into civil war, but actively engineered it as a means of his elevation to the role of Princeps. Added to this is the fact that Pompeius was a cautious commander who always studied his opponents and sought to understand them before committing to the fight. He would have done no less with Caesar, with whom he had worked closely in the past. Caesar could be summed up by his impatience and boldness; an asset on the battlefield but an impediment in politics.

Therefore, it is entirely possible to construct a scenario that from 51–50 BC, Caesar was working for a settlement (for his own benefit) and Pompeius was working towards a new civil war, with Caesar, ironically, cast as the villain. The events of early 49 BC forced an ambitious and inpatient commander, who had a large army a few days from Italy proper, into a situation where he only had two options: political and military irrelevance or the use of his army. Unsurprisingly, Caesar chose the latter, effectively making Pompeius the instigator of the crossing of the Rubicon.[5]

The Civil War in Italy – A Tale of Two Strategies

Whilst the events of the subsequent Italian campaign are not in dispute, the strategies of the two commanders are, especially that of Pompeius. Ironically, despite starting the civil war and being, in the eyes of many of his fellow oligarchs, the 'villain', Caesar would not have wanted these events to explode into a Republic-wide war engulfing the whole of the Mediterranean and Near East (as the First Civil War had done). His aims would have been to bring his opponents to the negotiating table and restore his political and military position, either by conducting a deal with

Pompeius or the rest of the non-Pompeian Senatorial oligarchy (a more enhanced version of what Pompeius himself had done in 71 BC).

Again, the whole strategy of the Italian campaign is dominated by two contrasting views of Pompeius; either the vastly experienced general who was taken by surprise that the impatient Caesar invaded Italy and thus was woefully unprepared, or the scheming Pompeius who had forced Caesar's hand and was counting on him to use force and wanted/needed the crisis to expand into a Republic-wide (and its empire) conflagration. Key to this is the question: did Pompeius want to defend Italy and more importantly Rome, or did he want them to fall to Caesar?

At the outbreak of the war, on paper, Pompeius had the greater forces in Italy, with two legions in the south against the one legion that Caesar had with him. Yet this simple view overlooks three clear facts: firstly, the two legions in Italy had come from Caesar and thus may not have been reliable; secondly, although Caesar had invaded Italy with just one legion, the others were not far behind; and thirdly, Caesar's legions were battle hardened from fighting in Gaul.

Thus having the military advantage, Caesar had two clear objectives. The first was to seize Rome and with it control of the Senate, and more importantly the Assemblies, with which he could have his outlawing overturned and his actions pardoned. The second was to stop Pompeius leaving Italy, by either negotiation or force, and retreating to either of his two powerbases – Spain in the Western Republic or the provinces and kingdoms of the Eastern Republic. Here Caesar was hampered by the one area of the military he was clearly deficient in, a navy, with Pompeius having control of the navies of the Adriatic and Spain.

Whilst Caesar had clear objectives, those of Pompeius are harder to discern. Again we are faced with the two clear schools of thought, the first being that Caesar's crossing of the Rubicon took him by surprise and that everything afterwards was a panicked response, including his inability to defend Italy, forcing him to flee across the Adriatic. This clearly underestimates Pompeius' political and military acumen, in that having boxed Caesar into a corner politically, he did not expect him to turn to his military, despite Pompeius knowing Caesar well and having the examples of his own career to hand.

The second school is that Pompeius expected Caesar to turn to a military response and was not caught off guard, and therefore deliberately chose not to defend Italy by stationing his legions in the south rather than between Cisalpine Gaul and Rome. If so, then this strategy was based on sound political and military reasons and was wonderfully cynical in its conception. Recent history had shown that Rome itself could not be defended, having fallen easily during the Civil War of 88 BC to Sulla and bloodily to Marius a year later. That being the case, to defend Rome Pompeius would need to face Caesar soon after he invaded Italy. This would have meant going into battle with untested legions in a hurried manner, which totally contradicted two aspects of Pompeius' art of war: preparation and caution.

Furthermore, whilst allowing Rome to fall to Caesar was a clear political risk and would result in the Assemblies overturning Caesar's outlawing and allow him to speak as the official voice of Rome, there were clear political benefits in terms of the deepening of the crisis and thus forcing the non-aligned factions of the Senate to make a choice. Even then, a number of Senators (such as Cicero) chose to continue to sit on the fence and vacated Rome for their summer villas in the country. Nevertheless, Caesar taking Rome would force a number of the Senate to back Pompeius as the only figure who could 'restore' the Republic, and would allow Pompeius to compare the fall of Rome to Caesar as akin to the fall of Athens to Xerxes in 480 BC.

All Pompeius had to do was to make a tokenistic show of defiance and then slow down Caesar enough to successfully organize an evacuation of Italy. The obvious question was where he and his allies would head for; westwards to Pompeian-held Spain or eastwards to Greece? Whilst he had legions in Spain, moving there himself would potentially find him bottled up, with the whole Eastern Republic – his traditional powerbase since the conquest of the Eastern War (74–62 BC) – open to Caesar. Thus Pompeius chose to evacuate eastwards and base himself in Greece, allowing him to tap into the wealth and manpower of the Eastern Republic whilst keeping Caesar cooped up in Italy. The only potential danger lay in Caesar's legions in Illyria, under the command of C. Antonius (see below).

Pompeius prepared a two-stage strategy: to slow Caesar down, but ultimately to evacuate Rome and Italy, if necessary, to ensure a wider victory in the war which must inevitably follow. Interestingly, we have corroboration of this theory from Cicero. Whereas his early letters had Pompeius abandoning Rome and then Italy for fear of Caesar's armies, he later confesses that it was part of a wider, preconceived Pompeian 'masterplan':

> 'Nor, indeed, did he [Pompeius] abandon the city because he was unable to protect it, nor Italy because he was driven from it; but his idea from the first was to stir up every land and sea, to rouse foreign princes, to bring barbarous tribes in arms into Italy, to collect the most formidable armies possible. For some time past a kind of royalty like Sulla's has been the object in view, and this is the eager desire of many who are with him. Do you suppose that some understanding between the two, some bargain has been impossible? Today it is still possible. But the object of neither is our happiness: both want to be kings.'[6]
>
> 'This "disgraceful" measure our friend Cnaeus [Pompeius] had contemplated two years ago.'[7]

This is a point that the eminent twentieth-century classicist and historian Syme found convincing:

> 'Furthermore, the whole strategy of Pompeius, distasteful if not inexplicable to many of his allies and associates, was simple and masterly. Caesar would be entrapped in Italy or entangled in a guerrilla war in Spain, while Pompeius returned to victory with all the armies and fleets of the eastern lands. Pompeius should have won.'[8]

The events that followed are analyzed in detail elsewhere,[9] but followed the expected pattern. Pompeius dispatched some junior officers north to try to recruit additional Italian forces before Caesar arrived, but these troops melted away when Caesar's battle-hardened veterans arrived. The only resistance came from L. Domitius Ahenobarbus (Cos. 54 BC), whom the Senate had appointed as successor to Caesar in the Gallic campaigns. He raised 10,000 men and made a stand at Corfinium, but was besieged by Caesar and abandoned by Pompeius, and was soon forced to surrender.

Pompeius, by contrast, was already in Capua when Caesar advanced into Italy, making a token show at negotiations before relocating to Brundisium (modern Brindisi, in the heel of Italy) with his legions to co-ordinate the evacuation of Italy.[10] In a clear demonstration of his priorities, Caesar sent men to secure Rome but bypassed it himself, pursuing Pompeius to Brundisium, clearly aware of the danger of allowing Pompeius (and the bulk of the Senate) to withdraw overseas. The first actual clash between the two architects of the Third Civil War thus came at Brundisium, when again Pompeius put on a show of defiance and ensured he was one of the last men to withdraw from the city under siege, safe in the knowledge that Caesar had no naval ability to challenge his control of the Adriatic and safe passage from the city.

So Caesar had his Pyrrhic victory, control of Italy and – most importantly – of Rome itself. However, whilst the Assemblies ensured that he was no longer an official enemy of Rome, he was now an impeccable one in the eyes of the majority of the Senatorial oligarchy and found himself inextricably caught in what would now be a long-drawn-out war.

Civil War in the Western Republic – Sardinia, Sicily and Africa

Caesar now found himself surrounded by Pompeian-controlled territory, as at this point he only held a block of territory comprising the two Gallic provinces, Italy and Illyria, with the rest of the Roman world controlled by Pompeian commanders or friendly allied kings. Always one to take the initiative, Caesar realized that he would need to gain control of the mid-Mediterranean territories (Sardinia, Sicily and North Africa) before Pompeius was able to shift his focus from the Adriatic and place Italy in a stranglehold.

To that end, he dispatched forces to Sardinia, under Q. Valerius Orca, immediately after capturing the evacuated city of Brundisium. Without a large Pompeian presence, the Sardinian inhabitants, having no wish to be caught in the crossfire, threw out the pro-Pompeius governor (M. Aurelius Cotta) and allowed the Caesarians to occupy the island unopposed. This initial success was repeated soon afterwards when C. Scribonius Curio was ordered to capture Pompeian-controlled Sicily, an island that was a far greater prize as it would have allowed Pompeius to place Italy under a naval siege (as actually happened under his son, Sextus, a decade later). The Pompeian commander was M. Porcius Cato, by now a sworn enemy of Caesar and one of the leading figures in the anti-Caesarian faction within the alliance Pompeius had built.

Yet for all his political reputation, which was far murkier in reality than the legend, Cato's military experience was limited. This soon showed when faced with an invading enemy, and despite being safely headquartered in the city of Syracuse – noted for its ability to withstands a siege – Cato chose to evacuate Sicily without a fight, handing Caesar a notable success and denting Pompeius' plans to keep Caesar bottled up in Italy. Cato withdrew with his forces to the island base of Corcyra (Corfu) and then the Pompeian forward base of Dyrrhachium, where Pompeius, quite understandably, kept him away from any commands of importance.

This run of Caesarian success initially continued with an attack on Roman North Africa by Curio, using Sicily as a springboard. The defenders' situation in North Africa was initially complicated by the overthrow of the Senatorially appointed governor, L. Aelius Tubero, by the Pompeian-supported P. Attius Varus, who had fled Italy and sought refuge there. Ultimately, however, this was to be a boon to the Pompeian cause, as Varus had served as Governor of Africa before and had close connections with the neighbouring allied Kingdom of Numidia, still the regional powerhouse. It was to be these links that proved so useful to the Pompeian cause, both in the short and medium terms. Rather than oppose the Caesarian attack, Varus withdrew to the capital of Utica and prepared for a siege, whilst sending word to the Numidian King Juba I. Whether driven by close links to Varus, wanting to ingratiate himself with Pompeius or inspired by hatred for Curio (for his Tribunician proposal of the previous year to annex Numidia), Juba threw his whole weight against Caesar and marched an army into Roman North Africa to destroy the Caesarian forces.

Aware that a Numidian force was approaching, but unsure of its true size, Curio saw the danger and withdrew to face it. The result was the Battle of Bagradas River. Initially, Curio met with success when his cavalry routed an advance force of Numidian cavalry. However, Curio made the ultimately fatal mistake of believing that the Numidian force that had been defeated was the main army and set off after it. To make matters worse, the Numidian commander, Saburra, learning of the Caesarian forces' advance, laid a trap for Curio and feigned retreat, thus reinforcing Curio's misconceptions.

At the appointed moment, the 'retreating' Numidian army turned and overwhelmed the advancing Romans (comprising a legion and a half), cutting them to pieces and hunting down the survivors. Curio was not one of the latter, falling in battle, with his corpse being identified and his severed head sent to Juba as a trophy. Caesar had been served his first defeat in the war, and Pompeius his first victory, and North Africa remained solidly Pompeian in what soon became a joint Pompeian-Numidian entity. At the time, the loss seemed a minor one to Caesar as North Africa remained a side show, but as events proved the following year (48 BC), it turned out to be an important defeat.

Notable throughout these initial campaigns is the absence of Pompeius himself, who left the three provinces (Sardinia, Sicily and North Africa) with limited manpower and sent no reinforcements. With the bulk of his western legions stationed in Spain, threatening Caesar's western flank and Gallic powerbase, he seemed in no mood to contest these 'middling' provinces.

Civil War in the Eastern Republic – Illyria

As well as not wishing to lessen his forces in Spain, Pompeius' primary attention was focused on securing his position in Greece and on the Adriatic. Despite withdrawing his Italian legions across the Adriatic and having overwhelming naval superiority, he faced one key danger: the Caesarian-controlled province of Illyria. It is often overlooked that Caesar had command of Illyria and had legionary forces stationed there, alongside his commands in the two Gallic provinces, and thus had a perfect springboard for an attack on Pompeius before he could secure his position in Greece. One of the reasons this is often neglected is that you will find no reference to it in Caesar's own commentaries on the civil war.[11]

Whilst the disaster in North Africa receives in-depth coverage from Caesar, mostly to point out that the defeat was due to 'perfidious foreigners' (the Numidians) rather than Pompeius himself, the Illyrian campaigns of 49 BC have no such treatment. This is on account of the fact that it was a second defeat of far greater strategic importance and one at the hands of Pompeius himself. Thus, the winner of the civil war – at least of its early years – wrote the history books and tried to erase this defeat. Despite this, there are enough references in other surviving sources to the campaigns which took place. Clearly, Pompeius needed to destroy this Caesarian bridgehead before Caesar could reinforce it, committing his whole naval and land resources to this end.

Command in Illyria fell to C. Antonius (brother of the Tribune M. Antonius), as a Legate of Caesar, with P. Cornelius Dolabella in command of Illyria's small fleet. Whilst Caesar had troops stationed in Illyria (at least three legions, according to Orosius)[12] and a fleet, they were dwarfed by the size of the Pompeian forces and more importantly by the Pompeian fleet, which effectively controlled the Adriatic. Command of the Pompeian Adriatic fleet fell to L. Scribonius Libo, who had been driven from Italy by M. Antonius. Florus preserves the best account of the campaign for Illyria and control of the Adriatic:

> 'For when Dolabella and Antonius, who had been ordered to hold the entrance to the Adriatic, had encamped, the former on the Illyrian coast and the latter on the shore near Curicta, at a time when Pompeius enjoyed a wide command of the sea, the latter's lieutenant-general Octavius [Scribonius] Libo suddenly surrounded both of them with large forces from the fleet. Famine compelled Antonius to surrender. Some rafts sent to his assistance by Basilus, as good a substitute as he could make for the lack of ships, were captured, as in a net, by means of ropes drawn along under the water, a new device on the part of some Cilicians in Pompeius' service. The tide, however, floated two of them off; but one of them, which carried troops from Opitergium, went aground on the shallows and provided an incident worthy of record in history. A band of barely 1,000 men withstood for a whole day the weapons of an army which had completely surrounded them, and when their valour procured no way of escape, at last, at the exhortation of the Tribune Vulteius, in order that they might not be forced to surrender, they fell upon one another and died by the blows of their fellows.'[13]

Dio also wrote about the Illyrian campaign:

> 'Marcus Octavius and Lucius Scribonius Libo, with the aid of Pompeius' fleet drove out of Dalmatia Publius Cornelius Dolabella, who was there attending to Caesar's interests. After this they shut up Caius Antonius, who had been desirous of aiding him, on a small

island, and there, after he had been abandoned by the natives and was oppressed by hunger, they captured him with all his troops save a few; for some had escaped in season to the mainland, and others, who were sailing across on rafts and were overtaken, made away with themselves.'[14]

Orosius adds some additional details, including the size of Antonius' force and the actions of the future historian Sallust:

'On the other hand, Dolabella, Caesar's supporter in Illyricum, was defeated by Octavius and Libo lost his troops and fled to Antonius. Basillus and Sallustius, each in command of a single legion, Antonius, who likewise had one legion, and Hortensius, who came to join them from the Inner Sea [Adriatic] all marched together on Octavius and Libo but were defeated by them. Antonius and his 15 cohorts surrendered to Octavius, and these were all taken to Pompeius by Libo.'[15]

Thus we can see there were two key phases of the campaign. The Pompeian fleet of Libo and Octavius first engaged with the Caesarian fleet of Cornelius Dolabella and defeated them, killing or capturing Dolabella's whole force. Appian reports that Pompeius seized forty of Caesar's Adriatic fleet.[16] The remaining Caesarian commanders, L. Minucius Basilus and C. Sallustius Crispus, then combined their forces with those of C. Antonius, creating an army of three legions. However, Antonius managed to become trapped with his army on an island and was starved into submission, with his troops all being transferred to Pompeius' army. Antonius was captured, but Sallustius and Basilus seem to have escaped.

Despite the scant details available to us, this Illyrian campaign was a major defeat for Caesar and a victory for Pompeius. In Africa, Caesar lost two newly formed legions, but in a strategically insignificant part of the world. Here, he lost at least three legions, probably established ones, and more importantly lost the only bridgehead he had on the eastern side of the Adriatic as well as his Adriatic fleet. Control of all lands east of the Adriatic now fell to Pompeius, as did control of the Adriatic itself, bottling Caesar up in the western half of the Republic and meaning that

Pompeius controlled access to the rich provinces and client kingdoms of the East.

Civil War in the Western Republic – Massilia and Spain

With Pompeius having retreated across the Adriatic and not yet having sufficient naval resources to force a crossing, Caesar was not in a position to bring the war to a swift conclusion, so he needed to change his plans to accommodate this. In the immediate term, this meant he needed additional finances to raise a larger army than the legions he had in Gaul, and there was only one place that this money could be acquired from quickly: Rome.

So Caesar finally returned to Rome himself and faced the People and the remnants of the Senate. Control of the Assembly meant that his outlawing was overturned and his actions pardoned. More importantly, control of Rome brought with it control of the monies lodged in the state treasuries in the temples, which Caesar sequestered for his forthcoming campaigns. Rome having been fed Pompeian propaganda about a bloodthirsty tyrant and his 'Gallic hoards', Caesar made a show of restraint and clemency, not that there were many of his opponents left in Rome. The only source of opposition came from a remaining Tribune (L. Caecilius Metellus) who had held to his oath of office and not left the city. Metellus attempted to intervene and use his Tribunician sacrosanctity to prevent the removal of the state treasures, but ended up being threatened with murder by Caesar.

Thus, despite his rhetoric of lenience and moderation, Caesar threatened, in public, to kill a Tribune of the People, one merely fulfilling the duties of his role; this coming despite all the rhetoric about having gone to war in the first place in defence of the rights of the Tribunes.[17] Caesar himself mentions Metellus, but naturally omits the death threats:

> 'Also L. Metellus, the Tribune, is put up by Caesar's enemies to thwart this proposal and to hinder everything else that he proposed to do.'[18]

A more revealing account can be found in one of Cicero's letters, when Cicero narrated an account he had received first-hand from a friend, Curio, who was one of Caesar's officers and present in Rome:

18   The Battle of Pharsalus (48 BC)

'…that in an access of anger Caesar had really wished the Tribune Metellus to be killed, and that it was within an ace of being done: if it had been done, there would have followed a serious massacre: that a great many people advised one: that Caesar himself was not by taste or nature averse from bloodshed, but thought clemency would win him popularity: if, however, he once lost the affection of the People, he would be cruel: he was, again, much disturbed by finding that he had caused ill-feeling among the populace itself by taking the treasury, and therefore that, though he had quite made up his mind to address the people before leaving Rome, he had not ventured to do so, and had started with very disturbed feelings.'[19]

It thus seems that Caesar narrowly averted a massacre of the People, but whilst he secured his financial position with a massive influx of monies, he soured his political position and confirmed to many within both the Senate and People that he was acting tyrannically. Having seen to the Senate and People and having secured the treasury, Caesar soon left Rome to go on campaign again, apparently wishing to spend no more time in Rome itself, playing politics, than he had to; an attitude which rather summed up Caesar's later career. Before he left, he placed M. Aemilius Lepidus in charge of the city and M. Antonius in charge of Italy, and ordered the construction of two fleets, one for the Adriatic and another for the Tyrrhenian Sea.

Building a new fleet would clearly take time and Caesar had no wish to be idle during that period. He understood that time was not on his side and that the longer he left Pompeius unchallenged in Greece, the greater a force could be assembled to oppose him. Yet without a fleet he could not reinforce his position in Illyria, unless he took the land route around the north of the Adriatic. However, that would mean marching through regions controlled by potentially hostile tribes, and even if he fought his way through, his forces would be in no condition to face those of Pompeius. With his lieutenants fighting to the south to secure Sicily and Africa, that left Caesar with two choices: he could wait in Italy and build up a larger army and navy, and inevitably be forced into the politics of Rome, or he could take the initiative in another region.

Lacking the ability to cross the Adriatic in force and the patience to spend the rest of the year in Italy expanding his forces to anticipate any Pompeian invasion from either the east or the west, Caesar chose to abandon Italy just three months after he invaded it and march on Pompeian held Spain. Spain had been a Pompeian stronghold since the latter stages of the First Civil War, when the Sullan faction dispatched Pompeius to reconquer it from the Cinnan general Sertorius. This longstanding association had been strengthened recently when Pompeius chose the two Spanish provinces as his consular command after his Consulship in 55 BC, receiving the right to rule it via Legates, meaning he could remain in Rome.

Crucially, Caesar only held the two major provinces, those of Italy and Gaul, both of which were vulnerable to attack: Gaul from the west (Pompeian Spain) and Italy from the east (Pompeian Greece and Illyria). Knowing Pompeius as he did, he would have been aware that he was unlikely to attack Italy before he had assembled his forces from across the East, so judged the main danger to be the threat from Pompeian Spain. Whilst Gaul was his powerbase, he had only just finished a decade-long programme of conquest and had already suffered a recent significant rebellion. This left the province vulnerable to any Pompeian armies marching into it from Spain and stirring up rebellion amongst the recently conquered Gallic tribes.

Consequently, Caesar marched nine legions towards Spain hoping to knock the Pompeian legions out of the war, allowing him to focus his subsequent campaigns entirely on the East. However, though tactically sound for Caesar, the move could easily have backfired and played into Pompeius' hands. The key resource that Pompeius needed was time, which he required to tap into the financial and military resources of the provinces and kingdoms of the East, to assemble a 'grand army' and defeat Caesar in a set-piece battle. If Caesar were to be tied down in Spain, then this removed the risk of Caesar attempting a mad dash across the Adriatic and disrupting these plans. Pompeius would thus have been planning for Caesar to be delayed by his Spanish armies for the rest of the year (49 BC) and into the following year. If this happened, then Pompeius would have a range of options, the two key ones being an invasion of Italy and subsequent march to Spain or, more likely, allowing Caesar to withdraw from Spain in 48 BC and face him in Greece.

So once again, Caesar required a short, sharp campaign to knock the Spanish armies out of the war and not get caught up in a drawn-out struggle, whilst Pompeius needed the opposite. However, the one outcome that Pompeius did not want was for Caesar to be cleanly defeated in Spain, or even worse killed, outcomes which would derail his whole civil war campaign, which was built around him being the only man who could defeat this existential threat to the Republic. Thus, his Spanish commanders would have been ordered to tie down Caesar, not defeat him, instructions which ultimately may have affected their ability to campaign effectively.

To further ensure Caesar would be tied down in the west, Pompeius contacted the city of Massilia (Marseilles), the key staging post to any land route from Italy to Spain, promising seaborne reinforcements if they opposed Caesar. Thus, unlike all the other cities he had encountered, Caesar found his path barred by Massilia and its new Pompeian commander, L. Domitius Ahenobarbus, the Senatorially appointed commander of Transalpine Gaul. Recognizing the danger of being bogged down into a protracted siege, Caesar continued his march on Spain, but was forced to leave behind three legions to besiege Massilia or face having a Pompeian staging post to the rear of his position, cutting him off from Italy. In consequence, Caesar's army had already been reduced by a third before he even reached Spain.

The subsequent Spanish campaigns have been covered in detail previously,[20] but the following is an outline of the key events and more importantly their implications. Facing Caesar and his six legions were three Pompeian commanders, the first two of which, L. Afranius (Cos. 60 BC) and M. Petreius (Pr. 64 BC), were both battle-hardened veterans. The third and final commander was an aging administrator, M. Terentius Varro. Of the three commanders, Afranius held three legions, Petreius and Varro two each, their combined seven legions numbering more than 35,000 men, all of whom had been serving in Spain for at least five years. They also had around 10,000 cavalry at their disposal, complemented by a large number of auxiliary troops from the natives of the region.

Pompeius sent a legate, L. Vibullius Rufus, with orders for his three commanders. Afranius was to meet the invasion head-on by intercepting the Caesarian army after it had cleared the Pyrenees. Petreius was to take his two legions to join him, and Varro was to defend the interior with his two legions. Afranius and Petreius had five legions to Caesar's six, but probably had orders to tie down Caesar rather than engage him in open battle. They chose to make their stand at the city of Ilerda in northern Spain.

The subsequent protracted campaign started badly for Caesar when his advance guard of three legions was nearly cut off and destroyed on the far bank of the River Sicoris before Caesar had even reached Ilerda. It was only fast thinking on his commanders' part, and perhaps a certain reticence on the part of the Pompeian commanders, that averted a disaster.

Nevertheless, the subsequent phases of the campaign seemed to play perfectly to Pompeius' strategy, with Caesar being seriously delayed at Ilerda. The first clash between Caesar and Afranius led to a Caesarian defeat at the city itself, with Caesar having to extricate his forces from a position in which one of his characteristic bold thrusts had left them. Caesar's position continued to deteriorate when a supply column from Gaul was attacked by Afranius, whose dominant position with its control of the river crossings meant his could cross at will the obstacle that separated the two armies.

Caesar's army was now effectively trapped with dwindling supplies, with Afranius ensuring that there was no way out for them and playing a waiting game. Caesar himself reports that Afranius and Petreius sent news of Caesar's plight back to Rome:

'Afranius and Petreius and their friends wrote to their partisans at Rome an amplified and exaggerated account of these events. Rumour added much, so that the war seemed almost finished. When these letters and messages were conveyed to Rome great crowds thronged the house of Afranius and hearty congratulations were offered. Many set out from Italy for Cn. Pompeius, some that they might show themselves the first to bring him such news.'[21]

According to Caesar's account, it was Afranius and Petreius who were exaggerating the situation Caesar found himself in. Dio, however, paints a different picture:

'Caesar, when things were taking this course, fell into desperate straits; for none of his allies rendered him assistance, since his opponents met and annihilated the separate forces as often as they heard that any were approaching, and it was with difficulty that he managed to obtain provisions, inasmuch as he was in a hostile territory and unsuccessful in his operations.'[22]

22 The Battle of Pharsalus (48 BC)

It seems that Afranius and Petreius certainly had Caesar tied down in the stalemate that Pompeius had demanded. Pompeius himself must have heard of this, as seen in Dio, with news being borne from Rome:

> 'The Romans at home, when they learned of this, renounced all hope of him, believing that he could hold out but a short time longer, and began to fall away to Pompeius; and some few Senators and others set out to join the latter even then.'[23]

Afranius and Petreius were now seemingly confident that all they had to do was wait and let hunger and the pressure tell on Caesar's legions, until such point as they mutinied or were starved into submission. It is not known if they considered an attack on Caesar's position, but that would have meant abandoning the strategic advantage given to them by holding the high ground and exposing themselves to Caesar's greater numbers.

However, as was custom with his military career, Caesar was always the most dangerous when in a seemingly losing position, and amazingly he was able to turn matters around and snatch victory from the jaws of defeat. With his military campaign having ground into a potential loss, Caesar clearly needed to change his tactics. This he did by constructing a fleet of troop transports and ferrying the bulk of his army back across the river unobserved, then fortifying the opposite bank. Having thus extricated himself from a potently dire situation, he was able to use his larger cavalry contingent (which had been reinforced from Gaul) to harass Afranius' foragers and put pressure back on the defenders.

Furthermore, realizing that he could not dislodge Afranius and Petreius from their position militarily, he set about undermining them politically and logistically. Freed from his dire position, he was able to communicate with the various native cities and tribes of the region, all of whom owed their allegiance to Pompeius, something which he seems not to have done to date.

Despite his military setbacks, Caesar was now able to convince a number of them to change sides, although the reasons for this are not clear in any surviving accounts. Dio puts it down to Afranius' boastful statements about his victories over Caesar, but this is far from convincing.[24] Certainly on a personal level, neither Afranius nor Petreius seemed to be what we could call charismatic, and Petreius later revealed a brutal streak which may well have been present here.

There may also have been some element of the naturally rebellious nature of the Spanish tribes, having earlier backed the rebel candidate in the First Civil War (Sertorius) against the 'official' Roman one (Pompeius). Furthermore, Pompeius having defeated Sertorius, there may have been lingering resentment which Caesar could have stoked. Naturally, Caesar himself does not state what inducements he offered them to switch. He does, however, say that the rumours of Pompeius coming to relieve Spain via North Africa (Mauretania as it was to become) were now widely believed to be false.[25] If Pompeius was not coming to Spain, then the immediate danger of disloyalty to the man was removed; all that was left was disloyalty to his subordinates.

Having alleviated the pressure he was under and turned the tables on Afranius and Petreius, Caesar was handed victory by the ineptness of his opponents, who took the disastrous decision to leave their strong position at Ilerda and retreat into the interior. As they should have expected, Caesar had no desire to allow them to retreat unchallenged. Indeed, faced with Caesar's superior numbers of cavalry, the retreat turned into a rout and then a disaster, with the Pompeian army trapped on a mountain with insufficient provisions, pinned down by Caesar.

With the morale of their Spanish forces deteriorating, Afranius and Petreius led their troops in a breakout, chased by Caesar's army until they were finally pinned down with their backs to the River Sicoris. Trapped and with morale destroyed, Afranius and Petreius chose to negotiate a surrender that left them free to leave Spain and rejoin Pompeius, but with Spain and its armies falling to Caesar.

With the loss of Afranius and Petreius, Pompeian Spain was reduced to the southern region commanded by M. Terentius Varro, who soon proved to be out of his depth when faced with the inevitable momentum that the Caesarian victory brought. With Caesar clearly on the ascendency in Spain and the Pompeian element reduced to just Varro, all of the main cities and tribes declared for Caesar and expelled their Pompeian garrisons, including the city of Gades, Varro's headquarters. Varro's situation deteriorated further when one of his two legions deserted his camp when they heard the news.

With his temporary headquarters lost, and with it access to the monies he had accumulated and the naval forces, Varro had no option but to make contact with Caesar and offer his surrender. Caesar dispatched a kinsman, Sex. Iulius Caesar, to take control of Varro's one remaining Pompeian legion, whilst Varro went to surrender in person to Caesar in Corduba. Caesar made for Gades to secure the Pompeian ships and the monies, and appointed Q. Cassius Longinus as the new Governor of Further Spain, leaving him with four legions.

Summary – Stalemate

From a losing position, Caesar had been able to turn the situation around and within a few months had secured control of Spain and its resources, bringing him mastery of the Western Republic (excepting North Africa). Upon hearing the news from Spain, Massilia ended its resistance and surrendered to Caesar, who returned to Rome in December and was able to organize the (closely controlled) elections for the magistrates of the following year. Perhaps the most important magistrate chosen was Caesar himself, who, with his customary lack of political acumen, had himself made Dictator.

Though he only held the office for eleven days to force through a programme of reforming legislation, the damage had been done; he had associated himself with the office last held by – and forever associated with – L. Cornelius Sulla, whose bloodthirsty rule after his victory in the First Civil War was notorious. Though an eminently practical choice, a wiser head would have avoided attaching himself to such a legacy. Pompeius had made a very public statement when he declined the office in 52 BC, brandishing his 'Republican' credentials. It was a choice which Caesar repeatedly returned to and one which ultimately led to his failure and death.

Nevertheless, Caesar ended the year where he started, back in Italy, no nearer to bringing the civil war to a conclusion. Yet he had escaped the trap which Pompeius had laid for him in Spain and, armed with a new fleet (albeit far smaller than that of Pompeius), was able to plan his campaigns for 48 BC which would bring the two protagonists face to face in battle for the first time.

Chapter Two

Pompeius Victorious – The Battle of Dyrrhachium (48 BC)

As we have seen, the dawning of a new year saw the Roman Republic still split into two, with the Western Republic controlled by Caesar and his faction and the Eastern Republic held by Pompeius and his supporters. Despite his capture of Italy and victory in Spain, Caesar still found himself dancing to Pompeius' tune. From the beginning, Pompeius had dictated the pace of this conflict; a long-drawn-out affair rather than a short, sharp one, ensuring that he was safely headquartered in Greece, whilst his lieutenants drew on the financial and manpower resources of the provinces and kingdoms of the Eastern Republic. For his masterplan to succeed, Pompeius needed to cleanly defeat Caesar in battle and thereby 'save' the Republic and earn his place as its guardian and protector (its Princeps). For Pompeius, this battle would only happen when his grand army had been assembled and he judged the time to be right. Well aware of his opponent's strategy, Caesar needed to disrupt Pompeius by quickening the pace and forcing him off his well-planned and leisurely timescale.

The Gamble - The Caesarian Invasion of the East (January 48 BC)

To upset Pompeius' plans, Caesar had to take yet another gamble, this time forcing a crossing of the Pompeian-controlled Adriatic and landing on the Illyrian/Epirote coast in force to re-establish the Caesarian bridgehead that had been wiped out the previous year. At the start of the year, Pompeius' forces were split into two, with neither ready to fight. His existing army in Greece was scattered across its winter quarters and the eastern army assembled by Metellus Scipio was wintering in Asia ready to cross the Bosphorus through Thrace and into Macedonia.

Caesar now saw a weakness he could exploit through an early attack across the Adriatic, rather than waiting for the winter weather to abate.

The risk, however, was that his attack could be disrupted or destroyed by either the weather or the Pompeian fleet. There was the additional danger that even if he landed successfully, he would be cut off from the Western Republic and trapped in Greece with no reinforcements.

Ever a man to take a military gamble, Caesar decided to force a winter crossing of the Adriatic and as early as 4 January launched his invasion of the east. Though he was taking an obvious chance on the weather, in many ways this would work to his advantage as his enemies would be less vigilant. As it was, Caesar also chose not to take the obvious route across the Adriatic from Brundisium to Apollonia (see Map 2), but went further south (nearer to the Pompeian naval headquarters at Corcyra) and landed just south of Oricum with, as Caesar himself informs us, seven legions, close to 30,000 men.

Having captured the element of surprise, Caesar then moved to secure naval bases on the eastern coast of the Adriatic, the cities of Oricum and more importantly Apollonia falling unopposed when the inhabitants refused to fight (a common theme in Roman civil wars). Caesar now had naval bases on both sides of the Adriatic, though the powerful Pompeian fleet stood between them. Furthermore, he had seven legions assembled in Epirus, whilst the Pompeian army was scattered in its winter quarters. Caesar now had the initiative in the war.

News reached Pompeius quickly, and he was soon marching towards Epirus from his capital city of Thessalonica in Macedonia. Realizing the danger, but also the opportunity, Caesar being trapped in Epirus, Pompeius immediately made for the Epirote coast and his winter headquarters of Dyrrhachium, using the Via Egnatia. The city of Dyrrhachium was the prize; the largest port on the Adriatic coast, the regional headquarters for Pompeius' army and the start of the Via Egnatia, which cut across Greece and Macedon. It was thus a key target for Caesar, and both generals were now engaged in a race for the city.

Geographically, Caesar was the nearer, but Pompeius was using the Via Egnatia and marched his army night and day to reach the city first and recover the initiative. Informed that Pompeius had beaten him in the race, Caesar checked his progress and halted at the River Apsus (the modern Seman). Having secured Dyrrhachium, Pompeius led his force south to the Apsus and camped on the opposite bank. For the first time since Brundisium in 49 BC, Pompeius and Caesar came face to face.

Accounts vary on what happened next, with Caesar stating that negotiations took place whilst Appian and Dio record skirmishes between the two forces.[1] What is clear is that no pitched battle took place, and again we can determine that it would have been Pompeius who would have been unwilling to fight, even though he apparently had the greater numbers. He understood that Caesar needed a victory over him and ideally access to Dyrrhachium as a base.

Pompeius, having blocked Caesar from Dyrrhachium, had no wish to jeopardize his masterplan on a hastily engaged battle, especially with all of his Eastern forces still in Asia. If he could avoid battle, then the momentum would swing back in his favour, with Caesar trapped in Greece without reinforcements or a supply line whilst Pompeius could order Metellus Scipio to cross from Asia into Greece. Consequently, Pompeius began another campaign to grind Caesar down.

We are not told by what number Pompeius' forces outnumbered those of Caesar; it may not have been by enough to be confident of victory (his army is likely to have been in the region of nine to ten legions). Furthermore, the current situation favoured Pompeius, with Caesar cut off from reinforcements whilst his own were crossing Greece. Pompeius was happy to sit back and contain Caesar until the situation swung decisively in his favour.

Caesar, by contrast, for once had to curb his natural boldness. Any reinforcements lay on the other side of Adriatic, and facing him was Pompeius Magnus himself, with a larger number of troops and a secure supply line to his base at Dyrrhachium. Though Caesar uncharacteristically chose a cautious approach, presumably as even he must have seen that he was outnumbered, he would also have realized – as would Pompeius – that time was not on his side. His rival had scrambled his forces from their winter quarters to counter Caesar's thrust, and every day more of these would have been converging on Dyrrhachium.

It was now a race to see which set of reinforcements could reach their commander first. The nearest geographically was the Caesarian army, commanded by Fufius Calenus, yet they were separated from their leader by the Adriatic and the Pompeian fleet, who now had a clear target. The Pompeian army of Metellus Scipio, who had crossed from Asia, were further away, marching across Thrace and Macedonia, presumably along the Via Egnatia. With both sides locked in stalemate across the

River Apsus, the focus of the war shifted once again to the Adriatic. If the Pompeian fleet could hold the Caesarian army at Brundisium, then Caesar would be cut off in Epirus, forcing him to either attack Pompeius or retreat before the army of Metellus Scipio arrived.

The Adriatic Campaign – Stalemate (February 48 BC)

Having failed to prevent Caesar from crossing the Adriatic, the Pompeian fleet commanded, by M. Calpurnius Bibulus (Cos. 59 BC), Caesar's former Consular colleague, had one clear aim: to prevent any further reinforcements from crossing, thereby bottling Caesar up in Epirus. Bibulus enacted a two-fold campaign; firstly blockading the recently captured Caesarian ports of Oricum and Apollonia on the eastern coast, and secondly – and more importantly – blockading Brundisium itself, which is perhaps what he should have done in the first place.

Stymied to both the north and the west, Caesar's natural restlessness came to the fore and he took one legion south to the coast opposite Corcyra, the Pompeian naval base, a show of force that achieved little. On the Pompeian side, a change of tactic was brought about by an enforced change of commander, when Bibulus died of disease and was replaced by L. Scribonius Libo (Cos. 34 BC), who decided to bolster his reputation by attacking Brundisium, either to capture the city or destroy the Caesarian fleet within its harbour. However, the attack was beaten off by M. Antonius, after which Libo seems to have slackened his blockade.[2]

The Breakthrough – The Antonine Invasion of the East (March/April 48 BC)

By late March/early April, Libo's blockade had slackened to the extent that Antonius launched his own invasion force across the Adriatic, the first the Pompeian fleet knew of it being when they passed Dyrrhachium. With Oricum and Apollonia under blockade, Antonius had no option but to sail north and land to the north of Dyrrhachium. The Caesarians now had Pompeius sandwiched between two hostile armies, with Antonius to the north and Caesar to the south. The second Pompeian failure to prevent Caesarian forces crossing the Adriatic had swung the initiative back to Caesar, as he now had a second army on the Adriatic coastline, one numbering at least four legions.

Though he now had more soldiers to hand, Caesar still faced the same two problems. The first was that he needed to bring Pompeius to battle and, if not defeat him, then at least drive him inland into mainland Greece, thereby establishing a secure bridgehead. The second problem was that he still had no clear supply line to the Western Republic, so did not have the resources to sustain a long campaign, other than by living off the land. An additional short-term problem was that although he had superior numbers overall, they were split across two forces and needed to be brought together to make the numbers tell.

Pompeius also realized this, and upon hearing of Antonius' crossing immediately set off north to meet and destroy him before he could establish a more permanent bridgehead or move south to link up with Caesar (see Map 2). Pompeius stole a march on Caesar by breaking camp at night, forcing his opponent to again engage in a race to see who could reach Antonius first. Winning that race, Pompeius laid a trap for Antonius, but the latter's scouts spotted it and Antonius drew to a halt; his scouts managed to evade Pompeius' forces and reach Caesar. Pompeius saw that he now either had to launch an attack on Antonius, with the danger of being held up long enough for Caesar to arrive at his rear and become trapped between the two armies, or withdraw. Ever the strategic thinker, Pompeius withdrew and ceded the immediate initiative back to Caesar.

Expanding the Campaign – The Civil War in Greece

Despite having succeeded in gaining additional forces with Antonius' four legions and seizing the initiative once again, Caesar still faced two fundamental problems. Pompeius and his troops, estimated at between eight and ten legions, were still close by, ready to contest any Caesarian move to secure the region but always avoiding open battle. Furthermore, time was on the side of Pompeius, with Metellus' Eastern army marching towards him, a secure forward base at Dyrrhachium, control of the Adriatic, an established supply line throughout Greece and Macedonia and control of the main route from the East (the Via Egnatia). Understanding this, Caesar made another roll of the dice, and no sooner had he gained numerical superiority through Antonius' forces than he voluntarily surrendered it by sending portions of his army into Greece and Thessaly:

> '[Caesar] sent into Thessaly L. Cassius Longinus with the legion of recruits, called the Twenty-seventh, and two hundred horse; into Aetolia, C. Calvisius Sabinus with five cohorts and a few horsemen; and he gave them special instructions, as the districts were close at hand, to provide for the corn supply. He ordered Cn. Domitius Calvinus to go into Macedonia with two legions, the Eleventh and Twelfth, and five hundred horsemen.'[3]

Caesar thus dispatched some three legions from his force to spread into Thessaly, Aetolia and Macedon. This meant that he went from having the largest army in Epirus to once again ceding the size advantage to Pompeius. Nonetheless, Calvisius was dispatched into Greece proper to try to secure some of the city states held by the Pompeian forces, and with it supplies for the main army, as well as possibly opening up new naval routes to Italy. Cassius was sent in Thessaly, again to secure territory and supplies and also possibly to support Domitius in his campaign against Metellus Scipio. Domitius was sent with two legions to try to slow or stop Metellus Scipio. Each commander met with contrasting fortunes, Calvisius Sabinus having the most success even though his force was the smallest.

There was now a series of parallel campaigns running during this period, in addition to the key one in Illyria between Caesar and Pompeius. Those in Greece proper were side shows, with a small Caesarian force contesting Pompeius' garrisons. With control of both ends of the Via Egnatia, the key ports of Dyrrhachium and Thessalonica and the supply routes to the East, Pompeius had no need of the Greek interior.

The campaign involving the Caesarian commander Cn. Domitius Calvinus (Cos. 53 BC) and the Pompeian Q. Caecilius Metellus Pius Scipio Nasica (Cos. 52 BC) was an important one. Domitius' task was clear (albeit far from simple): to stop, or more likely slow down, Metellus Scipio's Eastern army and deny Pompeius the reinforcements he was waiting for. Only then could Caesar force Pompeius from his cautious strategy and hopefully tempt him into battle. Unfortunately, the surviving sources for this period are far more interested in the manoeuvres between

Caesar and Pompeius than Domitius and Metellus, so we have little detail to go on.

What we do know is that Metellus' army was large and seemed to make slow progress; it took them months to arrive in Greece, let alone Illyria. From Antonius' invasion in late March/early April to the end of July (the final stages of the Battle of Dyrrhachium itself), Metellus' army had still not reached beyond Macedonia. It seems that this was down to the army's natural slowness, given its size, as well as its multiracial complexity and Domitius' harrying. We have two references to Metellus and Domitius meeting in battle, each ending in a Metellan victory, unsurprisingly neither from Caesar's own hand:

> 'The same winter Scipio, Pompeius' father-in-law, advanced with another army from Syria. Caesar's general, Caius Calvisius, had an engagement with him in Macedonia, was beaten, and lost a whole legion except 800 men.'[4]
>
> 'Lucius Cassius Longinus and Cnaeus Domitius Calvinus had been sent by him into Macedonia and Thessaly. Longinus had been disastrously defeated in Thessaly by Scipio.'[5]

So it seems that Domitius met Metellus head-on and was defeated, but was still able to recover and slow down his progression. There is a further reference to another clash between the Caesarian commander C. Calvisius Sabinus (Cos. 39 BC) and the Pompeian Faustus Cornelius Sulla (son of the Dictator and son-in-law of Pompeius himself), which also ended in a Pompeian victory.[6] Though the details of these campaigns elude us, we must keep them in mind when analyzing the subsequent battle between Caesar and Pompeius, as the expected arrival of Metellus' forces had a huge bearing on the strategic thinking of both commanders.

The Road to Dyrrhachium

Having failed to prevent Caesar from joining forces with Antonius, and having no wish to lose focus by trying to prevent these splinter Caesarian forces from pushing inland, Pompeius had withdrawn to a fortified position near Asparagium. The town lay close to Dyrrhachium on the River Genusus (modern Shkumbin) and was presumably on the Via

Egnatia, allowing Pompeius swift movement either to Dyrrhachium itself or further into Macedonia.

Caesar marched his army to Asparagium and arrayed it in battle formation. No details are given as to Pompeius' disposition or defences, but it seems that his position was too well fortified for Caesar to consider an attack. Thus, for the second time in the campaign, the armies of Caesar and Pompeius faced each other, but yet again there was no battle between them, with Pompeius in no mood to give battle without Metellus' reinforcements and Caesar apparently in no position to force him to do so.

Caesar once again determined on a fresh course of action, making an attack on the city of Dyrrhachium itself to force Pompeius to either come to the city's aid, and thus leave his position at Asparagium, or allow his Illyrian capital and nearest supply depot to fall into his rival's hands, providing him with his biggest port on the Adriatic.

Caesar had no wish to alert Pompeius as to his intentions, so set off by a circuitous route. Pompeius' scouts, however, soon determined that Caesar was making for Dyrrhachium, which forced Pompeius to break camp and try to intercept the Caesarian army, either barring its path or forcing it into battle. Once again it became a race between the two armies to see who could reach Dyrrhachium first. On this occasion it was Caesar who arrived there first, apparently with Pompeius' army in sight.

Having won the race, however, and forced Pompeius to move from his position at Asparagium, Caesar faced the question of what to do next? With Pompeius' army behind him, he could not lay siege to the city without becoming surrounded, nor would the city submit without a fight due to the large Pompeian garrison and it being surrounded by swampland.

Pompeius understood Caesar's predicament, and having moved his army to stop Caesar making an uncontested attack on Dyrrhachium was under no pressure to give battle. If anything, losing the race to the city seemed to confer more benefits for him. Had Pompeius' army reached the city first, then Caesar would have again been forced to change strategy and march off elsewhere. Now, Caesar had placed himself between the city and Pompeius' army. Whilst Pompeius still had no wish to give battle and would have allowed his opponent to move off unmolested, he deployed a new tactic, one which suited his campaigning style rather than Caesar's. Pompeius set about fortifying his position and occupied the high ground near the coastline of the bay, at a place known as Petra (see Map 4), allowing him access to the sea and to be supplied by his navy.

The tables had again been turned on Caesar, who still found Pompeius unwilling to give battle. Caesar now had a choice of withdrawing or becoming embroiled in an extended face-off. If he withdrew, Caesar had a range of options open to him. To the south lay Pompeius and his fortified position and to the east lay the Adriatic. This effectively left the north and Illyria, which was of no strategic significance, or the west and a push further into Macedonia, where his advance forces were holding the Pompeian army of Metellus Scipio. Yet uncharacteristically, Caesar chose to remain at Dyrrhachium and became drawn into what can only be seen as the ancient world's version of trench warfare.

Caesar later stated that he was worried this would become a drawn-out, prolonged campaign, for which he did not have the resources, with the Pompeian fleet controlling the coast.[7] Yet not only did he commit to this situation but he found himself fighting on Pompeius' terms – slow and grinding – rather than his own. Caesar himself provides no explanation for what was to be a near-disastrous decision, but it must have been borne out of frustration at his opponent's refusal to give battle. As a result, both sides settled down for what was seemed like a stalemate.

The Battle of Dyrrhachium – The Initial Skirmishes

As we have seen, it was Pompeius who was able to choose his ground first, occupying and securing an elevated location at Petra with access to the sea, which became the centre of his position. By doing so, he threw down the challenge to Caesar to either withdraw or attempt to force Pompeius into battle. It was perhaps a measure of Caesar's desperation that he chose the latter and tried to besiege an army holding a fortified position and with secure access to the coast. Caesar's most famous siege had been at Alesia in Gaul (52 BC), one of his most celebrated victories, but the circumstances of this siege were much different, including the Pompeian access to and control of the sea (see Map 4).

Nevertheless, Caesar had limited options at this point. Pompeius was clearly not intending to give battle until Metellus Scipio arrived, and if Caesar had moved his army away and targeted other cities or perhaps made an attack on Metellus, he would find himself shadowed by Pompeius' army, alert for any opportunity to trap him. Furthermore, Caesar was operating in hostile territory that had been under Pompeian control for over a year, and the further he moved into the interior of Greece or Macedon the worse this problem became.

It was for these reasons that Caesar chose to accept Pompeius' challenge and began to lay siege to his army. A major challenge for the siege was the territory itself. Again, the circumstances were as far from Alesia as could be found. The Bay of Dyrrhachium was not a flat one, but was mountainous (see the accompanying image of the Bay and the photographs in Veith's work),[8] so Caesar's siege lines would need to secure the various hilltops that surrounded Pompeius' army, a difficult task at the best of times, never mind when being contested by opposition forces.

To accomplish this, Caesar attempted to create a network of fortifications, stretching some 17 miles, to encircle Pompeius[9] and either starve him out or force the collapse of his army's morale and cause mass defections, the latter of which was seemed more likely given Pompeius' supply lines from the Adriatic. On the face of it, Pompeius had two options: he could attempt to withdraw from the encirclement or oppose it. He wanted to avoid a set-piece battle, and instead focus his forces on disrupting the building of the hilltop forts.

Pompeius could also have withdrawn his forces to the south-east of the bay, but as we discussed, he had no intention of ceding the initiative to Caesar once again, wanting him tied down and unable to besiege his military capital of Dyrrhachium.

Perhaps with one eye on keeping the whole of his army occupied, giving them no time to brood on their position, Pompeius set about building his own line of fortifications. Thus both sides threw up lines of fortifications around the Bay of Dyrrhachium (see Map 4), though we are not told how long this took.

In the meantime, Pompeius committed to disrupting Caesar's men from building their own fortifications, harrying them with long-distance weapons, though no casualty figures are given. Caesar himself provides a commentary on what subsequently descended into daily skirmishes between the two armies, each attempting to harry the other and prevent their fortifications from being completed.[10]

Whilst these minor clashes would not have inflicted heavy casualties in terms of the dead, they would certainly have resulted in an increasing number of injuries.¹¹ Despite this low-level skirmishing, both the Pompeian and Caesarian lines of fortifications were completed, though how long they took is not recorded. Both sides then settled down for a siege.

As previously stated, both sides suffered from supply issues in this unique situation. Caesar's forces, although they controlled access to wider Epirus and Greece, were themselves camped in a hostile country and had no clear supply lines to Caesarian-controlled territory or control of the seas. Pompeius's forces, meanwhile, had access to the Adriatic and being resupplied by sea, but were limited to what could be brought. Caesar's own commentary speaks of a constant stream of ships resupplying Pompeius' army, whilst his own army starved (though here we must be careful of dramatic license).¹²

Caesar's forces had dammed up all the streams that fed into the bay, meaning that Pompeius' army had limited access to fresh water other than what arrived by ship, and were forced to dig temporary wells on the territory they controlled. According to Caesar, this meant that although Pompeius' cavalry survived, the other pack animals perished. Overall, whilst both armies suffered from privations, they were able to endure their respective sieges and the stalemate was not broken by lack of food or water.

The Battle of Dyrrhachium – The Attack on Dyrrhachium

At some point, hoping to break the stalemate, Caesar seems to have switched his attention back to the city of Dyrrhachium, hoping to take it by a surprise attack and with the aid of sympathizers within the city. There is no account of this attack in Caesar's writings, other than reference to battles at Dyrrhachium. This may be down to an unfortunate gap in the surviving manuscripts, meaning that a portion of the text is lost to us. It is equally possible that even if we had a complete text, we would find no detailed description of the attack, due to it being a failure and apparently one that nearly cost Caesar his life. As we have seen throughout this period, Caesar did not like to dwell on defeats in his campaign histories, especially those in which he was personally involved. All we do have is an account by Dio:

'Upon Dyrrhachium itself Caesar made an attempt by night, between the marshes and the sea, in the expectation that it would be betrayed by its defenders. He got inside the narrows, but at that point was attacked both in front and in the rear by large forces which had been conveyed along the shore in boats and very nearly perished himself.'[13]

It seems that Caesar walked into an ambush and was nearly killed. Pompeian forces were waiting for him and had him pinned down between the marshes and the sea on a narrow strip of land. Although this is just a brief account in Dio, the implication is that Caesar had contact with supposed sympathizers inside the city who would open the gates at night and allow the Caesarian forces in. Caesar had already taken the cities of Apollonia and Oricum by betrayal from within rather than siege, and clearly hoped to emulate such tactics here.

However, it is clear that on this occasion the tactic backfired and the 'sympathizers' betrayed his plan to Pompeius, who rowed in additional forces to be stationed outside the city near the marshes to trap Caesar's night-time manoeuvre. We are not told how many men Caesar lost nor how he managed to escape, though Caesar does refer to three battles at Dyrrhachium on the same day. Yet it clearly resulted in a victory for Pompeius, even if Caesar chose not to acknowledge it for posterity.

The Battle of Dyrrhachium – The Battle of the Redoubts

Having foreknowledge of Caesar walking into a trap at Dyrrhachium, Pompeius seems to have planned an offensive campaign on the Caesarian fortifications while their leader was absent. With the two lines of fortifications complete, the situation was, as we have seen, vaguely reminiscent of trench warfare in the First World War, with opposing lines of defences and a no-man's land between them. This analogy is a helpful one, more so than that of a traditional siege, as Pompeius' forces were not trying to break out and escape. Rather than punch a hole in the fortifications where they were weakest, Pompeius chose to focus on what he saw was the key to the whole Caesarian defensive line – the garrisoned redoubts that anchored the defences.

The key to this strategy lay in a surprise attack by Pompeian forces on important redoubts and overwhelming them before reinforcements could arrive. We are told by Caesar that Pompeius chose three redoubts to attack, though not their locations. There is a gap in Caesar's accounts regarding the main Pompeian attack. Nevertheless, it seems that one such redoubt, which appears to have been to the north of Caesar's defensive line and near to his main camp, was being overwhelmed and Caesar's men on the point of defeat: 'In one of these fights in front of a redoubt Caesar's men were worsted.'[14]

Pompeius had hoped that with Caesar trapped in an ambush at Dyrrhachium, and possibly even dead, his main army would be in no position to launch a counterattack against this thrust. Unfortunately for Pompeius, the forces left at the main Caesarian camp were commanded by P. Cornelius Sulla (Cos. 65 BC), the nephew of the Dictator, who had chosen to follow Caesar in the civil war. Caesar's own account resumes at this point:

'Meanwhile P. Sulla, whom Caesar at his departure had put in charge of his camp, being informed of this came to the support of the cohort with two legions; and by his arrival the Pompeians were easily repulsed. In fact, they could not endure the sight or the onset of our men, and when the first of them had been overthrown the rest turned to flight and abandoned the position. But when our men followed, Sulla recalled them lest they should go too far in pursuit.

'As to the Pompeians, their situation caused them great difficulty in retreating; for, having advanced from unfavourable ground, they had halted on the top: if they were to withdraw by the slope, they feared the pursuit of our men from the higher ground, nor was there much time left before sunset, since in the hope of finishing the business, they had prolonged the action almost till nightfall. So Pompeius, of necessity and adapting his plans to the emergency, occupied a certain hill which was so far removed from our fort that a missile discharged from a catapult could not reach it. In this place he sat down and entrenched it and kept all his forces confined there.'[15]

Thus, the main Pompeian attack, led by Pompeius himself, was repulsed by Sulla and his two legions. We are not given the size of Pompeius' forces, though the casualties detailed by Caesar show it was probably more than a legion. Caesar's account also details the other two Pompeian attacks on the redoubts:

> 'At the same time there was fighting in two other places besides, for Pompeius had made attempts on several redoubts with the object of keeping our force equally scattered, so that succour might not be brought from the nearest garrisons. In one place Volcatius Tullus sustained with three cohorts the attack of a legion and drove it from its position; in the other the Germans went out of our lines, and after killing a number of men retired in safety to their comrades.'[16]

So all three Pompeian attacks were beaten off, with Caesar giving casualty figures for the two sides (which again must be taken with a pinch of salt):

> 'Thus six battles having taken place in one day, three at Dyrrhachium and three at the outworks, when account was taken of them all we found that about two thousand in number of the Pompeians had fallen, and very many reservists and centurions; among them was Valerius Flaccus, son of the Lucius who had governed Asia as Praetor; and that six military standards had been brought in. Of our men not more than twenty were lost in all the battles.'[17]

Dio paints a different picture:

> 'After this occurrence [the failed attack on Dyrrhachium] Pompeius took courage and planned a night assault upon the enclosing wall; and attacking it unexpectedly, he captured a portion of it by storm and caused great slaughter among the men encamped near it.'[18]

Overall, the clashes on this day (the date is not recorded) failed to produce a breakthrough, leaving the opposing armies still in a stalemate. Both commanders had been involved in the fighting and both could claim victories; Pompeius at Dyrrhachium and Caesar at his defensive line. Ironically, both were battles that the two commanders were not involved in; Sulla defeating Pompeius and an unknown Pompeian commander defeating Caesar. The result was that Caesar failed to take Dyrrhachium and Pompeius failed to destroy Caesar's fortifications.

Of the two men, however, it would probably have been Pompeius who was the more pleased, as his plan was to maintain the status quo and deny Caesar the initiative, whilst still waiting for the reinforcements with Metellus Scipio. Caesar's attack on Dyrrhachium had been betrayed and failed, and seemingly nearly cost him his life, whilst it was only due to the actions of P. Cornelius Sulla that Pompeius had not broken through his defensive lines and marched on his main camp. Caesar reports that after fending off these attacks he moved his army out of camp into the no-man's land and offered battle, perhaps showing his desperation. Pompeius marched his own army out of camp in an equal show of marital strength (and to maintain morale), but as usual refused to give battle.

The Battle of Dyrrhachium – The Decisive Clash

When dealing with the details of the final and decisive clashes of the Battle of Dyrrhachium, we inevitably encounter the issue that the most detailed account is the one written by the loser. Caesar's account begins to signal to the reader that a defeat is coming when he shifts the focus to a story narrating the treachery once again of 'perfidious foreigners'.

On this occasion it was two Gallic chieftains, Roucillus and Egus from the Allobroges tribe,[19] who defected from his army to Pompeius and apparently betrayed the best location to attack. In Caesar's mind it was this foreign treachery that cost him the battle, not Pompeius' tactical acumen in spotting a weak link in the fortifications, and nor could there be the possibility that the fault lay in Caesar's own tactical ability.

Naturally, Caesar chose to labour the point that Pompeius' army was the one feeling the pressure of the deadlock, stressing the supply issues he was facing, in this case a shortage of fodder for his cavalry, and that his army was suffering from defections to Caesar's army, but that prior to the Allobroges chieftains there were no defections from Caesars' army. Caesar's account dwells on the individual failings of the two Gallic chiefs, who apparently suffered from arrogance and avarice and were embezzlers.

We have a wonderful double standard here; when Pompeius' men defect to Caesar it is perfectly natural as his army was under pressure, but when Caesar's men go over to Pompeius it can't be because Caesar's army is under pressure and they believe he may lose; it has to be due to their personal moral defects. Cutting through this arrogance, the fact is that a large contingent of Caesar's Gallic allies abandoned his cause and defected to Pompeius. We are not given the size of this force, but Caesar himself admits that they left with 'a great retinue and many animals',[20] along with a considerable sum of money. It appears that after several months of deadlock at Dyrrhachium, the pressure was being felt on both armies, with both sides suffering from deflections.

Though the stalemate and delay had been more acceptable to Pompeius' overall strategy than that of Caesar, it seems that Pompeius again chose to take the initiative and planned a large-scale attack on Caesar's fortifications. Though he was still awaiting the arrival of Metellus, his army was struggling with supply issues and would inevitably be suffering from a morale problem, having been pinned in the Bay of Dyrrhachium for several months and perhaps becoming dubious about the arrival of Metellus. The high-profile defections of some of Caesar's Gallic allies would definitely have been a morale boost to Pompeius, and may have been the decisive factor in the timing of his assault, suggesting that morale in Caesar's army was just as fragile.

Having been repulsed in his attack on Caesar's redoubts, Pompeius chose a fresh target and highlighted where he believed Caesar's line to be weakest – where the fortifications met the sea to the south, furthest away from Caesar's main camp and on the opposite side of the bay to the city of Dyrrhachium (see Map 4). Pompeius was playing to his strengths and building on the success he had from the 'day of six battles', his only success having come when he used his fleet to carry troops to the marshes which surrounded the city of Dyrrhachium and ambush Caesar.

Pompeius chose to utilise his naval superiority again to ferry troops from his camp and attack the Caesarians in the rear. The attack was timed for dawn and Pompeius had, if we are to believe Caesar, sixty cohorts, or 30,000 men, though this is more than likely a serious exaggeration. The spot he chose had been identified by Caesar as a weak point and was in the process of being reinforced, which may well have spurred Pompeius' decision to attack before it was completed.

Pompeius then launched an overwhelming dawn attack on the Caesarian defences, from both the land and the sea, with only two cohorts of Caesar's Ninth Legion (less than 1,000 men) defending the seaward approach. Caesar himself details the attack:

Pompeius Victorious – The Battle of Dyrrhachium (48 BC)

'For two cohorts of the Ninth Legion being on sentry duty by the sea, the Pompeians suddenly approached at early dawn; at the same time soldiers conveyed round on shipboard began to hurl javelins at the outer stockade, the ditches were being filled up with earth, the Pompeian legionaries, having brought up ladders, were terrifying the defenders of the inner line with engines of every kind and missiles, and a great multitude of archers were being thrown around them on every side. But the osier coverings placed on their helmets protected them to a great extent from the blows of stones, which were the only weapon our men had. And so when our men were being hard pressed in every way and with difficulty holding their ground, the defect, mentioned above, of the line of entrenchment became observable and between the two stockades, where the work was not yet finished, the Pompeians, disembarking, took our men in the rear on both sides and dislodging them from each line, compelled them to take to flight.'[21]

It appears that the Pompeians landed with overwhelming force at dawn, taking the defenders by surprise and punching their way through a weak point in the Caesarian defences. On the previous occasion when Pompeians had broken through the defences, they were repelled by reinforcements from the nearest Caesarian camp. On this occasion, P. Cornelius Lentulus Marcellinus, the Caesarian commander of the Ninth Legion, also dispatched additional forces to try to force the Pompeians back, but these were overwhelmed by a combination of the sheer weight of Pompeian numbers (who on this occasion were attacking on flat ground) and the flight of the Caesarian defenders, making a sustained stand impossible. Having poured through the breach, the Pompeians made for the nearest Caesarian camp, that of Marcellinus and the Ninth.

A complete collapse of the Caesarian position was only prevented by the arrival of M. Antonius, who was the nearest Caesarian commander to the Ninth Legion, along with twelve cohorts (just under 6,000 men). He was supported by Caesar himself and additional reinforcements, having been alerted by pre-arranged smoke signals that a breach had occurred.

Again it seems that no pitched battle occurred, with the Pompeians happy to consolidate their newly won position, allowing Pompeius to build a fresh camp next to the sea and improve his supply lines. Likewise, Caesar appears to have accepted that he did not have sufficient forces to mount a counterattack and reclaim his defensive positions, given the strength of the Pompeian forces and their naval support. Caesar chooses not to provide the numbers of his troops lost in the engagement, a sure sign that they were extensive, merely saying that there was a great slaughter of his men. He does, however, provide an example of the fate of one unit, saying that 'all the Centurions of the first cohort were slain except the senior Centurion of the second maniple'.[22]

With Pompeius having broken through the Caesarian lines and improved his access to the sea, not to mention having gained a morale-boosting victory, Caesar was faced with two choices: he could either attempt to dislodge Pompeius or abandon the whole Dyrrhachium campaign. With no other viable option, he chose to continue with the campaign and made plans to try to evict the Pompeians from their newly won territory. This would need to be done quickly, before Pompeius was able to consolidate his control of the coastal area, improve his supply lines and undermine Caesar's whole 'trench warfare'/siege tactics.

To these ends, Caesar created a new forward base close to the Pompeian army and waited for an opportunity to counterattack. The chance came within a matter of days when Caesar's scouts reported that the Pompeians were creating a new forward base by enlarging a previously built smaller camp, it being manned by only one legion at the moment. Caesar determined on a surprise attack before the new camp could be finished, quietly amassing a force of thirty-three cohorts (just under 16,000 men, assuming they were at full strength). Caesar chose to lead the attack himself and provides a first-hand description.[23]

On the face of it, Caesar's strategy had succeeded, leading a characteristically bold surprise attack on the Pompeian forward camp and disrupting Pompeius' plans. Yet as was often the case, Caesar's boldness had left him exposed. Whilst he had some 15,000 men and possession of the half-built forward camp, the Pompeian legion, though pinned down and heavily outnumbered, continued to fight and contest possession of the camp. Caesar was now effectively in no-man's land, between his main army and that of Pompeius, and had not yet secured control of his newly won possession, though without Pompeian reinforcements that was clearly only a matter of time. When news of this attack and the fact that his legion still fought on reached Pompeius, he realized that this represented an opportunity. If he did nothing, then his legion would be destroyed and put to flight and he would lose his forward base, which would effectively reverse the gains he had recently made. Furthermore, he would have understood that this was one of Caesar's characteristic bold moves and that he did not have his full army present.

Consequently, Pompeius acted with uncharacteristic boldness and went on the counterattack, advancing on Caesar's position with five legions and cavalry (outnumbering Caesar by at least 10,000 men). Even if his defending legion had been overwhelmed, there was every chance that Caesar would still be exposed in advance of his main army and would not have had time to secure the forward base from a counterstrike.

Indeed, Pompeius found Caesar with fewer numbers and bottled up in the Pompeian camp rather than in the open field. The counterattack succeeded and the Caesarian army collapsed into a rout. Outnumbered and trapped in the camp, and with the surviving Pompeian legion there also attacking, they were denied the freedom of battlefield movement that they were so successful at utilizing. Fearful of being bottled up and overwhelmed, the morale of Caesar's legion collapsed and his surviving soldiers fled back to the safety of their lines, joined by Caesar himself.

Caesar had suffered a clear defeat, with his army routed. Unlike the setback during the night attack on the city of Dyrrhachium, this one was in full sight of both armies. Caesar provides casualty figures for the defeat, which once again we must treat with caution, admitting to losing nearly 1,000 men and thirty two military standards.[24]

Non-Caesarian Accounts – A Greater Defeat?

As is often the case, Appian's account (written centuries later) contains some significant, and possibly illuminating, differences from Caesar's own version of events. Appian (or whoever his source was)[25] mostly glosses over the detail of the original battle and focusses on the rout, which continued far beyond that recorded by Caesar. In Caesar's account, he is defeated in Pompeius' camp and his army flees, but seemingly is not pursued and makes it safely back to his own lines with minimal casualties. However, according to Appian, not only does Caesar's force from the camp fail to recover their morale and make a stand, but reinforcements drawn from the rest of Caesar's army also lost their discipline and refused to defend Caesar's camp from the advancing Pompeian army.[26]

As this version has Caesar's reinforcements refusing to make a stand and seemingly the whole army in that sector fleeing, Pompeius was allowed to advance unopposed. Another key difference in Appian's account is that this continued lack of resistance led to a 'great slaughter' of Caesar's forces, far more than the 1,000 casualties Caesar himself reports. Though Appian's account was written several hundred years later, he would have been using earlier (and possibly contemporary)[27] sources, and certainly ones not written from the Caesarian point of view. Whilst Appian frequently presents differing versions of battles found in other accounts, on this occasion he is describing events that are noticeably absent from Caesar's own writing.

Caesar details the defeat and rout – he had no alternative, given the number of witnesses and eyewitness accounts, as well as Pompeius' own dispatches – but naturally plays down its impact. So whilst his own attack on Pompeius' camp was defeated, he suggests the wider effects were limited. Yet in the Appianic version, defeat in Pompeius' camp turns into a general rout of his whole army (at least in the southern sector) and his men leave his camp undefended.

Appian also details that Caesar did not institute widespread sanctions, such as decimation, but rather 'he reluctantly punished a few'.[28] Furthermore, Appian presents what purports to be a verbatim discussion between Caesar and his officers about the wisdom of a subsequent attack on Pompeius, who now controlled the south of the bay, and about whether the whole campaign at Dyrrhachium was a mistake, something understandably not found in Caesar's own works:

> 'He privately admonished his friends that it was necessary first for the soldiers to recover from the very great alarm of their recent defeat, and for the enemy to lose something of their present high confidence. He confessed also that he had made a mistake in encamping before Dyrrhachium where Pompeius had abundance of supplies, whereas he ought to have drawn him to some place where he would be subject to the same scarcity as themselves.'[29]

Aside from Appian, our main source for this period is Dio, in whose account the battle is noted by its absence. As we have seen earlier, Dio includes a description of Caesar's failed attack on Dyrrhachium, but seems to combine Pompeius' subsequent night attack on the walls with the final battle:

> 'After this occurrence Pompeius took courage and planned a night assault upon the enclosing wall; and attacking it unexpectedly, he captured a portion of it by storm and caused great slaughter among the men encamped near it.
>
> 'Caesar, in view of this occurrence and because his grain had failed, inasmuch as the whole sea and land in the vicinity were hostile, and because for this reason some had actually deserted, feared that he might either be defeated while watching his adversary or be abandoned by his other followers.'[30]

Plutarch's account of Pompeius does mention the battle and has the same quote as Appian:

> 'In these skirmishes Caesar was for the most part victorious and carried the day; but once he narrowly escaped being utterly crushed and losing his army, for Pompeius made a brilliant fight and at last routed Caesar's whole force and killed two thousand of them. He did not, however, force his way into their camp with the fugitives, either because he could not, or because he feared to do so, and this led Caesar to say to his friends: "Today victory would have been with the enemy if they had had a victor in command."'[31]

Thus, we can see that Plutarch and Appian seem to have shared the same source for this information. We also find an expanded version of this clash in Plutarch's biography of Caesar:

> 'There were constant skirmishes about the fortifications of Pompeius, and in all of them Caesar got the better except one, where there was a great rout of his men, and he was in danger of losing his camp. For when Pompeius attacked not one of Caesar's men stood his ground, but the moats were filled with the slain, and others were falling at their own ramparts and walls, whither they had been driven in headlong flight.

'And though Caesar met the fugitives and tried to turn them back, he availed nothing, and when he tried to lay hold of the standards the bearers threw them away, so that the enemy captured thirty-two of them.'[32]

Plutarch adds further detail to the rout with a story of how close Caesar himself came to being killed, again naturally not found in Caesar's own account:

'Caesar himself, too, narrowly escaped being killed. For as a tall and sturdy man was running away past him, he laid his hand upon him and bade him stay and face about upon the enemy; and the fellow, full of panic at the threatening danger, raised his sword to smite Caesar, but before he could do so Caesar's shield-bearer lopped off his arm at the shoulder.'[33]

Plutarch repeats the famous quote about Pompeius not taking Caesar's camp, though on this occasion he adds detail that there were men within:

'So completely had Caesar given up his cause for lost that, when Pompeius, either from excessive caution or by some chance, did not follow up his great success, but withdrew after he had shut up the fugitives within their entrenchments, Caesar said to his friends as he left them: "Today victory would have been with the enemy, if they had had a victor in command."'[34]

Plutarch's account also has Caesar ruminating on the decisions he had made in the campaign:

'Then going by himself to his tent and lying down, he spent that most distressful of all nights in vain reflections, convinced that he had shown bad generalship. For while a fertile country lay waiting for him, and the prosperous cities of Macedonia and Thessaly, he had neglected to carry the war thither, and had posted himself here by the sea, which his enemies controlled with their fleets, being thus held in siege by lack of provisions rather than besieging with his arms. Thus his despondent thoughts of the difficulty and perplexity of his situation kept him tossing upon his couch, and in the morning, he broke camp.'³⁵

As always, we must lament the loss of Livy and his narrative of these events. Nevertheless, we do have Orosius, a much later source but one believed to have been based on Livy:

'Meanwhile at Dyrrhachium, a large number of Oriental Kings came bringing support for Pompeius. When Caesar arrived, he besieged Pompeius in vain, for although he dug a ditch fifteen miles long, the seas lay open to Pompeius. Pompeius destroyed a strongpoint by the sea guarded by Marcellinus and killed Caesar's garrison posted there. Caesar set out to take Torquatus and his single legion by storm. Pompeius, realising his allies' danger, concentrated his forces there, upon which Caesar abandoned his siege and immediately marched against him. Torquatus then sallied forth and attacked his rearguard. This led to Caesar's troops panicking at their sudden danger and they fled, while Caesar vainly tried to rally them. Pompeius, whom Caesar admits was the victor, then recalled his army. 4,000 of Caesars' troops, 22 centurions, and a good number of Roman knights were killed in this battle.'³⁶

As is usually found with Orosius, we have additional details not found in other accounts. Whilst we have the key attack by Pompeius on the coastal fort, guarded by P. Cornelius Lentulus Marcellinus, we also have further details for the subsequent battle. Orosius seems to confirm that the Pompeian legion which was holding the forward base was commanded by L. Manlius Torquatus. More importantly, he preserves a crucial difference to the account of the subsequent battle found in Caesar's writing. Here, it is Caesar who broke off the siege of the base and marched on Pompeius, rather than Pompeius' forces attacking Caesar whilst he was still in the base. Orosius says Caesar was undone by Torquatus attacking his forces from the rear whilst he was confronting Pompeius, and it was this that caused his army to panic and rout. In this tradition, therefore, it was Caesar's decision to break off the siege and confront Pompeius that was responsible for the defeat, not his army being caught in unfavourable topography.

Orosius, who does have a good reputation for reporting accurate losses – thanks to the sources he used – has the highest figure for numbers killed amongst the Caesarian forces, at more than 4,000. So once again we can see a variant tradition at play amongst the histories written of this period that has Caesar clearly defeated.

The Impact of the Battle

Analyzing the impact of the Battle of Dyrrhachium depends to an extent on which account you choose to follow, as they vary from the minor reversal in Caesar to the major defeat in Appian. What is clear, however, is that whatever version is followed, Caesar's strategy of besieging Pompeius in the Bay of Dyrrhachium had failed. Pompeius had broken through Caesar's siege lines to the south of the bay, by the sea, and established a forward base which had then been secured, having driven off Caesar's counterattack. If we follow the Appianic tradition, then Caesar's entire army in the area had been driven off, leading to the total collapse of Caesar' siege lines in the south of the bay.

We either have Pompeius securing a bridgehead through Caesar's lines, or Pompeius driving a massive hole through them. In either event, Pompeius' army would now have a clear route through to open countryside beyond the bay, rendering Caesar's attempts at a siege null and void. The critical issue would be what happened next for the two armies, both of which had endured the privations of several months of siege warfare. Yet it would have been clear to everyone there that Pompeius was the victor, as Caesar himself begrudgingly admits:

> 'In this battle Pompeius received the appellation of Imperator. To this title he adhered and afterwards allowed himself to be saluted as such, but he was never wont to use the ascription in his dispatches, nor did he display the insignia of the laurel on his fasces.'[37]

Summary – Advantage Pompeius

Ultimately, whilst the victory at Dyrrhachium was a bonus, it did not change Pompeius' overall strategy. This still called for awaiting the arrival of his Eastern army commanded by Metellus Scipio, and only then facing

Caesar in a set-piece battle to give him the victory he needed over the 'enemy of the Republic' and cement his position as its saviour.

Nevertheless, Dyrrhachium must have greatly heartened Pompeius and convinced him that his strategy was a sound one. During the course of the Dyrrhachium campaign, Caesar had been defeated twice, first during the ambush at Dyrrhachium itself and then in the battle for the southern camp. On both occasions, Caesar's boldness had cost him victory and nearly his life. This would have emphasized in Pompeius' mind that he could exploit Caesar's boldness in a way that his subordinate commanders had failed to do in Spain, and that if he continued his policy of 'giving Caesar enough rope' then he would surely hang himself. Furthermore, Pompeius had now seen first-hand that Caesar's army had broken and fled, something which he would surely factor into plans for any future encounters.

Plutarch reveals that the 'Pompeian' Senate assembled after Dyrrhachium to discuss the future of the campaign, and that a number of the Senators, seemingly led by L. Afranius, advocated an invasion of Italy, just across the Adriatic from the Pompeian position.[38] Though Italy and Rome did stand underdefended, with the bulk of Caesar's legions in Greece, this clearly did not fit in with the Pompeian masterplan and thus was ignored by Pompeius.

The majority of the sources focus on Caesar in the aftermath of the battle, but we can surmise that Pompeius would have re-established his supply lines by land and then awaited the next move by Caesar, confident that time and the momentum of the campaign were on his side.

The opposite was true for Caesar. His immediate priority would have been to regroup his army and calm the legions that had not been present at the battle (which represented the majority of his army). Once that had been achieved, then he needed to rethink his whole strategy.

Dyrrhachium had not merely been a defeat on the battlefield; it had seen his whole strategy of a lightning attack across the Adriatic and an early battle with Pompeius – before Metellus arrived – collapse into a months-long siege which ended with a portion of his army being very publicly routed. He had been drawn into playing out Pompeius' strategy rather than his own. His forces in Greece had met with some success, but mostly due to the Pompeians falling back, and his efforts to slow Metellus had also been successful, but the arrival of Pompeius' reinforcements was now expected sooner rather than later.

Caesar was stuck holding onto fortifications that had now been breached to the south and thus rendered useless, knowing that Pompeius, despite his victory, would still not face him in open battle until Metellus Scipio arrived. When Metellus did arrive, if Caesar held onto his position at Dyrrhachium, it would be he that would be under siege. Caesar had also seen how a portion of his army would react to fighting on such terrain, when they had broken and fled. Consequently, Caesar needed to change the dynamics and regain the momentum that defeat at Dyrrhachium had cost him.

Section II

The Pharsalan Campaign (48 BC)

Part II

The Paraetacene Campaign (318 BC)

Chapter Three

From Dyrrhachium to Pharsalus

Tactical Reappraisals in the Aftermath of Dyrrhachium

As we have seen, the first battle between Pompeius and Caesar had resulted in a victory for Pompeius and a chastening defeat for Caesar. Yet the fundamentals of the campaign remained unchanged for both sides. Of equal importance was the psychological and reputational impact on the two commanders, their armies and supporters. The wider impact of this clash of arms was lessened given that the subsequent battle at Pharsalus came just a month later.

i) Caesar's Strategy after Dyrrhachium

Though defeated at Dyrrhachium, in many ways the loss allowed Caesar to reset his campaign and return to his original aims. He had invaded Epirus and Illyria in January 48 BC to disrupt Pompeius' preparations and bring him to battle before he had had a chance to assemble his whole army, and thus fight on his own terms, not those of Pompeius. Yet Caesar had allowed himself to be dragged into a protracted siege which had gone on for months and was taking as big a toll on his own army as it was on Pompeius', especially given that Pompeius controlled both the city of Dyrrhachium and the Adriatic. In short, he had yet again fallen into Pompeius' trap and had lost all the momentum of his initial thrust. Caesar naturally does not take the blame himself for this; his autobiographical account of the campaign exonerates him and blames his own army, whom he later forgives:

> 'The loss that had been sustained should be attributed to the fault of anyone rather than himself. He had given them a favourable situation for fighting, he had gained possession of the enemy's camp, he had expelled and overcome them in fighting. But whether it was their own nervousness or some blunder, or even a chance of fortune

that had interrupted a victory already won and within their hands, they must all exert themselves to repair by their valour the damage they had sustained.'[1]

Yet with the siege broken, Caesar now had a chance to reset his campaign, re-inject some vigour and once again seize the initiative he had squandered at Dyrrhachium. In truth, he had few other options. He was operating in Pompeian-dominated territory – though the majority of the locals would not have cared one way or another, so long as they were left alone – and he was cut off from the Caesarian-controlled Western Republic by Pompeius' control of the Adriatic. In short, he could not have retreated back to Italy even if he had wanted to. Had he even been able to do so, such a move would have been disastrous both militarily and politically.

Trapped in Greece and effectively sandwiched between two Pompeian armies (Pompeius to the west and Metellus Scipio to the east), he had no option – other than surrender – but to revert to his strategy of disrupting Pompeius' masterplan by knocking out one of the two armies before they had a chance to combine. Having failed to beat Pompeius' army, the only realistic option was to head east and try to bring Metellus' army to battle without getting trapped between them. If he could defeat Metellus, whose army was the weaker of the two given its non-Roman composition, then he could throw Pompeius' plan into chaos and force his rival to either face him directly, on his own, or change tactics completely, buying Caesar valuable time to regroup.

ii) Pompeius' Strategy after Dyrrhachium

Pompeius, on the other hand, had no need to change strategies when his masterplan was reaping such rich rewards. Although the unexpected arrival of Caesar and his army in Epirus had disrupted his plans, the subsequent months had taken the momentum out of Caesar's campaign and restored parity. His own army had certainly suffered at Dyrrhachium, but the losses were worth it when he gained his unexpected victory over Caesar, enhancing his reputation and demonstrating to all, especially those on his own side, that his tactics were the right ones.

His masterplan called for Caesar to be defeated in battle, but Dyrrhachium had not afforded him the circumstances to destroy Caesar's army, as much of it was not present on the southern part of the bay where his minor victory was gained. He needed a grander stage for his victory; one that would be seen by all his allies, Roman and non-Roman alike. Only then would he be able to claim that he had saved the Republic from the 'monster' and cement his unquestioned role as its Princeps. To accomplish that, he believed that he needed the overwhelming support of the additional forces that Metellus was bringing from the East. There was no need to jeopardize his strategy by fighting Caesar before he felt he was ready.

Yet it is possible to see that the victory at Dyrrhachium actually worked against Pompeius, as he would have been perfectly happy to stay there, rooting Caesar to the spot until he was trapped by the arrival of Metellus. Thus, the effect of the victory and the rout of Caesar's forces was slightly tarnished by the fact that Caesar was once more on the offensive and planning an attack on Metellus. Pompeius now faced the difficult balancing act of trying to ensure that Caesar was prevented from attacking Metellus without being brought into battle himself.

Several sources raise the alternative strategy that Pompeius, having defeated Caesar, should have invaded Italy instead of chasing his rival, and in all cases this is ascribed to his commander, L. Afranius.[2] Given Afranius' failures in Spain the previous year, when he had thrown away a potential winning situation against Caesar and lost his armies and the province without a battle, we can well believe that he thought this was the best tactic.

The civil war was never about who controlled Rome, which is why Pompeius so casually discarded it in 49 BC. In fact, Rome having fallen to Caesar only strengthened Pompeius' hand. For Pompeius, the civil war was instead about making Caesar appear the greatest threat to the Republic since Hannibal (or at least Sulla, ironically) and then defeating him in battle. Abandoning Greece and leaving Caesar free to defeat Metellus and the eastern kings, thereby allowing Caesar unchallenged access to the East, all for the hollow prize of holding Italy and Rome, seemed a certain way to invite defeat. So Pompeius moved to link up with the army of Metellus and then face Caesar in battle. Ultimately, this strategy proved to be one of the greatest cases of 'beware of what you wish for' in history.

iii) The Hidden Campaign of Metellus Scipio

One of the fundamental problems of studying the whole campaign in 48 BC is the almost complete absence of detail about Metellus Scipio and his army. All the later surviving sources focus on Pompeius and Caesar; the only surviving contemporaneous source is Caesar himself, and again Metellus was not his focus. This naturally narrows the focus of the whole campaign and does not allow us to see it in its entirety. If not careful, we are reduced to studying a play where one of the key characters is waiting in the wings for his cue and is only referred to 'off-stage'.

That Caesar disrupted the timescale for the joining of the two armies by invading in January 48 BC is clear. Under Pompeius' original plan, Caesar would be wintering in Spain, tied down by Afranius and his fellow commanders. Their collective incompetence and his navy's inability to maintain a blockade on the Adriatic meant that Caesar was in Greece before the two armies had combined. Pompeius was able to communicate with Metellus and order him to set off immediately, after wintering in Asia, but that westward march took time.

The stalemate at Dyrrhachium would have given Metellus the time he needed, but for the fact that, as we have seen, Caesar sent a portion of his army into Macedonia to slow him down. We know that a clash took place between the Caesarian army (commanded by Cn. Domitius Calvinus) and Metellus, and that seemingly Metellus was victorious. However, the subsequent failure of Metellus to arrive at Dyrrhachium between April and July speaks volumes. Either the victory had been less clear-cut than the sources allude to, or, more likely, Domitius continued to slow Metellus' army down.

Nevertheless, despite being slowed down, it is clear, given how quickly he subsequently joined up with Pompeius, that Metellus was nearing Dyrrhachium when Pompeius launched his final decisive attack there. It is also clear that Domitius' army remained between Metellus and Dyrrhachium; according to Caesar, the two sides had been camped facing each other for several days when the news of Dyrrhachium reached them.[3]

It seems that one the dangers facing Metellus came from the propaganda emanating from the aftermath of the Battle of Dyrrhachium. According to Caesar, the Pompeians spread the news that he had been totally defeated and his army destroyed,[4] and for propaganda purposes we can see the logic in this. The danger, of course, lay in Metellus coming to hear such news, meaning he would not have been prepared for a full-scale attack by Caesar's (clearly still intact) army. As it happens, it seems that this danger was averted by Pompeius sending messengers to Metellus directly, informing him of the details of events at Dyrrhachium and that Caesar was now heading in his direction. Presumably, Metellus was also warned not to engage with Domitius, but to detach himself from their standoff, avoid Caesar and join up with Pompeius.

The Greek Campaign – The Four Armies

Thus there were now four Roman armies locked in a strange pattern. On the extremes of this campaign lay the two Pompeian armies, with Pompeius in the west and Metellus in the east, each trying to link up with the other whilst avoiding the two Caesarian armies. Between them lay the army of Caesar, heading eastwards, trying to link up with Domitius and bring Metellus to battle without getting sandwiched between him and Pompeius (see Map 3). Domitius' army lay to the east of Caesar, with orders to link up with his commander but not let Metellus get away.

i) The Withdrawal from Dyrrhachium
The first problem that faced Caesar was to extricate his army from the entrenched positions around Dyrrhachium Bay and set off into the interior of Greece without suffering further casualties at the hands of Pompeius. Whilst Pompeius would not want to engage Caesar in a set-piece battle, he would take great delight in attacking a retreating army, inflicting further casualties and damaging its morale.

We have Caesar's own account of his army's withdrawal, which took place at night to try to avoid detection.[5] Caesar utilized the few strategic assets he had in Epirus and Illyria, notably the handful of coastal cities he had taken in the early months of 48 BC, which he still held, and which whilst blockaded by sea were still open on the landward side. The nearest and strongest of these cities was Apollonia.

Under cover of darkness, Caesar dispatched his baggage train with one legion to set out to cover the short distance to Apollonia, which lay to the south (see Map 3). They were soon followed by the bulk of the army, leaving two legions behind in camp to create the impression that Caesar's troops were still at rest.

However, this ruse seems to have been anticipated by Pompeius, who soon broke camp with his army in pursuit. With Caesar having a head start and travelling lightly, due to the baggage train having gone on ahead, he hoped he could outpace Pompeius' army. Pompeius responded by sending ahead a cavalry force (of unknown size) to catch up with and engage Caesar's rearguard. Despite the swiftness of his retreat, Caesar's army was slowed down crossing the River Genusus (the modern Shkumbin), which was where Pompeius' cavalry caught up with the rearguard.

ii) The Clash at the River Genusus – A Taste of Things to Come

Wasting little time, Pompeius' cavalry attacked Caesar's rearguard, but either word got to Caesar or, as seems more likely given the composition of the force, he had anticipated problems at the river and had kept additional troops in reserve for just such a circumstance:

> 'But when they [Caesar's army] reached the River Genusus, with its difficult banks, the cavalry following up engaged and hindered the rearguard. Caesar opposed his own horsemen to them, mixing with them four hundred light-armed front-rank men, who gained such success that, engaging in a cavalry skirmish, they repelled them all, slaying many, and withdrew unhurt to the main body.'[6]

This clash is noteworthy in two aspects. Firstly, in the immediate context, Pompeius' pursuit was beaten off and Caesar's men were able to continue their withdrawal in safety. The second point to note is the composition of the force Caesar used to beat off Pompeius' cavalry, an interesting mixture of cavalry and lightly armed infantry, which proved so effective against them. Given the turning point in the battle which followed, it is tempting to look back to this clash and see the genesis of the concept that Caesar seems to have developed, namely a method of negating Pompeius' superior cavalry numbers. The key seems to have been the adoption of specialist anti-cavalry tactics by mixing lightly armed soldiers, presumably with javelins, amongst his own cavalry, creating a blended force.

iii) A Short Game of Cat and Mouse

Though Caesar had defeated Pompeius' cavalry attack on his rearguard, he had only bought himself a short respite as his rival's army still shadowed his movements. Caesar himself sets out the manoeuvres that followed in subsequent days.[7] Both sides reoccupied the fortifications they had left behind from the pre-Dyrrhachium period of the campaign, and Caesar constantly had to use darkness or ruses to try and gain a time and distance advantage over the pursuing Pompeius. Caesar states that by such ploys he was able to keep his army clear of the pursuit, and it seems that Pompeius' cavalry did not attempt to attack Caesar's rearguard again.[8]

Caesar adds that after four days Pompeius gave up his pursuit.[9] This was a sensible move on Pompeius' part, as he had been unable to inflict any casualties on Caesar's army and was in danger of playing 'follow the leader' and being drawn into adopting Caesar's tactics rather than his own. It must have been clear to Pompeius that Caesar was heading for the few cities he held, the largest being Apollonia, and not striking directly inland into Thessaly in search of Metellus and Domitius.

Though justified in terms of attending to his wounded, strengthening the garrisons of the cities he held and ensuring the loyalty of these places (given that news of the defeat at Dyrrhachium would have reached them), this move cost Caesar time.[10]

Having gauged Caesar's intentions and being unable to inflict any meaningful damage on Caesar, Pompeius changed tactics, broke off the pursuit and set off inland into Thessaly himself, having no need to replicate Caesar's delay to secure his position or waste time trying to assault those cities loyal to Caesar. Caesar had to delay briefly in Apollonia, as he states, to deposit his wounded, pay his troops and strengthen his garrisons. This meant leaving behind up to 4,000 of his troops:

> '… leaving a garrison of four cohorts at Apollonia, one at Lissus, and three at Oricum, and depositing at various places those who were suffering from wounds.'[11]

iv) A Dangerous Four-way Dance
Both Caesar and Pompeius had set out eastwards through Epirus into Thessaly in a strange game of hide and seek, with four armies caught in a complex web of manoeuvres, simultaneously trying to link up with their opposite numbers whilst trying to prevent their opponents from doing so, with four sets of scouts and messengers searching for the other forces. For Caesar, the ideal outcome would have been to link up with Domitius and then attack Metellus before Pompeius arrived, though he would probably have attacked Metellus with or without Domitius. The intentions of

Pompeius are less clear; would he have preferred to attack Domitius first or link up with Metellus?

Thus, two armies were heading eastwards, two heading westwards, all seemingly on a collision course and trying to co-ordinate with their opposite numbers. Having abandoned the pursuit of Caesar, Pompeius technically had a head start, but had further to travel and had the issue of Domitius likely being between himself and Metellus.

Having abandoned pursuit of Caesar, Pompeius could more easily reach the Via Egnatia and use it to march rapidly inland. Whilst we are not explicitly told this, Caesar does state that Pompeius marched towards Candavia, itself on the Via Egnatia.[12] Caesar, avoiding Pompeius, seems to have travelled further southwards, not using the one Roman road in the region. The problem for Caesar's strategy is that of the four armies, he was now last in line, behind Pompeius, Domitius and Metellus. Not only did this make combining with Domitius more difficult, but it also meant that it was highly unlikely that he would be able to attack Metellus before he met up with Pompeius, thus collapsing his initial strategy within days.

Caesar reports that this set of manoeuvres nearly resulted in disaster for his forces when Domitius, apparently having broken away from shadowing Metellus (perhaps having heard the news of Dyrrhachium), was marching directly into the path of Pompeius (perhaps also using the Via Egnatia). Caesar records that a catastrophe was only averted when Domitius' scouts encountered Allobrogan scouts employed by Pompeius, having defected from Caesar during the Battle of Dyrrhachium:[13]

> 'But the Allobroges, friends of Roucillus and Egus, who, as we have explained, had deserted to Pompeius, having seen on the route some scouts of Domitius, either by reason of their old intimacy because they had waged war together in Gaul, or in the elation of vainglory, set before them everything that had happened, and told them of the departure of Caesar and the arrival of Pompeius. Domitius, who was scarcely four hours ahead, receiving this information from them, escaped his peril thanks to the foe.'[14]

It seems that thus forewarned, Domitius avoided marching straight into the army of Pompeius, which would have resulted in his destruction, and was able to swing southwards into Thessaly, on a parallel course to the direction of Caesar's travel (see Map 3). So the two Caesarian armies were now to the south, whilst the Pompeian armies were to the north. Given the shorter distances involved, the Caesarian armies were now seemingly able to coordinate their directions and joined together in Thessaly at the town of Aeginium (see Map 3).

This short period of manoeuvrings thus resulted in mixed fortunes for Caesar. On the one hand, the army of Domitius had avoided being destroyed by Pompeius and had been able to unify with him once more, adding anything up to two legions.[15] On the other hand, his plan to confront Metellus was now in ruins and he would not be able to prevent the two Pompeian armies from also uniting. Nevertheless, this meant that Pompeius would now be confident enough to face Caesar in battle, heavily outnumbering him.

v) Waiting for Pompeius – The Sack of Gomphi

With his armies united and with the Pompeian armies still to the north, Caesar seems to have changed tactics once again. Rather than immediately move northwards to prevent the Pompeian forces from uniting, Caesar seems to have now preferred to remain in Thessaly and await the arrival of Pompeius and Metellus. To this end he set about securing the resources of the region for his army and building up his forces' strength.

Caesar moved to secure the city of Gomphi, on the Thessalian-Epirote border, a place of strategic significance that guarded the route between the two provinces and dominated the plains of Thessaly. The city had previously been attacked by Rome during the Second Romano-Macedonian War (198 BC) to secure dominance of the region. Throughout the campaign to date, the cities of the region, even those with Pompeian garrisons, had chosen to remain neutral in the war and admit whichever Roman army was nearest, rather than risk an attack. On this occasion, however, reflecting the perceived shift in power brought about by Caesar's defeat at Dyrrhachium, the prefect of Gomphi, Androsthenes, chose to refuse Caesar entry (thereby gaining the favour of Pompeius) and braced the city for a siege.

More importantly, he sent urgent messengers northwards to find Pompeius and Metellus and reveal the location of at least Caesar's army, if not both Caesarian armies. Upon hearing this news, it seems that both

Pompeius and Metellus turned southwards to attempt to intercept their enemies.

With Gomphi being barred to him, Caesar was determined to make an example of the city and let his men vent some of the frustration that had been building since Dyrrhachium. The city fell within a day and was sacked by Caesar's troops, who according to several sources became roaringly drunk and in no fit state to continue, something which Caesar omits from his own account.[16]

With the fate of Gomphi in their minds, none of the other cities or towns in western Thessaly provided any further resistance, meaning Caesar was able to gather food and resources for his army. We know that once recovered, they continued their journey south and took the city of Metropolis (see Map 3). Caesar made no move towards the north of Thessaly and the approach of the two Pompeian armies.

Even in his autobiographical account of the campaign, Caesar does not provide us with an insight into his thinking, yet we can speculate. Having abandoned the strategy of attacking Metellus before he could combine with Pompeius, and being on the backfoot in this campaign, he seemed determined to gamble everything on one battle with Pompeius, which he now must have acknowledged would only happen when Pompeius combined with Metellus. Having that in mind, all that remained was to rebuild the strength and morale of his army and to search for a suitable battleground. He decided that it would be on the plains of Thessaly where he would meet his fate, and thus prepared for the arrival of Pompeius and Metellus.

vi) An End to the Prelude – The Pompeian Armies Unite

Having failed (narrowly) to locate the army of Domitius, Pompeius must have been moving towards Metellus when messengers reached him from Gomphi. Given how close he had been to Domitius, his own scouts may well have been following Domitius' trail to the south. As is usual in this campaign, we have no detail on Metellus' movements, or whether he was prioritizing looking for Domitius and Caesar over meeting with Pompeius. What we are told, by Caesar, is that Metellus struck southwards first, being the nearest, and marched away from the Via Egnatia into Thessaly.

He presumably took the coastal route, crossed onto the eastern end of the Thessalian plain (see Map 3) and headquartered his army at Larissa, the largest city in Thessaly. It was here that he waited for the arrival of his son-in-law Pompeius, rather than move against Caesar. Pompeius and his army duly arrived several days later, and finally, nearly seven months since the unexpected arrival of Caesar in Illyria in January, Pompeius' masterplan came to fruition and the two halves of his army united.

The problem Pompeius now faced, and one which is ignored by our surviving sources, was the amount of time available to him to unify the two very different elements of his army: the Roman legions of Pompeius and the eastern forces of Metellus. The issue here was that although Pompeius had more than twice Caesar's numbers, he needed time to unify them into a coherent fighting force. So although it seemed that the long-awaited clash between Pompeius and Caesar – eighteen months since the crossing of the Rubicon – would take place on the plains of Thessaly, there remained the key question of where and when.

Committing to Battle

i) The Choice of Pharsalus – Caesar's New Plan

Unfortunately, thanks to the poor state of the surviving sources, we are far from clear on both where and when that momentous clash would be. What we do know is that the battle took place on the plain of Pharsalus, which lay east of Metropolis (Caesar's last recorded position) and south of Larissa (the site of Pompeius' two armies). Exactly where on the plain this battle happened remains a mystery to this day (see Chapter Four).[17] The clearest statement we have about the location is when Appian mentions that it was fought 'between the city of Pharsalus and the River Enipeus'.[18]

One of the problems we have is that there were two cities thus named in antiquity, old and new Pharsalus,[19] and a number of the later accounts refer to the battle being fought near old Pharsalus (Palaepharsalus).[20] The key issues relating to the site of the battle have been covered in detail by Morgan.[21] Another key aspect to the battle site is just who chose it? Here, surprisingly, Caesar sheds no light on the matter, his narrative jumping from his preparations in Metropolis to the two armies drawing up to face each other. The only source that does mention the choice of Pharsalus and the timescale is again Appian:

'After seven days of rapid marching Caesar encamped near Pharsalus.'[22]

Both of Appian's statements are revealing. Firstly, he implies that it was again Caesar taking the initiative and marching from Metropolis towards the Pompeian armies at Larissa. The second point to note is that he did so at speed. This takes us back to Caesar's original plan post-Dyrrhachium, in which he seemingly wanted to defeat Metellus' army before it had a chance to combine with Pompeius. Interestingly, there must have been a short period when Metellus' arrival in Thessaly revived this plan, with Pompeius being some days behind him and coming from further north on the Via Egnatia. Yet had Caesar advanced all the way to Larissa to confront him, Metellus would have either hunkered down for a siege or withdrawn to the north.

As it turned out, and as Caesar may have expected – assuming his scouts were searching for Pompeius' army – this window of opportunity was only a short one and Pompeius soon arrived in Thessaly. Yet there was still a chance for Caesar to strike quickly. He had spent the last seven months trying to bring Pompeius to battle before the two armies combined, and although they now physically occupied the same location, he would have realized that it would take some time for Pompeius to achieve this unification of his forces in practice; there was still a slight, albeit diminishing, window in which to force the battle, before Pompeius had accomplished this amalgamation to his satisfaction.

This would account for the rush towards Pompeius' position and the initial reluctance of Pompeius to fight that are reported in most of the major surviving sources. He did not yet judge his unified army to be sufficiently combined; it was not that he did not want to face Caesar in battle. Thus it seems that Caesar again gambled on disrupting Pompeius' masterplan, even at this late stage, and threw down the gauntlet to his rival once more by going on the offensive and advancing towards him, choosing the site for their clash and making a very public offer of battle.

ii) Pompeius' Dilemma

Here we see the horns of Pompeius' dilemma. After seven months, his two armies were finally united, and Caesar was offering battle despite being outnumbered nearly two to one. Furthermore, he now not only had the majority of the Senate in his entourage, but also most of the kings and representatives from Rome's Eastern Empire, an empire he had forged only two decades earlier.[23] But had he had sufficient time to combine the two very different halves of his army in order to face Caesar and his veterans? He may have had the numbers, but could they be relied upon to fight as a cohesive army?

His original plan had been only to fight Caesar when this 'grand army' had been forged together as a single force and properly trained in unified manoeuvres, with the language problems alone being many. This plan had called for Caesar to be tied down in Spain or trapped in Italy, not advancing towards him in Thessaly. Throughout the year, he had been able to stall Caesar by refusing to fight him and then tying him down in the months-long siege at Dyrrhachium.

However, the reasons he must have used to explain his actions – waiting for Metellus and the Eastern army – were now exhausted, and on paper he now had an army twice the size of Caesar's. Furthermore, Caesar had already been defeated once and his army routed (at least in the view of the Pompeians). Pompeius was now seemly trapped by his own masterplan. Due to his early political manipulations and subsequent propaganda, Caesar was seen as the enemy of the Republic; another bloodthirsty tyrant who would overthrow the Republican system and create a bloody tyrannical rule. Pompeius had been chosen to defeat the menace and 'save the Republic', using Caesar's corpse as a steppingstone to a more subtle form of sole rule, as Princeps; first amongst equals.

Yet the months he required to unify the various elements of his army into one cohesive fighting force had now been reduced to days, and the pressure on him – from both his own plan and from others – would have been intense. Nevertheless, there was only ever going to be one person who would determine when Pompeius was ready to fight, and that was himself.

iii) Did Pompeius have to Fight Caesar at Pharsalus?

There is a well-known historical tradition represented in many of the surviving sources that Pompeius did not need to fight Caesar at Pharsalus, and that he was pressured into it against his better judgement. We have no way of knowing when this tradition started or even its original source – Caesar being the only surviving contemporaneous source – but we do know of other contemporary histories written by Pompeian allies. The intent of this tradition is clear enough; to exonerate Pompeius, the Roman Alexander and 'defender of the Republic', from being defeated by Caesar, seemingly so easily and so comprehensively, and allowing the Republic to fall to the 'tyrannical clutches' of Caesar.

According to this school of thought, it was not Pompeius' fault, but that of his allies who forced the battle on him, against his better judgement; if they had only listened to him, then the Republic would have been saved. As we have seen, this is a pipe dream on both counts. Pompeius needed to defeat Caesar in battle; there was no other way if he wanted to assume sole power in Rome himself. Furthermore, Pompeius was not the sort of man who would be pressured into anything he had not decided upon himself. Yet did this mean that Pompeius was chomping at the bit to attack Caesar immediately? This must ultimately sit behind the reported reluctance to rush to Pharsalus and give battle. As is common, both Appian and Plutarch (first/second-century AD writers) repeat this tradition:

> 'Although this was the best possible advice Pompeius disregarded it and allowed himself to be persuaded by those who said that Caesar's army would presently desert to him on account of hunger, or that there would not be much left of it anyway after the victory of Dyrrhachium. They said it would be disgraceful to abandon the pursuit of Caesar when he was in flight, and for the victor to flee as though vanquished. Pompeius sided with these advisers partly out of regard for the opinions of the eastern nations that were looking on.'[24]
>
> 'With these and many similar speeches they forced Pompeius from his settled purpose, a man who was a slave to fame and loath to disappoint his friends, and dragged him into following after their own hopes and impulses, abandoning his best laid plans.'[25]
>
> 'For Pompeius himself was cautious about hazarding a battle for so great a stake, and since he was most excellently provided with everything necessary for a long war, he thought it best to wear out and quench the vigour of the enemy, which must be short-lived.'[26]

As we have seen, the arguments put forward by the historians and their sources, namely that Caesar's army would desert him or be starved into submission, are nonsense. Caesar's army had recovered from the defeat at Dyrrhachium, which had only affected a certain part of his force, not the whole (most not having been present). The danger of starvation was not a likely one either, given the example Caesar had made of the city of

Gomphi and that thereafter no other town or city would fail to supply his army.

Furthermore, Pompeius had twice the number of troops as Caesar and seven times as many cavalry to feed. If Caesar's army was allowed to roam Greece unchecked, then it could live off the land. Had Pompeius continued to shadow Caesar but failed to give battle (adopting Fabian tactics), this would have shown Caesar's army that Pompeius feared them, enhancing their morale whilst undermining that of Pompeius' own army and political supporters.

So did Pompeius need to fight Caesar and defeat him in battle? The short answer is yes, as without a decisive victory over the enemy of the Republic he would not be able to cement his position as saviour of Rome. As for whether Pompeius needed to fight Caesar here in Thessaly, again the answer must be yes, as allowing Caesar to withdraw would seem weak and jeopardize his position as undisputed leader of the non-Caesarian Republic.

But did that mean that he needed to fight Caesar here and now at Pharsalus? That is something that only Pompeius knew, based on his understanding of the readiness of his newly unified army. Ultimately, the decision was Pompeius' alone, and he seems to have judged the prize to be worth the risks, although that would not have stopped him from worrying about the readiness of his whole army. Pompeius therefore ordered his army from Larissa to the plains of Pharsalus and camped some 30 *stades* (3–4 miles) away from Caesar, apparently occupying some high ground, foothills of the nearby mountains.[27]

iv) The Standoff

Even at this late stage, Pompeius did not seem to be in a rush to engage Caesar, no doubt using the time to assess the competence of his army in its first full battle formation. Whilst Caesar apparently occupied the plain of Pharsalus, Pompeius took a more cautious approach and took up a defensive position on the foothills (according to Caesar),[28] giving him the tactical advantage. This position gave Pompeius the initiative and placed the decision whether or not to fight firmly in his own hands. If Caesar wanted to force the issue and attack him, he would have to do so against a defensive position on hilly ground and against a superior force, something he was not likely to do.

What followed was a series of cat and mouse manoeuvres which seem to have gone on for several days, though we are not told exactly how long; Caesar merely states 'subsequent days'.[29] According to Caesar, he took the initiative each day and marched his army towards Pompeius' position, but in such a disposition that Pompeius would have to leave the safety of the hills and fight on the plain:

> 'And so he [Caesar] led his army out of the camp and drew up his lines, first of all in a position favourable to himself and some little distance from the camp of Pompeius, but on subsequent days advancing away from his own camp and pushing his line up to the foot of the hills held by the Pompeians.'[30]

Pompeius, by contrast, was in no rush to fight Caesar on his own terms, and so held off, not leaving the safety of the foothills his army was occupying:

> 'Pompeius, who had his camp on the hill, kept drawing up his line on the lowest spurs of the mountain, apparently always waiting to see whether Caesar would approach close up to the unfavourable ground.'[31]

Such events suggest that Pompeius was waiting to see how far (literally in this case) Caesar would go. Caesar himself admits that each day he got a little closer to Pompeius' camp. Here we have a microcosm of the whole campaign to date, with Caesar impatient for battle and Pompeius patiently waiting until he judged the time was right, seeing whether his opponent would make a mistake. Furthermore, the longer Pompeius held Caesar at Pharsalus, the stronger his position would be. As Appian points out, Pompeius had ensured that his logistical operation would keep his army well stocked, with resources pouring in from across Greece:

> 'Pompeius' supplies came from every quarter, for the roads, harbours, and strongholds had been so provided beforehand that food was brought to him at all times from the land, and every wind blew it to him from the sea. Caesar, on the other hand, had only what he could find with difficulty and seize by hard labour.'[32]

Caesar's army had no such logistical structure and would have been burning through the supplies he had taken from the cities along the way – Gomphi, Metropolis – forcing his army to forage at night to avoid Pompeius' cavalry. Indeed, Appian tells us: 'That same night three of Caesar's legions started out to forage.'[33] Thus, whilst Pompeius' men were well supplied and fresh, Caesar's forces had to spend their nights searching for food, tiring them out before the next day. Once again, it seemed that Caesar found himself dancing to Pompeius' tune.

v) The Initial Skirmishes

Whilst a full-scale battle had so far been avoided, there were clashes between the two forces. Caesar is once more the only source for these encounters, but according to him there was a skirmish between the two sets of cavalry in the days before the battle:

> 'For even on those days he fought a successful cavalry skirmish and killed among some others one of the two Allobrogians who, as we explained above, had deserted to Pompeius.'[34]

Again we have no details as to numbers, and Caesar's narrative is clearly boasting about the new method he was using to fight Pompeius' superior cavalry:

> '[Caesar] gave orders that lightly equipped youths from among the first-rank men, with arms selected with a view to fleetness, should go into battle among the cavalry, so that by daily practice they might win experience in this kind of fighting also.'[35]

As he had previously demonstrated at the clash by the River Genusus, Caesar here compensated for his inferior numbers of cavalry by creating a mixed cavalry/infantry unit, which seemingly scored a second minor victory. It is tempting to see Caesar here advertising his new anti-cavalry tactics to Pompeius and believe that the latter should have taken note. Yet we do not know how much of Caesar's narrative reflected the situation at the time and how much had been rewritten with the benefit of hindsight. Furthermore, we only have Caesar's word that his forces were successful. Nevertheless, it does appear that Pompeius' cavalry were not overwhelming the smaller number of Caesar's horsemen, even in small clashes.

vi) Pompeius' Final Decision

It is not clear, even from Caesar's own narrative, how long this game of cat and mouse went on, but it seems to have been several days. As always, Caesar had been eager to give battle, even though he had fewer troops. In truth, Caesar had little option but to gamble on a battle, believing that the cohesion and experience of his troops would count more than the number of Pompeius'. Yet again, Pompeius had refused to accept the offer of battle, leaving Caesar cut off from his powerbase in the Western Republic.

As we have seen, however, Pompeius' whole political strategy lay in defeating Caesar in battle and being seen to have done so (by the Senate and now the leaders of Rome's Eastern allies). Whilst tactically he could have strung out this standoff for longer and continued to wear down Caesar, politically he could no longer do so. Having drawn up his army on the plain of Pharsalus, he gained himself a few extra days to grind down Caesar logistically and enhance the cohesion of his new hybrid army, but at some point he had to accept battle.

Whilst Caesar must have worried that Pharsalus would prove to be another anti-climax, with Pompeius continually refusing to give battle, it seems that Pompeius had finally determined that Pharsalus would be the place he would crush Caesar's 'rebellion'. However, in typical fashion, he was refusing to be rushed into it, with time still on his side. It appears that it was Caesar who now 'blinked' first and made preparation to break camp and march away from Pharsalus. Caesar's own account explains his thinking:

> 'Caesar, thinking that Pompeius could by no means be enticed out to a battle, judged that his most convenient plan of campaign was to move his camp from that place, and to be always on the march, with the view of getting his supplies more conveniently by moving camp and visiting various places and at the same time of meeting with some opportunity of fighting on the route, and of wearing out the army of Pompeius, which was unaccustomed to hard work, by daily marches.'[36]

Plutarch also records these events:

> "At break of day, Caesar was about to decamp and move to Scotussa."[37]
> 'However, Caesar did not expect to fight on that day, but began to break camp for a march to Scotussa.'[38]

In his explanation, Caesar emphasizes the logistical constraints he was under. Plutarch's accounts are notable for stating Caesar's intended destination, the city of Scotussa, which lay to the north-east of Pharsalus, near which was the battlefield of Cynoscephalae, site of the famous Roman victory in 197 BC, their first in mainland Greece.

All accounts seem to agree that Caesar was genuinely intending to march off, having given up on the prospect of fighting at Pharsalus. Yet it is tempting to wonder whether Caesar was also tempting Pompeius. It is notable that on this occasion, Caesar chose to set off in daylight, having previously used the cover of night to move away from the army of Pompeius whenever they had been facing each other to avoid exposing his troops on the march to a Pompeian attack when they were most vulnerable.

It is worth speculating that Caesar was now offering Pompeius such an opportunity; to attack him when he was breaking camp and supposedly at his most vulnerable. If so, there could be a two-fold benefit: he would finally tempt Pompeius into battle, seemingly on his own terms, but he could also have prepared his army for just this set of circumstances, being ready to form up for battle the moment Pompeius moved and thus not be taken by surprise.

We will never know what Caesar's actual intent was. What we are certain of, however, is the outcome: Pompeius finally decided the time had come to give battle and ordered his army to be deployed. Having judged Pharsalus to be the right place and time for his destruction of Caesar's army – even though Caesar had actually chosen the location – Caesar's decision to break camp and prepare to move off was the final spur Pompeius needed.

There were two reasons why Pompeius finally decided to act. Firstly, as detailed above, he could hardly deploy his newly unified army at Pharsalus only to allow his opponent to wander off unmolested. This would be a public demonstration to his supporters in the Senate and from the East, as well as his troops, that he did not believe he could defeat Caesar. Secondly, it would allow him to fight Caesar again at the time of his own choosing, when Caesar was breaking camp and setting off on the march. Consequently, Pompeius took what was ultimately to be the most career-defining decision he ever made and committed his army to battle at Pharsalus.

vii) The Timing of the Deployment

Though Pompeius had committed to giving battle, perhaps intending to catch Caesar unawares, he seems to have given away his intention to do so by deploying his army before Caesar had finished breaking camp. Caesar's account has Pompeius always intending to give battle that day, it being seemingly a coincidence that it was the day Caesar chose to break camp and leave Pharsalus. Other accounts have Caesar's scouts noticing the movement in the Pompeian army whilst Caesar's forces were breaking camp:

> '[Caesar's] soldiers were taking down their tents and sending on ahead the beasts of burden and servants, when the scouts came in with a report that they saw many shields moving to and fro in the enemy's camp, and that there was a noisy movement there of men coming out to battle. After these, others came announcing that the foremost ranks were already forming in battle array.'[39]
>
> 'But just as the tents had been struck, his scouts rode up to him with tidings that the enemy were coming down into the plain for battle.'[40]

So we have Pompeius' forces deploying too early if they were hoping to catch Caesar's army off-guard and on the march. Given the quality of Pompeius as a general, we can rule out a mistake, even one caused by having to rouse such a large army. That leaves us with deliberate intent: Pompeius wanted Caesar to see him deploying his army, again announcing that the battle was to take place at a time of his choosing. Though it would have been a tactical advantage to wait until Caesar's army was on the march, this would perhaps not have fitted the 'narrative' that Pompeius was weaving; he needed to be seen to defeat Caesar face-to-face rather than by attacking him on the march. Thus, once Pompeius' scouts had seen that Caesar was breaking camp, he decided to immediately deploy his army.

There remain two other interesting possibilities. The first is that spies – or traitors – in Caesar's camp informed Pompeius that Caesar intended to leave the next day, so he was forewarned and ready for an early deployment. The other possibility is that Caesar's army made a very obvious show of breaking camp, unlike the previous times that Caesar had disengaged from Pompeius when the two armies had faced each other. The process were very obvious and perhaps slower than it should have been if Caesar was in a hurry to avoid being caught on the march.

Nevertheless, we cannot with any certainty state which of the commanders was ultimately responsible for the decision to fight that day. Was Pompeius panicked into it by Caesar abandoning his position or was he lured into it by Caesar deliberately baiting him by pretending to break camp? Or was Caesar genuinely not expecting to fight that day, himself being caught out, perhaps undermined by Pompeius having foreknowledge of this? We will never know for sure, but that should not halt speculation. The important point was that, after eight months, battle between Pompeius and Caesar had been agreed upon.

Summary – Right Place, Wrong Time?

On what now equates to 9 August 48 BC, after eighteen months of manoeuvre and counter-manoeuvre, the two architects of the Third Civil War finally faced off against each other. Though this had been the culmination of Pompeius' masterplan – a set-piece battle in front of the assembled Senate and foreign kings; a showcase for him to defeat the 'enemy of the Republic' and burnish his credentials to be its guardian – the timing was far from ideal for him.

Pompeius had got what he wanted, but the manner by which it had been achieved was not perfect. The original plan seems to have been to tie Caesar down in Spain, then in early 48 BC to assemble his grand army at leisure, integrating his existing forces in Greece with Metellus' troops from the East. Whilst Pompeius had the advantage of numbers, he had not had the time to integrate his army and battle-test them with a short local campaign before facing Caesar at a time and place of his choosing.

Here had lain Caesar's main chance to disrupt Pompeius' strategy and force his hand, which he did through his gamble in crossing the Adriatic in January and then pushing into the Greek interior after defeat at Dyrrhachium. Cut off from his powerbase in the Western Republic and having suffered defeat at Dyrrhachium, this was Caesar's last gamble, finally forcing Pompeius into battle before he was ready. He had to trust that his own smaller but more integrated army could counter the overwhelming size of Pompeius' forces, and that his tactics would nullify his opponent's superior numbers of cavalry and archers.

Chapter Four

The Battle of Pharsalus (Palaepharsalus) (48 BC)

After eighteen months of cat and mouse, the rival Roman oligarchs finally committed to battle on 9 August 48 BC. However, before we can analyze the battle itself, we must first examine the strengths and composition of the armies and their disposition on the battlefield.

The Size and Composition of the Two Armies

The first and most obvious point is that Pompeius' army outnumbered Caesar's by two to one:

> '[Pompeius'] forces amounted to forty-five thousand men, and about two thousand reserves who had come to him from the beneficiaries of his former armies.'[1]

> '[Caesar] had eighty cohorts posted in his lines, making a total of twenty-two thousand men; seven cohorts he had left as a protection for the camp.'[2]

> '[Pompeius' cavalry] were seven thousand to Caesar's one thousand. The numbers of the infantry also were unequal, since forty-five thousand were arrayed against twenty-two thousand.'[3]

> '[Caesar's] army, then, consisted of about 22,000 men and of these about 1,000 were cavalry. Pompeius had more than double that number, of whom about 7,000 were cavalry. Some of the most trustworthy writers say that 70,000 Italian soldiers were engaged in this battle. Others give the smaller number, 60,000. Still others, grossly exaggerating, say 400,000. Of the whole number some say Pompeius' forces were half as many again as Caesar's, others that they were two-thirds of the total number engaged.'[4]

Appian's statement about the variations of the number of troops in the battle is borne out by several other late surviving sources. Orosius has Caesar's army at a little under 30,000, with near equal numbers of cavalry,[5] whilst Florus has an amazing and unlikely total of 300,000 men on the battlefield.[6] It is not often in ancient history that we have a surviving account of troop numbers from one of the generals involved, and it is interesting that despite this account being available in ancient times, we still see a wide divergence of troop numbers in later writers, even amongst the handful that survive. Such a divergence has implications for studying other battles where we do not have a surviving account.

Ignoring these outliers, it seems that Pompeius had some 45,000 infantry and 7,000 cavalry against Caesar's 22,000 infantry and 1,000 horsemen. Caesar was heavily outnumbered, and we can see why Pompeius had refused to be diverted from his strategy of waiting for Metellus Scipio and the eastern reinforcements before committing to battle.

It was not only the numbers that were different, as the composition of the two armies also varied greatly. Appian provides the best account of the two armies,[7] there being clear differences between them. He has Caesar's troops as the traditional Italian legionnaires, whilst those of Pompeius are more cosmopolitan and representative of Rome's wider empire, from the Spanish West to the Syrian East); a clash, as it were, between the past and the future of the Roman army:

'However that may be, each of them placed his chief reliance on his Italian troops. In the way of allied forces Caesar had cavalry from both Cisalpine and Transalpine Gaul, besides some light-armed Greeks, consisting of Dolopians, Acarnanians, and Aetolians.'[8]

'From Greece he [Pompeius] had Lacedaemonians marshalled by their own kings, and others from Peloponnesus and Boeotians with them. Athenians marched to his aid also.

'Besides the Greeks almost all the nations of the Levant sent aid to Pompeius: Thracians, Hellespontines, Bithynians, Phrygians, Ionians, Lydians, Pamphylians, Pisidians, Paphlagonians; Cilicia, Syria, Phoenicia, the Hebrews, and their neighbours the Arabs; Cyprians, Rhodians, Cretan slingers, and all the other islanders. Kings and princes were there leading their own troops: Deïotarus, the tetrarch of Galatia, and Ariarathes [Ariobarzanes], King of

Cappadocia. Taxiles commanded the Armenians from the hither side of the Euphrates; those from the other side were led by Megabates, the lieutenant of King Artapates."[9]

More important than the ethnic make-up of Pompeius' army was its military composition. Though Pompeius had double the numbers of Caesar, it was not a case of 45,000 legionaries facing 22,000. A large portion of the army of Pompeius – it is impossible to determine just how many – were lightly armed archers and slingers. This meant that the fighting strengths of each army were different, which would affect the nature of the battle.

In terms of legionary strength, Pompeius probably still had more legionaries than Caesar, but not the overwhelming advantage that we may think of. Pompeius' clearest tactical advantages lay in his far greater resources in terms of cavalry and distance weaponry (archers and slingers). Consequently, he would fight a battle that emphasized range and speed rather than a straight stand-up legionary confrontation. The opposite is therefore true of Caesar, who needed a battle that negated those Pompeian strengths and to get the two armies entangled face to face.

The Disposition of the Two Armies

Caesar provides us with an eyewitness account of the disposition of the two armies (see diagram below), starting with that of Pompeius:

> 'On the left wing were the two legions which had been handed over by Caesar at the beginning of the civil strife by decree of the Senate, one of which was called the First, the other the Third. At that place was Pompeius himself. Scipio occupied the middle of the line with the Syrian legions. The Cilician legion, united with the Spanish cohorts, which, as we explained, had been brought over by Afranius, was stationed on the right wing. These legions Pompeius regarded as the strongest under his command. The rest he had interposed between the centre and the wings and had made up the number of one hundred and ten cohorts.
>
> 'Seven remaining cohorts he had placed on garrison duty in the camp and the neighbouring forts. A stream with difficult banks

protected his right wing; for which reason he had stationed his whole cavalry and all his archers and slingers opposite the enemy on the left wing.'[10]

Caesar then offers a breakdown of his own forces:

'Caesar, observing his previous custom, had posted his Tenth Legion on the right wing, and his Ninth on the left, though it had been seriously attenuated by the Dyrrhachian battles. To this legion he added the Eighth, so that he almost made the two into one, having given orders that the one should support the other. He had eighty cohorts posted in his lines, making a total of twenty-two thousand men; seven cohorts he had left as a protection for the camp. He had placed Antonius in command on the left wing, P. Sulla on the right, and Cn. Domitius in the centre. He himself confronted Pompeius.'[11]

Nevertheless, the best description of the battlefield (its original source still unidentified) comes from Appian, likely utilizing the works of Asinius Pollio:[12]

'Leaving 4,000 of his Italian troops to guard his camp, Pompeius drew up the remainder between the city of Pharsalus and the River Enipeus opposite the place where Caesar was marshalling his forces. Each of them ranged his Italians in front, divided into three lines with a moderate space between them, and placed his cavalry on the wings of each division. Archers and slingers were mingled among all. Thus were the Italian troops disposed, on which each commander placed his chief reliance. The allied forces were marshalled by themselves rather for show than for use.

'There was much jargon and confusion of tongues among Pompeius' auxiliaries. Pompeius stationed the Macedonians, Peloponnesians, Boeotians, and Athenians near the Italian legions, as he approved of their good order and quiet behaviour. The rest, as Caesar had anticipated, he ordered to lie in wait by tribes outside of the line of battle, and when the engagement should become close to surround the enemy, to pursue, to do what damage they could, and to plunder Caesar's camp, which was without defences.'[13]

The key problem with Appian's description is that it fails to mention which city of Pharsalus the battle took place near; the old or the new? Even more problematically, Caesar fails to mention either of them, only ever describing the clash as 'the battle fought in Thessaly'.[14] The author of the *Alexandrine War*, usually attributed to Caesar, uses the phrase 'achieving success at Palaepharsali [Old Pharsalus]'.[15] Furthermore, Frontinus in his work on military stratagems, clearly states that it was Old Pharsalus:

> 'In the battle against Caesar at Old Pharsalus, Cnaeus Pompeius drew up three lines of battle, each one ten men deep, stationing on the wings and in the centre the legions upon whose prowess he could most safely rely on and filling the spaces between these with raw recruits. On the right flank he placed six hundred horsemen, along the Enipeus River, which with its channel and deposits had made the locality impassable; the rest of the cavalry he stationed on the left, together with the auxiliary troops, that from this quarter he might envelop the troops of Caesar. Against these dispositions, Caius Caesar also drew up a triple line, placing his legions in front and resting his left flank on marshes in order to avoid envelopment.'[16]

Cicero, however, the only other contemporaneous source who mentions the name of the battlefield, uses Pharsalus on a number of occasions throughout his works:

> '… you had been in the Battle of Pharsalia.'[17]
> '… concerning that most lamentable Battle of Pharsalia?'[18]
> '… what was that drawn sword of yours doing in the Battle of Pharsalia?'[19]

Thus, even the ancient sources are not in agreement over where the battle took place. If we add to this the lack of agreement over the modern locations of these ancient cities, then it is unsurprising that a definitive battle site has never been determined with any unanimity, with various locations being discussed. There have been numerous academic discussions on the location of the battle,[20] with the best summary coming from Morgan, who favours modern Kirni as the most viable site.[21] The location of the battlefield is not just a matter of archaeological speculation, but is critical

The Battle of Pharsalus (Palaepharsalus) (48 BC)

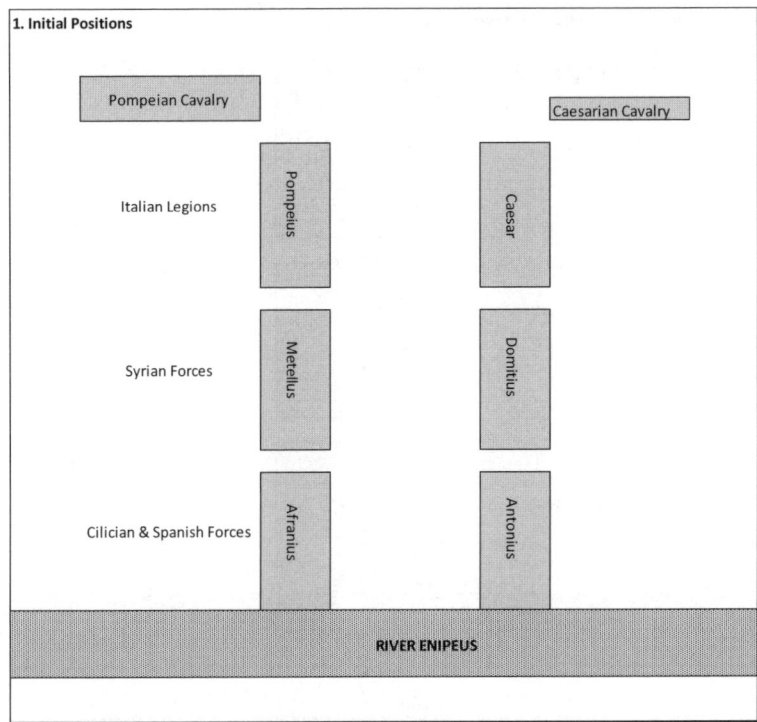

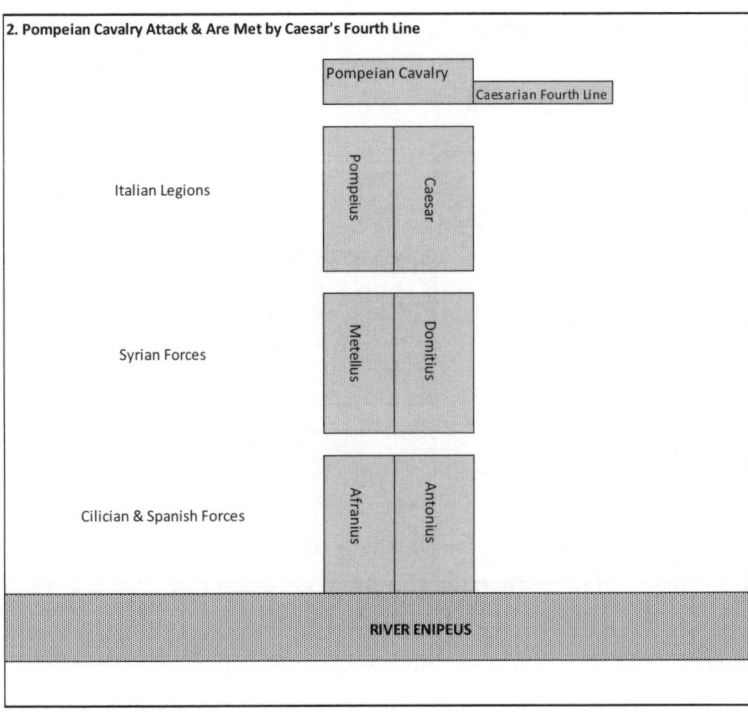

80 The Battle of Pharsalus (48 BC)

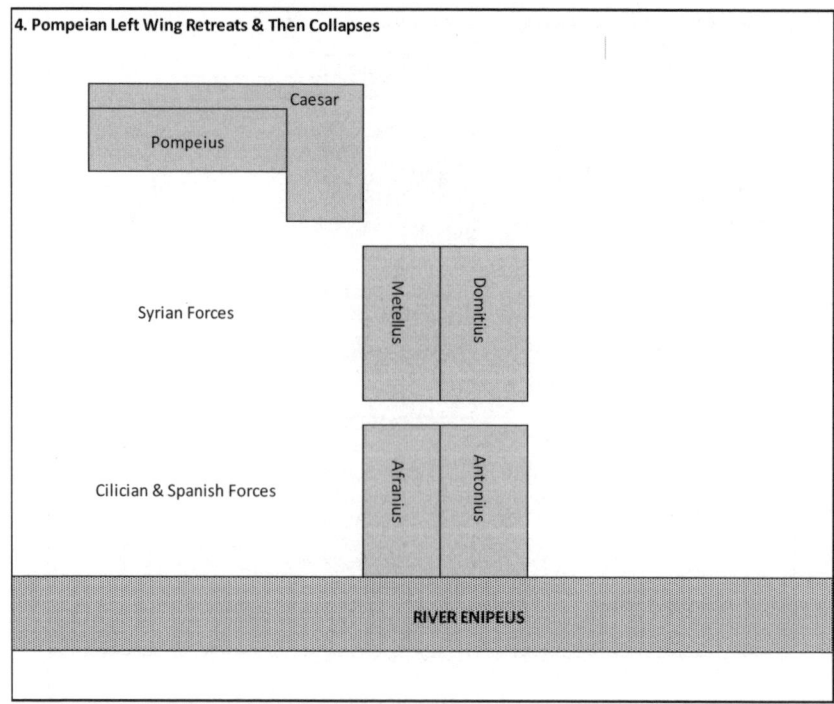

to understanding the topography of the battle site, without which we must fall back on the ancient and contrasting accounts.

There are further interesting differences between the accounts of Appian (Pollio) and Caesar. In terms of the dispositions, Appian goes on to say that Pompeius changed the disposition of his army when he saw Caesar take command on the right wing, moving his cavalry to face them on his left wing (see diagram).[22] Yet not only does Appian say that this was Caesar's custom, and thus we should have expected Pompeius to anticipate it, but Caesar's account has Pompeius place his cavalry on the left wing to avoid the river on his right flank.

Another interesting divergence concerns Pompeius' cavalry and his archers and slingers, which in Caesar's account are focused on Pompeius' left wing, facing Caesar, whilst Appian notes that the cavalry were split between the two wings whilst the archers and slingers were dispersed throughout. This seems to hinge on the location of the armies in relation to the River Enipeus. In Caesar's first-hand account, the river is on Pompeius' right, guarding his right flank but also restricting the movement available, hence the loading of the left wing. In the source account Appian used, however, the river does not seem to figure in terms of the disposition of the armies, it merely being in the vicinity. Modern discussions have centred around whether the battle took place north or south of the river.[23]

These dispositions were crucial to the flow of the battle which followed. With his right flank guarded/hampered by the river, Pompeius heavily loaded his left wing, apparently with the two sections of his army that he believed would give him the winning advantage, namely his cavalry and archers/slingers. Equally, Caesar placed his two weakest legions (the Eighth and the Ninth) on his left wing (by the river) and his strongest forces on his right, commanded by himself. The topography of the battle site thus seems to have dictated the flow of the subsequent battle, with neither side wanting to fight by the river, ensuring that the main flow of the battle would take place on the opposite flank (Pompeius' left, Caesar's right).

Caesars' Fourth Line

It was faced with this certainty, that the battle would be fought on his right flank, the left being protected by the river, that Caesar introduced what was to be the winning tactical disposition. With both armies drawn up into three lines of troops, he introduced a fourth line:

> 'At the same time, having noticed the arrangements mentioned above, fearing lest his right wing should be surrounded by the multitude of cavalry, he hastily withdrew individual cohorts from the third line and out of these constructed a fourth line, stationing it opposite the cavalry, explaining what his object was and reminding them that the day's victory depended on the valour of these cohorts. At the same time he commanded the third line and the whole army not to join battle without orders from himself, saying that when he wished this to be done, he would give the signal with a flag.'[24]
>
> 'When Caesar perceived this movement, he placed 3,000 of his bravest foot-soldiers in ambush and ordered them, when they should see the enemy trying to flank him, to rise, dart forward, and thrust their spears directly in the faces of the men because, as they were fresh and inexperienced and still in the bloom of youth, they would not endure injury to their faces.'[25]
>
> 'But seeing that the enemy's cavalry were arraying themselves over against this point, and fearing their brilliant appearance and their numbers, he ordered six cohorts from the furthermost lines to come round to him unobserved, and stationed them behind his right wing, teaching them what they were to do when the enemy's horsemen attacked.'[26]
>
> 'On the right he placed his cavalry, among whom he distributed the fleetest of his foot-soldiers, men trained in cavalry fighting. Then he held in reserve six cohorts for emergencies, placing them obliquely on the right, from which quarter he was expecting an attack of the enemy's cavalry. No circumstance contributed more than this to Caesar's victory on that day; for as soon as Pompeius' cavalry poured forth, these cohorts routed [them].'[27]

Thus, Caesar (if we are to believe Appian's numbers) weakened his right flank by placing nearly 15 percent of his forces as an emergency reserve, should his right flank be overwhelmed by Pompeius' cavalry. As we have seen demonstrated on several occasions, Caesar had been developing a specialist infantry force for fighting cavalry, and Frontinus drew particular attention to this. On two previous occasions, at the withdrawal from the River Genusus and in skirmishing at Pharsalus in the days before the battle (see Chapter Three), Caesar's new cavalry fighting force and tactics had proved successful, so we can see that Caesar had been preparing to negate Pompeius' cavalry advantage for some time.

It is worth speculating on the role of the Battle of Carrhae, just some five years before, where Crassus (Caesar's former mentor) had seen his army destroyed by superior cavalry numbers.[28] Pompeius had nothing like the number of the Parthian cavalry, but there were enough Roman survivors to provide eyewitness accounts, many of whom may well have been in the Caesarian entourage.

Whatever the case, both Caesar and Pompeius believed that the superior Pompeian cavalry on the Pompeian left/Caesarian right would be the critical element of the battle. If they could overwhelm Caesar on the right, then they could turn on the Caesarian centre and push it towards the river and annihilation. Equally, if the cavalry could be turned, then Caesar could advance on the open left flank of Pompeius and do the same. In consequence, both commanders threw everything into this flank of the battle. Of the two, however, it seems that it was only Caesar who developed a back-up plan for this flank buckling under pressure.

The Standoff and the First Attack of Crastinus

As we have seen, throughout this campaign, and even with both armies drawn up on the plains of Pharsalus, there was a reluctance for them to engage. Having finally agreed to accept the offer of battle, Pompeius still exercised caution. We can clearly see the tactics that Pompeius was utilizing: awaiting the Caesarian attack, blunting it and then, when Caesar's forces were being worn down, hitting them hard on the left flank with his superior cavalry numbers. Caesar criticized these tactics as overly cautious,[29] but Pompeius wanted Caesar to come to him and his army to wear itself out whilst fully committed all along the line, allowing for the greater impact of his own cavalry attack. Furthermore, given such a multinational army, any Pompeian attack ran the risk of a disorderly advance rather than a coherent one.

With Pompeius still refusing to take the bait and attack first, Caesar gave the orders to advance, knowing that this was again playing to Pompeius' strengths. If Pompeius' lines could be broken, then that would have been a bonus, but what was more likely was that it would hold, with the Pompeian front line primarily being well-trained Roman legionaries. If Caesar's army was thus fully committed, it would be exposed to a Pompeian cavalry attack on his right flank. To avoid defeat, Caesar's right flank needed to hold, or his fourth line had to come to its rescue. So Caesar ordered his army to attack, seemingly in the belief that he was playing to Pompeius' battleplan, but with his own back-up plan of the fourth line as a standby. Caesar names the centurion who led the initial attack:

> 'There was in Caesar's army a reservist, C. Crastinus, who in the previous year had served under him as first Centurion in the Tenth Legion, a man of remarkable valour.
>
> 'At the same time, looking at Caesar, he says: "Today, General, I will give you occasion to thank me alive or dead." Having said this, he ran forward first from the right wing, and about one hundred and twenty picked men of the same cohort, serving as volunteers, followed him.'[30]

Crastinus' attack, though brave, turned out to be foolhardy:

> "Also Crastinus, whom we have mentioned above, was slain by a sword-stroke in his face while fighting with the utmost bravery.'[31]
>
> 'But after cutting his way through the first rank, and while he was forging onwards with great slaughter, he was beaten back by the thrust of a sword through his mouth, and the point of the sword actually came out at the back of his neck.'[32]
>
> 'The javelin of Crastinus was noted as that of the man who started the battle, and the strangeness of the wound which he received; he was found among the dead with a sword thrust into his mouth, showing the zeal and rage with which he had fought.'[33]

Stalemate

We are given no timings, but it is clear that the early stages of the battle went according to how Pompeius envisaged it. The Pompeian front line held the Caesarian attack and the two armies then engaged in the standard pattern of combat, albeit between two evenly matched sides using the same tactics and equipment:

> 'Nor indeed did the Pompeians fail to meet the emergency. For they parried the shower of missiles and withstood the attack of the legions without breaking their ranks, and after discharging their javelins had recourse to their swords.'[34]

We can discount the lazy narrative that Caesar's army had the advantage in terms of experience against the inferior quality of Pompeius' foreign army. Legionary fought legionary, and the discipline of both sides held. What is interesting is that hardly any of the surviving accounts describe any advantage held by the Pompeians in terms of range weapons during these early exchanges, despite them having far more archers and slingers. Certainly, they don't seem to have blunted the Caesarian charge, perhaps indicating that they were being held in reserve. The only source that does refer to this is Dio, and even then the account is vague:

> 'The Pompeians surpassed in cavalry and archers; hence they would surround troops at a distance, employ sudden assaults, and retired after throwing their opponents into confusion; then they would attack them again and again, turning now to this side and now to that.'[35]

None of our surviving sources detail how long this stalemate continued, but at this point the battle was following the pattern that both commanders expected, with a deadlock between the two Roman armies and no obvious advantage to either side. At this early stage, the Pompeian numbers could not be brought to bear, given that they were fighting defensively. Neither commander would have expected their opponent's line to be broken so soon, and Pompeius must have been satisfied that his less-experienced army had held. It seems that both men were waiting for the inevitable; the Pompeian cavalry attack on the Caesarian right/Pompeian left, which both anticipated as being the decisive manoeuvre.

The Turning Point – The Pompeian Cavalry Attack and Caesar's Fourth Line

We don't know how long Pompeius left it before the order for the cavalry attack was given. Caesar's account implies that it was not long after first contact, but Plutarch says the following:

> 'After Crastinus had fallen, the battle was evenly contested at this point; Pompeius, however, did not lead up his right wing swiftly, but kept looking anxiously towards the other parts of the field, and awaited the action of his cavalry on the left, thus losing time.'[36]

Pompeius would have wanted to wait to ensure that his hitherto untested front line held the Caesarian attack and that Caesar's army was fully committed. When thus satisfied, Pompeius gave the order and threw the whole weight of his cavalry, archers and slingers at Caesar's right flank, not simply because that was where Caesar himself was but it being the only wing that had sufficient space for such an attack and for turning the wing onto the centre. Pompeius thus deployed what both sides considered to be his greatest strength and started the key phase of the battle:

> 'At the same time the horse on Pompeius' left wing, according to orders, charged in a body, and the whole multitude of archers poured forth. Our cavalry, failing to withstand their attack, gradually quitted their position and retired. Pompeius' cavalry pressed forward all the more eagerly, and deploying by squadrons began to surround our lines on their exposed flank.'[37]
>
> 'Then, as the cavalry were a little in advance of the infantry, they charged each other. Those of Pompeius prevailed and began to outflank the tenth legion.'[38]
>
> 'These at last deployed their squadrons with a view to envelop Caesar, and to hurl back upon their supporting lines the horsemen whom he had stationed in front, only a few in number.'[39]

As predicted by both sides, Caesar's right flank buckled in the face of this cavalry and projectile onslaught, with Caesar's own mounted force being no match for Pompeius' superior numbers. At this point, had the battle followed the traditional path, the Tenth Legion, no matter how battle hardened, would have been slaughtered or turned and collapsed back into the Caesarian centre, allowing the Pompeian cavalry to encircle Caesar's army and complete its annihilation. However, having anticipated this eventuality, and with his right flank in danger of collapse, Caesar deployed his fourth line, his specially trained cavalry fighting units, which he calculated would be sufficient to counter the superior numbers and momentum of Pompeius' cavalry.

This tactic was clearly a gamble and was by no means certain to be successful. Though the tactic had been deployed on two previous occasions in the recent campaign, both were on a much smaller scale and there was no certainty that it would have similar results against such large numbers and in a full-blown battle situation. The presence of Pompeius' archers and slingers in large quantities added an extra unknown factor to this clash. Nevertheless, Caesar had been training his men for such an eventuality and many of them had already been tested in anti-cavalry fighting.

They would also carry the element of surprise, though we might argue that this Caesarian counter should have been anticipated. The great unknown element in this tactic was the quality of the Pompeian cavalry. Other than their numbers, we have little detail of their composition or experience, apart from the two occasions they had lost skirmishes to Caesar's forces in the days before the battle. Yet those would not have been a true indication of how the whole body of cavalry would react in a full-scale battle. In short, this Caesarian counter, and ultimately the battle itself, would hinge on whether nearly 3,000 infantry could withstand the charge of up to 7,000 cavalry, and not only check their momentum but actually turn them back.

There were three possible outcomes to the mounted assault: the Pompeian cavalry might overrun Caesar's fourth line and collapse his right wing, the fourth line could beat off the Pompeian horsemen but they would regroup and retreat in good order, covered by the archers and slingers – ensuring a stalemate – or the fourth line might rout the cavalry, forcing them to collapse and exposing the slingers and archers and Pompeius' left flank. Caesar preserves the best description of this critical clash, though Appian and Plutarch provide some additional detail:

'Caesar, observing it, gave the signal to his fourth line, which he had composed of six cohorts. These advanced rapidly and with colours flying attacked Pompeius' horse with such fury that not one of them stood his ground, and all, wheeling round, not only quit the position but forthwith in hurried flight made for the highest hills. When these were dislodged all the archers and slingers, left defenceless, without support, were slain.'[40]

'Caesar then gave the signal to the cohorts in ambush and these, starting up suddenly, advanced to meet the cavalry, and with spears elevated aimed at the faces of the riders, who could not endure the enemy's savagery, nor the blows on their mouths and eyes, but fled in disorder. Thereupon Caesar's men, who had just now been afraid of being surrounded, fell upon the flank of Pompeius' infantry which was denuded of its cavalry supports.'[41]

'But Caesar gave a signal, his cavalry retired, and the cohorts drawn up to oppose the enveloping movement ran out, three thousand men, and confronted their enemies, and standing close by the horses, as they had been directed, they thrust their javelins upwards, aiming at the faces of the riders. These, since they were without experience in every kind of fighting and did not expect or even know anything about such a kind as this, had neither courage nor endurance to meet the blows which were aimed at their mouths and eyes, but wheeling about and putting their hands before their faces, they ingloriously took to flight.'[42]

None of the surviving sources provide any figures for causalities on either side, but they do not seem to have been heavy (see below). Caesar's gamble had paid off handsomely, with results at the high end of his expectations. Not only did Caesar's fourth line withstand the charge of Pompeius' cavalry, but with their new tactics of attacking the riders at close quarters with their *pilum* and aiming for their faces – the horsemen wore open-faced helmets – forced them to retreat. Stalemate turned into victory when the cavalry were seemingly unable to regroup and dispersed from the battlefield, betraying their inexperience. This left the advancing Pompeian slingers and archers totally exposed to the swiftly advancing Caesarian forces, which overwhelmed and massacred them.

The Battle of Pharsalus (Palaepharsalus) (48 BC) 89

Thus, in one short manoeuvre – we do not know its duration, but it cannot have been a long-lasting encounter – Pompeius' mounted attack was not only neutered, but destroyed, along with the two elements of his army which were his strongest: his cavalry and projectile units. With those eliminated, the encounter became a straight infantry battle.

The Turning Point – the Race to Redeploy

Though Pompeius' attack had been defeated, this did not automatically mean that he had lost the battle. That would be won by whichever commander reacted most quickly to the events on this far wing of the battlefield. Pompeius needed to bolster his now-weakened left wing, whilst Caesar needed to press home his advantage on his right. Ultimately, it seems to have come down to which commander was able to better utilize his remaining resources, and in this the smaller and more compact nature of Caesar's army appears to have been the critical factor. Caesar provides the key narrative for the tactics used, naturally taking delight in sticking the knife into Pompeius' reputation:

> 'With the same onslaught the cohorts surrounded the left wing, the Pompeians still fighting and continuing their resistance in their lines, and attacked them in the rear. At the same time Caesar ordered the third line, which had been undisturbed and up to that time had retained its position, to advance. So, as they had come up fresh and vigorous in place of the exhausted troops, while others were attacking in the rear, the Pompeians could not hold their ground and turned to flight in mass.
>
> 'Pompeius, when he saw his cavalry beaten back and that part of his force in which he had most confidence panic-stricken, mistrusting the rest also, left the field and straightway rode off to the camp.'[43]

Plutarch later repeated much of Caesar's account, with his usual added dramatical flourishes:

> 'When Pompeius, on the other wing, saw his horsemen scattered in flight, he was no longer the same man, nor remembered that he was Pompeius Magnus, but more like one whom Heaven has robbed of

his wits than anything else, he went off without a word to his tent, sat down there, and awaited what was to come, until his forces were all routed, and the enemy were assailing his ramparts and fighting with their defenders.'[44]

Interestingly, Appian preserves a variant account that has Pompeius initially stand his ground and try to rally his men:

'When Pompeius learned this, he ordered his infantry not to advance farther, not to break the line of formation, and not to hurl the javelin, but to open their ranks, bring their spears to rest, and so ward off the onset of the enemy. Some persons praise this order of Pompeius as the best in a case where one is attacked in flank, but Caesar criticises it in his letters. He says that the blows are delivered with more force, and that the spirits of the men are raised, by running, while those who stand still lose courage by reason of their immobility and become excellent targets for those charging against them. So, he says, it proved in this case, for the tenth legion, with Caesar himself, surrounded Pompeius' left wing, now deprived of cavalry, and assailed it with javelins in flank, where it stood immovable; until, finally, the assailants threw it into disorder, routed it, and this was the beginning of the victory.'[45]

Caesar certainly has no reason to portray Pompeius as anything other than a beaten man, but the account of Appian is the one that rings more true here. Seeing his attack on the left destroyed, he realized the vulnerability of that wing, stopped his army's advance and ordered it to adopt defensive tactics to try to counter the Caesarian advance.

Yet it is Caesar who provides us with the details of the factors that finally swung the battle in his favour. Robbed of their cavalry and archers, Pompeius' left wing was weakened and Caesar's Tenth Legion, led by himself, was able to surround Pompeius' flank and attack it in the rear before Pompeius had the chance to bring up any reinforcements from his reserves. It was Caesar who was able to deploy his reserves more quickly, using his third line, which had been held in reserve, to press home the advantage and stop Pompeius utilizing his greater manpower.

It was here that the size and nature of the two armies came to play its critical part, as did the topography. It is important to stress, however, that simply because Caesar won the encounter on his right wing did not automatically mean he had won the battle. He certainly was winning on the right wing, but Pompeius could have saved the day if he had been able to deploy his greater manpower more quickly. However, Caesar, with the smaller and more cohesive army, was able to react more swiftly and adapt to the changing circumstances of the battle; hence the renewed offensive across the line, putting pressure on the rest of Pompeius' army and stopping him from reinforcing their left.

Despite the greater reserve of manpower in Pompeius army, much of it was multi-national and seemingly not able to deploy as quickly. Furthermore, with the river on the Pompeian right, there was no room for a counter flanking manoeuvre on the opposite wing. Due to the unknown nature of the battle site, arguments continue over how wide or deep the river was and whether it was the formidable barrier it seems to have been.[46] All Caesar's army had to do was hold its left and centre in a stalemate and let the battle's focus remain on the Caesarian right.

The Pompeian Retreat

If we are to believe Caesar's account, then the Pompeians soon collapsed into flight and Pompeius himself left the field to sit in his tent, a 'broken man'. Although this account has the key points in it, it naturally condenses the timescale to make his victory all the more overwhelming. However, Appian again preserves a variant account that paints the final stages of the battle in a different light, with a more drawn-out and thus less overwhelming victory:

> 'As Pompeius' left wing began to give way his men even still retired step by step and in perfect order, but the allies who had not been in the fight, fled with headlong speed, shouting, "We are vanquished," dashed upon their own tents and fortifications as though they had been the enemy's, and pulled down and plundered whatever they could carry away in their flight. Then the rest of Pompeius' Italian legions, perceiving the disaster to the left wing, retired slowly at first, in good order, and still resisting as well as they could; but when

the enemy, flushed with victory, pressed upon them they turned in flight.'[47]

Pompeius having failed to reinforce his embattled left wing, the conclusion of the battle must have been clear for all experienced soldiers and commanders to see. With the bulk of his army pinned down, the left wing, surrounded on three sides, would eventually be overwhelmed, yet in Appian's account they were initially able to retreat in good order, with discipline maintained. Though Appian contains the familiar Roman (or Greco-Roman) trope about the bravery and discipline of Italian solders as opposed to their 'perfidious and cowardly' Eastern allies, who fled the field, there may well in this case have been some truth in the matter.[48]

We do not know how long Pompeius' left wing was able to maintain a disciplined retreat, nor how many men were killed or injured in doing so. What is clear is that at some point the growing attrition rate amongst Pompeius' left wing, with most men probably suffering multiple stab wounds, saw their discipline finally crack and retreat turned into flight. According to Appian's account, it was only with this final collapse of his left wing that Pompeius quit the field of battle, accepting the inevitable that he had been defeated.

With the total collapse of the Pompeian left wing, the rest of the army would have realized that the battle was lost too, and their orderly retreat would also have turned into full-blown flight. Appian adds that Caesar then ordered that the fleeing Roman troops in the Pompeian forces should not be hunted down, but granted amnesty, a tactic to ensure that their flight did not become a defiant last stand:

> 'Thereupon Caesar, in order that they might not rally, and that this might be the end of the whole war and not of one battle merely, with greater prudence than he had ever shown before, sent heralds everywhere among the ranks to order the victors to spare their own countrymen and to smite only the auxiliaries.'[49]

With the Pompeian army now in full flight and Pompeius himself having quit the battlefield, the victory belonged to Caesar.

The Final Pompeian Stand

Yet there was one more clash still to come, a number of the Pompeians having retreated to their fortified camp at one end of the Pharsalian plain. Though Caesar had won the battle, he clearly had not yet won the war, and the bulk of the Pompeian soldiers – and more importantly their commanders – had avoided the heaviest fighting on the left wing and were able to retreat unmolested. Caesar now wanted to take the Pompeian camp, and hopefully Pompeius himself and thus end the civil war. Caesar provides an account of his attack on the Pompeian camp, which he times at noon, finally providing us with some measure of time for how long the battle took (from first light and allowing time for the deployment and subsequent standoff), the Pompeian retreat seemingly having taken some time.

> 'The camp was being zealously defended by the cohorts which had been left there on guard, and much more keenly still by the Thracians and barbaric auxiliaries. For the soldiers who had fled from the battlefield panic-stricken in spirit and exhausted by fatigue, many of them having thrown away their arms and their military standards, were thinking more of further flight than of the defence of the camp. Nor could those who had planted themselves on the rampart stand up any longer against the multitude of javelins, but, worn out by wounds, quit their position, and forthwith all, following the guidance of centurions and military tribunes, fled for refuge to some very lofty hills that stretched up to the camp.'[50]

Having apparently given orders for the slaughter of any foreign auxiliaries they could find, it should not have come to a surprise to Caesar that the Pompeian auxiliaries fought so hard. It seems that the Caesarian assault on the camp was a full-blow one on the ramparts which faced the battlefield, rather than an encirclement. It is not clear what role Caesar's cavalry played, as they are recorded as chasing certain men who fled the camp (see below), but others eluded them, most notably the main prize:

> 'When our [Caesarian] men were now circulating within the rampart, Pompeius, procuring a horse and tearing off his insignia

as Imperator, flung himself out of the camp by the decuman gate [the main gate of the camp] and, putting spurs to his horse, hurried straight off to Larisa.'[51]

Thus Caesar's men stormed the Pompeian camp, but Pompeius took flight and slipped out of their commander's reach, ensuring that the war would continue. It seems to have been a disappointing end to Caesar's greatest victory to date.

Casualties

Though the day now belonged to Caesar, as we have seen, Pharsalus was hardly a crushing victory. Only Pompeius' left wing had been heavily defeated, with the rest of the army, and all its commanders, able to retreat in good order (see Chapter Six). This is reflected in the comparatively low number of casualties, for which we have two contemporary sources, Caesar and Asinius Pollio:

> 'In this battle he [Caesar] lost not more than two hundred from the ranks, but about thirty brave centurions.
>
> 'Of the Pompeian army about fifteen thousand appeared to have fallen, but more than twenty-four thousand surrendered, for even the cohorts which had been on garrison duty in the forts surrendered to [Publius] Sulla; many besides fled to the neighbouring communities. There were brought to Caesar from the battle one hundred and eighty military standards and nine eagles.'[52]

Appian, quoting Asinius Pollio, provide us with a much lower figure for Pompeian deaths and warns against those who provide an exaggerated total:

> 'The losses of Italians on each side, for there was no report of the losses of auxiliaries, either because of their multitude or because they were despised, were as follows: in Caesar's army, thirty centurions and 200 legionaries, or, as some authorities have it, 1,200; on Pompeius' side ten Senators, among whom was Lucius Domitius, the same who had been sent to succeed Caesar himself in Gaul, and

The Battle of Pharsalus (Palaepharsalus) (48 BC) 95

about forty distinguished knights. Some exaggerating writers put the loss in the remainder of his forces at 25,000, but Asinius Pollio, who was one of Caesar's officers in this battle, records the number of dead Pompeians found as 6,000.'[53]

Pollio's account is also found in Plutarch:

> '[Asinius Pollio] also says that most of the slain were servants who were killed at the taking of the camp, and that not more than six thousand soldiers fell.'[54]
>
> 'The rest of his legions also fled, and there was a great slaughter in the camp of tent-guards and servants; but only six thousand soldiers fell, according to Asinius Pollio, who fought in that battle on the side of Caesar.'[55]

These differing accounts can be reconciled if we recall that Pollio states that the figures he quoted were for Italians only, and not the auxiliaries. This would tally with Pompeius' losses on his left wing and Caesar's apparent clemency towards Italian soldiers during the retreat. So despite this being a titanic clash between two Roman armies, casualties were not as heavy as one may expect, or as later historians and commentators would allude to. The only heavy fighting was on the Pompeian left wing, which may well account for the 6,000 men killed, with the destruction of the foreign archers and slingers and any other foreign auxiliaries in the retreat accounting for the other 9,000 deaths we find in Caesar's account. Naturally, many later historians and commentators wanted to exaggerate the losses to make them tally with what they saw as a turning point in Roman history:

> 'The limits set to a work of this kind will not permit me to describe in detail the battle of Pharsalia, that day of carnage so fatal to the Roman name, when so much blood was shed on either side, the clash of arms between the two heads of the state, the extinction of one of the two luminaries of the Roman world, and the slaughter of so many noble men on Pompeius' side.'[56]
>
> 'Of Pompeius' followers who were not destroyed on the spot some fled whithersoever they could, and others were captured later on.

'Of the Senators and knights, however, he put to death all whom he had previously captured and spared, except some whom his friends begged off; for he allowed each friend on this occasion to save one man.'[57]

Yet despite its reputation as a major battle, Pharsalus not only saw comparatively few deaths among the soldiers, but also amongst the Pompeian elite. The most notable casualty on the day was L. Domitius Ahenobarbus, the long-term opponent of Caesar's who had twice been defeated by him (at Corfinium and again at Massilia). He was the commander of the Pompeian left wing which collapsed under attack from Caesar, but seems to have survived long enough to reach the camp. Caesar (who no doubt took delight in this) records his subsequent death:

'L. Domitius in his flight from the camp to the mountain was slain by the cavalry, his strength having failed him from fatigue.'[58]

Cicero (unsurprisingly given his vitriolic abuse of the Caesarian commander) lays the death at the hands of none other than M. Antonius:

'… you had been in the Battle of Pharsalia as a leader; you had slain Lucius Domitius, a most illustrious and high-born man; you had pursued and put to death in the most barbarous manner many men who had escaped from the battle, and whom Caesar would perhaps have saved, as he did some others.'[59]

The poet Lucan provides a much more dramatic description of this, including a final conversation between the two men as Domitius lay dying:

> 'Still faintly throbbed within Domitius' breast,
> Thus finding utterance: "Yet thou hast not won
> Thy hateful prize, for doubtful are the fates
> Nor thou the master, Caesar; free as yet,
> With great Pompeius for my leader still,
> Warring no more, I seek the silent shades,
> Yet with this hope in death, that thou subdued
> To Magnus and to me in grievous guise
> Mayst pay atonement." So he spake: no more
> Then closed his eyes in death.'[60]

Though Domitius may have been a committed enemy of Caesar, he was hardly one of the leading Pompeians, and seems to have been the only Pompeian leader cut down in the aftermath of the battle. This was a fact that would come back to tarnish Caesar's victory at Pharsalus (see Chapter Six).

Summary – How Great a Victory?

Thus ended the Battle of Pharsalus, whose reputation as a titanic clash between Rome's two leading generals for the 'soul' of the Roman Republic seems to far outstrip the reality. Many subsequent historians chose this battle as the moment that the Republic ended, much as today the same is often said of the Battle of Actium (31 BC). Yet having examined the battle, it is difficult to assess the scale and impact of Caesar's victory.

We can see that the key elements to Caesar's victory were three-fold. Firstly, he developed tactics to counter Pompeius' cavalry superiority and tested them before the battle. Secondly, he reacted more quickly than his opponent to the success on the wing and was able to drive home this advantage and convert it into a wider victory on the battlefield. Thirdly, there is the matter of the choice of battle site, beside the River Enipeus. Regardless of whether the battle was fought to the north or south of the river (here the north is favoured), its location anchoring one wing prevented Pompeius from using his superior cavalry numbers on both wings and therefore allowed Caesar to focus his anti-cavalry formation on just the one wing, rather than having to spread them on both and be overwhelmed on one or the other. So the topography of the battle site played considerably to Caesar's strengths.

Caesar was aided by Pompeian weaknesses, starting with the battle site, though in Pompeius' case that would only have been in hindsight. Fighting on one wing actually allowed Pompeius to concentrate his full cavalry might in one place to deliver what he hoped to be a knockout blow. The Pompeian weakness only came to the fore when the knockout blow failed, and here there were two key issues. Firstly, there was the failure of the cavalry to reform after they had been attacked, perhaps showing the dangers of using 'foreign' cavalry (though we know nothing of their pedigree, and it had worked well at Carrhae). The second failure was not to react quickly enough to this Caesarian victory on the wing, which again seems to have been caused by the size and composition of the Pompeian army, being too large and too multi-national in nature to respond in time.

Again, we are brought back to the question of whether Pompeius agreed to battle too quickly, before he had time to integrate the two main elements of his army, the Italian legionaries in Greece and the Eastern army of Metellus Scipio. As seen in Chapter Three, Caesar had forced the pace and harried Pompeius, giving him only a few weeks between his two armies combining and the subsequent battle. Had Metellus arrived earlier or Pompeius delayed, then this unwieldly army may well have been forged into a more cohesive and disciplined body, allowing them to resist the Caesarian tactics. It is one of history's greatest 'what ifs'. With this in mind, Caesar's victory at Pharsalus was not inevitable.

However, whilst it is indisputable that Caesar won the day, we need to assess whether the battle deserves its great reputation and what its wider impact was on the Third Civil War. Ultimately, Pharsalus became the last battle between Pompeius and Caesar, but that was not on account of what happened in the battle, but by default, with the subsequent death of Pompeius. It was his death that greatly increased the mythology of the battle and enhanced its reputation, whilst lessening that of Dyrrhachium. Had Pompeius not been murdered during his retreat (see Chapter Six), then there would have been subsequent battles between the two and Pharsalus' reputation too would have diminished to the level we find in Caesar's own account; merely a 'battle in Thessaly'.[61]

Though he was successful on the battlefield, the immediate scale of his victory was a far lesser one than Caesar might have imagined. Pompeius' army was not destroyed and the bulk of his forces were able to retreat. Furthermore, despite later sources depicting a massacre of Caesar's opponents, the only notable casualty was L. Domitius Ahenobarbus, and he was hardly in the first order of key figures of the Pompeian factional alliance. Clearly, this battle had not brought Caesar victory in the wider war.

However, perhaps the greatest impact of this victory was on the narrative of the Third Civil War itself. Caesar began the war as the rebel, the 'traitor' who invaded his own country for personal gain (albeit having been manipulated into it by his skilled opponent). Ranged against him were the bulk of the Senatorial oligarchy (the 'true' Republic, at least in their own eyes) and their champion Pompeius, a man who was well known to have his own eyes on ruling the Republic. Throughout 49 BC and up to this point in 48 BC, Caesar was a rebel and the underdog; an upstart general who, though he had achieved success against the Gauls, would seemingly be no match for the 'Roman Alexander'. None of Caesar's successes in Italy or Spain in 49 BC had done anything to change this narrative. Indeed, his position deteriorated rapidly in 48 BC when his gamble to cross the Adriatic failed so spectacularly at the Battle of Dyrrhachium.

Having been defeated by Pompeius at Dyrrhachium, expectations were thus even higher before Pharsalus, which was expected by the bulk of the Senate, Rome's allies and probably even the People of Rome to spell the end of the upstart Caesar and his rebellion. This gave Caesar's victory a far greater psychological impact. The favourite was defeated, and the outsider became the new favourite in the eyes of everyone but his most ardent opponents. It was this role reversal that ultimately led to Pompeius' murder on an Egyptian beach, as those who had backed him looked on in horror as it seemed that they had backed the loser and scrambled to prove their loyalty to the new favourite.

Thus, the Battle of Pharsalus did indeed mark a turning point in the history of the Third Civil War, as it was the moment that Caesar switched from underdog to favourite. Questions of legitimacy are pointless in a civil war, as yesterday's rebel becomes tomorrow's ruler and the winner writes the history books. From Pharsalus onwards, however, Caesar became the leading figure of the Republic – might, rather than right – and the greatest impact of this was on Rome's allies.

The provinces and kingdoms that composed Rome's Eastern Republic had all initially thrown themselves in to support Pompeius, not due to historical ties but because they were attaching themselves to the most likely man to succeed. After Pharsalus, they found that they had seemingly attached themselves to the loser, which they feared would spell disaster for them. Pompeius may have survived, but without an army for protection there was nothing between them and Caesar.

The Pompeian 'grand army' was dissipated after Pharsalus and was never reconstituted. No matter what ties of patronage bound the kings and governors of the Eastern Republic to Pompeius, he was now seen as the loser; until he could reverse that position, he would find few friends. This was the key consequence of the Battle of Pharsalus; the balance had swung in Caesar's favour, no matter how temporarily. It did not mean that Caesar's ultimate victory was inevitable, merely that on 10 August 48 BC he was in the lead. The key to the outcome of the Third Civil War would be whether Pompeius could not only survive the immediate aftermath, but recover from his defeat and regain the initiative.

Section III

Aftermath & Consequences (48 BC)

Chapter Five

The Impact of Pharsalus on the other Campaigns

Whilst the Battle of Pharsalus was clearly the main clash in the war between Pompeius and Caesar, it was by no means the only one, as there are details scattered across the various surviving sources of further campaigns (on both land and sea) conducted by the Pompeian faction, mostly against the Caesarians. Not only does this provide us with additional information of the wider civil war which was raging across the Roman world – though at this point limited to the Western Republic – but the details we have show the impact of Pharsalus on the wider war, as when news of the battle reached the other commanders all their campaigns were halted.

Cato and the Parthinian Campaign

Though now a legendary figure, we must be careful when assessing the status of M. Porcius Cato at the time. Although descended from a noble ancestry, his family had spent the previous hundred years as a solid, if unspectacular, Consular family. Cato himself had failed to reach the Consulship, and though a prominent figure of his generation was clearly not part of the Pompeian inner circle. Cato had become the figurehead of the other wing of the Pompeian alliance, those amongst the Senatorial elite who backed Pompeius as the best of a bad lot; a man who could hold together the Republic, but one who was not to be trusted.

It is therefore no surprise that we find Pompeius did not take Cato with him as he marched in pursuit of Caesar, instead leaving him in charge of Dyrrhachium. Furthermore, Cato had spectacularly failed to hold Sicily the previous year (see Chapter One), and his military record was dubious at best. Dio presents us with two principle reasons why Cato was left behind:

'It came about in this way. Cato had been left behind at Dyrrhachium by Pompeius to keep an eye out for any forces from Italy which might try to cross over, and to repress the Parthini, in case they should begin any disturbance. At first, he carried on war with the latter, but after Pompeius' defeat he abandoned Epirus, and proceeded to Corcyra.'[1]

Here we can see Cato's dual role, which perfectly encapsulates Roman military activity during civil wars, both fighting the opposing Roman faction and continuing to subdue native populations. Having already seen one Caesarian army force its way across the Pompeian-controlled Adriatic, Pompeius had no wish to see reinforcements arrive and catch him in a pincer movement whilst he was chasing after Caesar. Unfortunately, we do not know the size of the force that was left with Cato, but it must have amounted to several legions.

Both men must have been fairly confident that the blockade of the Adriatic would hold, especially as the Pompeian navy launched a fresh attack on Brundisium (see below). This would allow Cato to take his legions in a punitive expedition against the Parthini, the largest Illyrian tribe of the region, who dominated the western end of the Via Egnatia. We are not told of any particular incident that provoked this campaign, but the fiercely independent tribe may well have taken the opportunity of the chaos caused by the Third Civil War to assert their independence or raid neighbouring towns and cities. It is also possible that Caesar used agents to stir them into action.

Given the short time that elapsed between Pompeius leaving Dyrrhachium and the Battle of Pharsalus – just a month – Cato can have made little progress in this campaign, especially if the Parthini took to the mountains to avoid battle. It is unsurprising that Cato found out about events at Pharsalus so quickly, as doubtless a number of survivors would have headed for his army, especially those from the non-Pompeian section of the factional alliance.

With the dissolution of Pompeius' 'grand army', Cato's legions represented the main Pompeian military force still active in Greece. Nevertheless, the Parthinian campaign was abandoned in less than a month and Cato marched for Corcyra, the main Pompeian military base in Greece.

Possible bust of C. Marius.

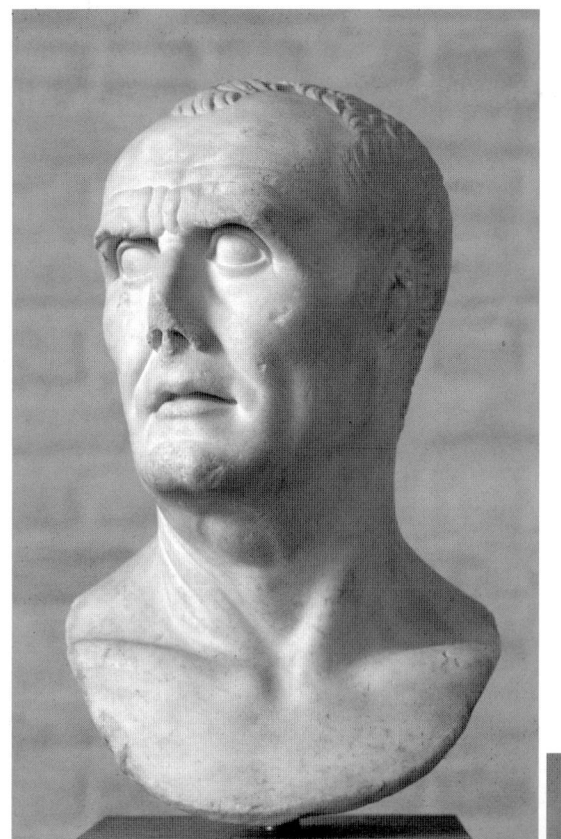

Bust of L. Cornelius Sulla.

Bust of Cn. Pompeius Magnus.

Possible bust of M. Licinius Crassus.

Bust of C. Iulius Caesar.

Bust of M. Tullius Cicero.

Bust of M. Antonius.

Bust of M. Porcius Cato.

Bust of Sex. Pompeius.

Coin of Q. Caecilius Metellus Scipio.

Bust of Juba I of Numidia.

Coin of Bocchus II of the Mauri.

Coin of Deiotus of Galatia.

Coin of Pharnaces II of Pontus.

Plain of Pharsalus.

River Enipeus. (*Robin Rönnlund via Wiki Commons*)

The Pompeian Naval Campaigns

Following the victory at Dyrrhachium, and with Caesar moving inland, the Pompeian navy was freed from being tied down on the Adriatic coast and could return to offensive operations. To this end, we hear of the commissioning of two new naval campaigns to extend Pompeian domination of the Western Republic and strengthen the dominant position they held in Greece.

i) Brundisium

The first and most important campaign was a renewed attack on the Caesarian port of Brundisium. Caesar is the source that best preserves the details of this Pompeian naval campaign:[2]

> 'At the same time D. Laelius reached Brundisium with the fleet and occupied the island lying over against the Brundisian port, as we have shown that Libo did previously. In the same way Vatinius, who was in charge of Brundisium, having covered over with a deck and carefully equipped some rowing-boats, enticed out the ships of Laelius and captured in the narrows of the harbour one quinquereme which had been brought out too far and two smaller ones and also by placing pickets of cavalry here and there took measures to prevent the sailors from getting water. But Laelius, finding the time of year more suitable for navigation, brought up supplies of water for his men from Corcyra and Dyrrhachium in merchant-vessels, and, until news was brought of the battle fought in Thessaly, he was not deterred from his purpose, nor could he be driven to leave the port and the island either by the disgrace of losing his ships or by the want of necessaries.'[3]

We can see three key purposes behind this attack. The first represents the most immediate need for the Pompeians, namely to ensure that there would be no further Caesarian reinforcements crossing the Adriatic and coming to Caesar's aid. The second represented the opposite, to ensure that once defeated, Caesar would be unable to retreat across the Adriatic in any force should he escape the Pompeian army. The third reason would be thinking ahead, namely to secure Brundisium as the landing point for a victorious Pompeian army crossing back into Italy.

However, the Pompeians were not successful in their attack against the city, which was defended by the Caesarian commander P. Vatinius. When news of the defeat at Pharsalus reached him, Laelius presumably broke off the attack and returned to the main Pompeian fleet for fresh orders, though this is not explicitly stated. Now more than ever, with Caesar victorious and in a position to dominate mainland Greece, control of the Adriatic would be vital if Greece was to be held for the Pompeians.

ii) Sicily

The second major naval campaign demonstrates a wider Pompeian concern for control of the Western Republic and highlights a strategic plan for cementing what they believed would be their victory in Greece and translating that into control of Rome's possessions in the West. The previous year has seen Caesar strengthen his control of the Western Republic, adding Italy, Spain and Sicily to his domination of Gaul, leaving the Pompeians only Africa. Of these three regions, it was Sicily that was the most vulnerable to the Pompeian navy, and its conquest would help encircle Italy. Furthermore, Sicily seems to have been the location of the main elements of the Caesarian navy that were not in Brundisium. On this occasion, the Pompeian commander was C. Cassius Longinus, veteran of the First Romano-Parthian War and a future assassin of Caesar. Caesar again presents us with details of this campaign:

> 'About the same time C. Cassius came to Sicily with the Syrian, Phoenician, and Cilician fleets, and as Caesar's fleet was divided into two parts, the Praetor P. Sulpicius at Vibo being in command of one half, and M. Pomponius at Messana of the other, Cassius hurried with his ships to Messana before Pomponius could learn of his approach, and finding him in a state of disorganisation, with no surveillance and no fixed order of battle, with the aid of a strong and favourable wind he sent against the fleet of Pomponius some merchant-ships loaded with pine, pitch, tow, and other combustibles and burnt all thirty-five ships, of which twenty were decked. Such terror was caused by this action that, though there was a legion on guard at Messana, the town was scarcely defended, and had not some news of Caesar's victory been brought, just at that time, by relays of horn, many were of [the] opinion that it would have

been lost. But news having most opportunely arrived, the town was defended.

'Cassius departed thence to Vibo to the Sulpician fleet, and our ships having been moored to the shore in the same way as before, Cassius, with the advantage of a favourable wind, sent down some merchant-vessels prepared for burning, and the fleet having caught fire on each wing, five ships were consumed. And when the fire, through the greatness of the wind, spread more widely, some soldiers on the sick list, who had been left from the veteran legions to guard the ships, could not brook the ignominy, but of their own accord boarded the ships and let loose from the land; and making an attack on the Cassian fleet, they captured two quinqueremes, in one of which was Cassius himself, but he was taken off by a boat and escaped; besides this two triremes were sunk. And not long after news arrived of the battle fought in Thessaly,[4] the result being that the Pompeians themselves believed it, for up to that time they thought it was an invention of Caesar's envoys and friends. So these events having become known, Cassius departed with his fleet from this district.'[5]

There is also a brief passage in Dio:

'And his example was followed by Caius Cassius, who had done very great mischief both in Italy and in Sicily and had overcome a number of opponents in many battles both on sea and on land.'[6]

It appears that the attacks on the two Caesarian fleets at Sicily were far more successful, with Cassius using fireships to destroy the Caesarian vessels, though he himself was nearly captured in a counterattack. Once again, further successes were only prevented by news reaching them of the defeat at Pharsalus, at which point Cassius took the fleet to the eastern Mediterranean (see Chapter Six), perhaps necessitated by the fleet being eastern in origin and the crews wanting to return to home waters.

iii) Oricum
Though absent from Caesar's narrative, there were two other naval campaigns continuing throughout this period which predated the

Battle of Dyrrhachium, but which were brought to a halt when news of Pharsalus reached the participants. The first was commanded by Cnaeus Pompeius (the Younger), the eldest son of Pompeius. He had been placed in charge of the Egyptian Pompeian fleet and was campaigning against the Caesarian-held city of Oricum on the Epirote coast.

The city had a wider strategic significance to the Pharsalan campaign. Were Caesar to be defeated (as the Pompeians expected) and not killed or captured in the battle itself, then Pompeius would need to ensure that his opponent had no port to retreat to; and if he did, then to ensure that it was blockaded to prevent his flight across the Adriatic. On this occasion, it is Dio who preserves a description of the campaign:

> 'Cnaeus Pompeius first sailed about with the Egyptian fleet and overran the district called Epirus, almost capturing Oricum. The commander of the place, Marcus Acilius, had blocked up the entrance to the harbour by means of boats loaded with stones and about the mouth of it had raised towers on either side, both on the land and on freight-ships. Pompeius, however, had divers scatter the stones that were in the vessels, and when the latter had been lightened, he dragged them out of the way, freed the passage, and then, after putting heavy-armed troops ashore on each half of the breakwater, he sailed in. He burned all the boats and most of the city, and would have captured the rest of it, had he not been wounded and caused the Egyptians to fear that he might die. When now, his wound had been cured, he did not continue to assail Oricum, but journeyed about pillaging various places and once vainly made an attempt upon Brundisium itself, as did some others. He was thus occupied for a time; but when his father had been defeated and the Egyptians on receipt of the news sailed home, he betook himself to Cato.'[7]

We can see that the Pompeian fleet once again met with mixed success, with the city of Oricum ultimately holding out. Before the Pharsalan campaign, Pompeius seems to have broken off the siege, which would not have served the wider strategic objectives detailed above. When news of the defeat reached him, his Egyptian fleet deserted him – a clear sign of the shifting allegiances of Rome's allies – forcing him to return to Corcyra and the regrouping of the Pompeian faction (see Chapter Six).

iv) Salonae

The final campaign for which we have some detail is one that had been ongoing since 49 BC. Again, it is not covered by Caesar's account, but as previously noted,[8] this whole campaign – in which Caesar's existing forces in Illyria were defeated – is ignored by Caesar. This particular campaign was commanded by M. Octavius, as we are told by Dio:

> 'Later Octavius also joined them. After sailing into the Ionian Sea and arresting Caius Antonius, he had conquered several places, but could not take Salonae, though he besieged it a very long time. For the inhabitants, having Gabinius to assist them, vigorously repulsed him and finally along with the women made a sortie and performed a remarkable deed. The women let down their hair and robed themselves in black garments, then taking torches and otherwise making their appearance as terrifying as possible, they assaulted the camp of the besiegers at midnight. They threw the outposts, who thought they were spirits, into a panic, and then from all sides at once hurled the fire within the palisade, and the men, following them, slew many while they were in confusion and many who were still asleep, promptly gained possession of the camp, and captured without a blow the harbour in which Octavius was lying. They were not, however, left in peace. For he escaped them somehow, gathered a force again, and after defeating them in battle besieged them. Meanwhile, as Gabinius had died of some disease, he gained control of the whole sea in that vicinity, and by making descents upon the land ravaged many districts. This lasted until the Battle at Pharsalus, after which his soldiers, as soon as a force sailed against them from Brundisium, changed sides without even coming to blows with them. Then, destitute of allies, Octavius retired to Corcyra.'[9]

The role of Gabinius – the former Pompeian commander who now fought for Caesar – is confused and contradicted by other accounts, which have him dying the following year (see Chapter Seven). Again we see a similar pattern, with the Pompeian fleet unable to successfully besiege a coastal city in Illyria/Epirus. The other interesting point of this passage is the reference to a Caesarian force being dispatched from Brundisium after Pharsalus and the lifting of Laelius' siege. Given that Dio's account is questioned as to its conflating of events (around Gabinius' death), there would be some question as to the timing of this force being dispatched. Nevertheless, once again we find evidence of the Pompeian naval forces deserting, on this occasion changing sides altogether, when news of Pharsalus reached them. This led to another Pompeian commander retiring to Corcyra to regroup.

Summary

It is possible to see both the breadth and scope of Pompeian military activity that was taking place at the time of the Battle of Pharsalus, and that when the result of the battle became known, all was brought to a sudden halt, with campaigns being abandoned. The news of Pharsalus forced the majority of commanders to return to Corcyra to regroup and plan the next stage of the campaign. The obvious exception was Cassius and his Eastern fleet, who set off for Asia Minor, presumably to join up with Pompeius and provide him with much-needed reinforcements that could block Caesar crossing the Bosphorus (see Chapter Six).

The other obvious factor arising from these events was the reaction of Pompeius' eastern naval forces. Whilst the Syrian, Phoenician and Cilician fleets followed Cassius to Asia Minor, it seems they had little stomach to keep fighting in the west and wanted to return home after the defeat of their patron, much as the eastern armies had done. As events soon proved (see below), their loyalty quickly collapsed. A more immediate defection was the Egyptian fleet, which seemingly mutinied and deserted Pompeius' son, Cnaeus, and returned home, all of which boded poorly for Pompeius' cause in the east. We are not told the composition of Octavius' fleet, which seems to have been more Roman-based as they did not return home but defected straight to Caesar.

However, it is apparent that none of the Pompeian naval commanders followed their fleets in either returning home or immediately switching sides to Caesar. Aside from loyalty to Pompeius (or dislike of Caesar), it is likely that the news they received had been 'filtered' to downplay the severity of the defeat (as happened with Labienus in Dyrrhachium – see Chapter Six). Consequently, with their commander (and in many cases patron) still alive, the war was still very much active and they needed to return to their headquarters to receive their new orders.

Chapter Six

Responding to Victory, Recovering from Defeat

Having reviewed the impact of the Battle of Pharsalus on the peripheral campaigns, we must now return our focus to Greece itself following Caesar's defeat of Pompeius, and the critical events that took place in the immediate aftermath and did so much to shape the rest of the civil war.

As we have seen, against all odds, Caesar had emerged victorious and destroyed the myth of Pompeian invincibility, seeming to completely overthrow the narrative of the Third Civil War to date. Whilst it is undeniable that the Caesarian victory at Pharsalus was a major psychological blow, as evening fell on the day of the battle, both generals could reflect that perhaps it was not as major a turning point as they would have hoped or feared.

What Next for Caesar?

In terms of achieving his objectives, Caesar had enjoyed a near-perfect day. Not only had he avoided annihilation at the hands of Pompeius, but he had scored a major victory, effectively dissipating Pompeius' grand army. Yet though Caesar found himself master of the battlefield, it had to be acknowledged that this battlefield was in the midst of enemy territory and he was still separated from his core territories in the Western Republic by the Pompeian fleet.

Furthermore, the battle had been more a psychological victory than a military one. The Pompeian army had only suffered between 6,000 and 15,000 casualties, the majority of whom were from the foreign elements of the army, with another 20,000-plus taken prisoner. Crucially, there had only been ten Senators killed, the most notable of whom was Caesar's old enemy L. Domitius Ahenobarbus. Whilst this must have been a satisfying moment of personal revenge for Caesar, in the wider scheme of the civil war it was insignificant. Pompeius and all of his key lieutenants, including Metellus Scipio, had escaped from the field of battle unharmed.

Caesar was now faced with what seems to have been a familiar problem for him – how could he convert success on the battlefield into success in the wider campaign? The Pompeian army was dispersed and Pompeius in flight, effectively giving Caesar military control of mainland Greece and Macedonia, with only scattered Pompeian garrisons and the retreating elements of his enemy's army to oppose him. Yet no matter the size of the victory on the day, the position that Caesar fought from – outnumbered, in Pompeian dominated territory and without control of the surrounding seas – limited his ability to build on that success.

Critically Caesar needed to follow up the battle with a strategy – both military and political – which would transform his battlefield success into victory in the civil war. His enemies needed to be killed, captured or prevented from rebuilding their military capacity. The problem Caesar faced was that although he had won a battle, he would only be the victor in the war if his enemies accepted the fact that they had lost; therefore, the question was whether his victory had enhanced his reputation in their eyes or merely made it worse?

What Next for Pompeius (Magnus no more)?

Pompeius had endured a disastrous day at Pharsalus, the worst in his career as all his worst fears had come true. He had not just been defeated but had been publicly defeated, with the myth of his military invincibility shattered in front of both the Senate and the Eastern kings. Pompeius the Great was now Pompeius the mortal. The only crumbs of comfort were that the bulk of his army had not been destroyed, he himself had evaded capture, he was in what was still (nominally at least) Pompeian-controlled territory and his fleet had control of the seas. Furthermore, though he would clearly be unable to hold Greece or Macedon, his armies still held Africa to the west and the Eastern Republic.

He clearly needed to evade capture, leave Greece and find a base from where to rebuild. His whole masterplan, which he had been working towards for eighteen months, was in tatters due to Caesar having emerged victorious on the battlefield. Yet Caesar's victory was not so overwhelming as to shatter the basic tenets of the narrative that Pompeius had spent so long budling. Caesar was still viewed as the 'enemy of Rome' who had attacked his own city for personal glory, and if anything this victory merely enhanced that 'bogeyman' image. If Pompeius could convince the two elements of his powerbase – the Senatorial oligarchy and the Eastern kings – that this loss was a blip and that the situation could be recovered, then his plan could well be put back on track. He had to raise a new army, defeat Caesar and 'save' the Republic, although that task was now much harder. As it turned out, only one of those elements was carried out.

The Two-Pronged Pompeian Retreat – The Leaders

Given that the battle took place in central Greece, the Pompeian army and their commanders had two viable options for where to retreat once they had secured enough distance from any pursuing Caesarian cavalry: westwards, towards the key Pompeian ports of Dyrrhachium and Corcyra and the security of the Pompeian fleet, or eastwards towards the Pompeian capital of Thessalonica and then into Asia Minor and the Eastern Republic. These two avenues posed a significant problem for Caesar in choosing which to tackle first.

As it was, it was Pompeius who made the running, with Caesar following in his wake. Pompeius faced the problem of whether to choose safety with his fleet – the only remaining source of military superiority he had over Caesar – or safety in the East, with less tangible military forces but more potential for future success. If he had chosen his fleet (as his son famously did), then he would have short-term security but would expose his eastern powerbase to Caesarian attack, thereby jeopardizing his longer-term chances of success. Yet if he selected his eastern powerbase, he would be exposing himself militarily in the short term and gambling that he could rebuild his forces before Caesar overwhelmed him.

In the end, Pompeius gambled on retreating eastwards and the potentially greater rewards of securing himself in his eastern powerbase, hoping that his fleet would fight on in the West and keep Caesar cut off from Italy and delaying his rival from pursing him eastwards. The other gamble that Pompeius was taking, which he would have been well aware of, was that on this occasion he was arriving in the East as an individual, not at the head of a great army or navy; would this lack of immediate military force be sufficient to command the loyalty of the Eastern kings? Velleius and Plutarch add some detail as to who accompanied Pompeius during his eastwards retreat, which ties in with a statement of Appian, who does not name his four companions:[1]

> 'Pompeius fled with the two Lentuli, [L. Cornelius Lentulus Crus and P. Cornelius Lentulus Spinther) both ex-consuls, his own son Sextus, and [M.] Favonius, a former Praetor, friends whom chance had gathered about him as his companions.'[2]
>
> '... all whom Pompeius wished to have with him, these were the two Lentuli [L. Cornelius Lentulus Crus and P. Cornelius Lentulus Spinther) and [M.] Favonius.'[3]

We will never know for certain whether there was any co-ordination of the Pompeian retreat, organized in the short time as the battle turned inexorably against them. Yet it is noticeable that the Pompeian commanders split their retreats to maximum effect, and we may speculate that this was by design rather than accident. The most notable retreat was that by Pompeius' father-in-law and second-in-command, Q. Caecilius Metellus Scipio, who did not join his son-in-law in retreating eastwards, despite his having come from there with his eastern army, but moved westwards towards the Pompeian-held coastal cities and naval base of Corcyra.

Thus, in a reversal of the previous eighteen months, Pompeius went east whilst Metellus headed west, ensuring that both regions had a significant Pompeian commander. Appian and Dio preserve details of the flight of the Pompeian leaders, the majority of whom made for the Pompeian island stronghold of Corcyra (modern Corfu):

> 'Lucius Scipio, Pompeius' father-in-law, and the other notables who had escaped from the Battle of Pharsalus, more prudent than Pompeius, hurried to Corcyra and joined Cato, who had been left there with another army and 300 triremes. The leaders apportioned the fleet among themselves, and Cassius sailed to Pharnaces in Pontus to induce him to take up arms against Caesar. Scipio and Cato embarked for Africa, relying on Varus and his army and his ally, Juba, King of Numidia. The elder son of Pompeius, together with Labienus and Scapula, each with his own part of the army,

hastened to Spain and having detached it from Caesar, collected a new army of Spaniards, Celtiberians, and slaves, and made formidable preparations for war. So great were the forces still remaining which Pompeius had prepared.'[4]

'It came about in this way. Cato had been left behind at Dyrrhachium by Pompeius to keep an eye out for any forces from Italy which might try to cross over, and to repress the Parthini, in case they should begin any disturbance. At first, he carried on war with the latter, but after Pompeius' defeat he abandoned Epirus, and proceeding to Corcyra with those of the same mind as himself, he there received the men who had escaped from the battle and the rest who had the same sympathies. Cicero and a few other senators had set out for Rome at once, but the majority, including Labienus and Afranius, who had no hope in Caesar, the one because he had deserted him, and the other because after having been pardoned by him he had again made war on him, went to Cato, put him at their head, and continued the war. Later Octavius also joined them.'[5]

Not only do these extracts detail the battle plans of the Pompeians, which we will dissect later, but they show the strength that the Pompeians still possessed. Frontinus preserves a unique account of the exploits of one of the Pompeian elite, T. Labienus, Caesar's former lieutenant. He chose not to go to Corcyra, but to the key Pompeian city of Dyrrhachium:

'Titus Labienus, after the Battle of Pharsalus, when his side had been defeated and he himself had fled to Dyrrhachium, combined falsehood with truth, and while not concealing the outcome of the battle, pretended that the fortunes of the two sides had been equalised in consequence of a severe wound received by Caesar. By this pretence, he created confidence in the other followers of Pompeius' party.'[6]

Cicero confirms the movements of Labienus:

'In fact, a few days later Labienus reached Dyrrhachium in flight from Pharsalus, with the news of the loss of the army.'[7]

So Labienus shored up support for the Pompeian cause in Greece by masking the result of the battle. In answer to the riddle of when is a defeat not a defeat, the Pompeian solution was to deny it ever was a defeat. Given the confusion and the two possible directions the retreating Pompeians could have taken, it would have been possible to keep up this illusion for at least the first key week. To those in the West, the Pompeian army was in the East, and vice versa. Even when eyewitness accounts from the survivors who had surrendered (see below) were heard, it would still have been possible to counter this by admitting that Caesar had indeed won the day, but that tales of the size of the victory were mere Caesarian propaganda. The important aspect is that the Pompeian cause did not collapse in the immediate aftermath of the battle, the Pompeian leaders being given time to stabilize their faction and plan their next moves, aided by what we will see was the relative inactivity of Caesar.

Key to this stabilization was perhaps the most noticeable aspect of the Pompeian retreat: how few of the elites surrendered to Caesar. Caesar had pursued a longstanding policy of clemency that would have been hard to transmit during the chaos of the battle itself and the immediate aftermath. Yet in the days that followed, only two notable men sought Caesar's pardon, neither of them from amongst the first rank of Pompeian supporters. The first was to become the most infamous, M. Iunius Brutus, not only a supposed scion from one of the Republic's founding families[8] but a man rumoured to be Caesar's illegitimate son. Plutarch records his flight and subsequent surrender:

> 'After the defeat at Pharsalus, when Pompeius had made his escape to the sea and his camp was besieged, Brutus went out unnoticed by a gate leading to a place that was marshy and full of water and reeds and made his way safely by night to Larissa. From thence he wrote to Caesar, who was delighted at his safe escape, and bade him come to him, and not only pardoned him, but actually made him a highly honoured companion.'[9]

The other was the notoriously battle-shy former Consul and author, M. Tullius Cicero (Cos. 63 BC). Cicero's record in this war speaks for itself. Despite on paper being an enthusiastic supporter of Pompeius, he remained in Italy after the Caesarian conquest, only latterly joining

Pompeius in Greece in mid-49 BC. Though present at both the Battles of Dyrrhachium and Pharsalus, he excelled himself by taking part in neither, being 'ill' on the day of the battle. The *Periochae* of Livy summed up his inaction thus:

> 'Cicero remained in Pompeius' camp, because there was never a man less suited to war than he.'[10]

Despite said 'illness', Cicero was still able to take an enthusiastic part in the retreat and reached the safety of Dyrrhachium, where his lack of eagerness for continuing the fight nearly cost him his life:

> 'However, after the Battle at Pharsalus, in which Cicero took no part because of illness, had been fought, and Pompeius was in flight, Cato, who had a considerable army and a large fleet at Dyrrhachium, asked Cicero to take the command in accordance with custom and because of his superior consular rank. But Cicero rejected the command and was altogether averse to sharing in the campaign, whereupon he came near being killed; for the young Pompeius and his friends called him a traitor and drew their swords upon him, and that would have been the end of him had not Cato interposed and with difficulty rescued him and sent him away from the camp. So Cicero put in at Brundisium and tarried there, waiting for Caesar.'[11]

Cicero himself admits his keenness for the path of peace:

> 'But even after the army was lost, I, who had at all times been an adviser of peace, but who, after the Battle of Pharsalia, urged everyone not to lay aside, but to throw away their arms ...'[12]

For the majority of the others, however, there could be no such accommodation. Though we can never probe into the minds of the men involved, the Pompeian elite was composed of two distinct elements, as has been commented on earlier. Firstly there was the Pompeian faction itself, men who were tied by family or patronage to Pompeius, the most notable examples being Metellus Scipio (his father-in-law) and Faustus Cornelius Sulla (his son-in-law). The other element comprised those who were not natural Pompeian supporters but believed that he was the best option to 'save' the Republic from an aspiring tyrant such as Caesar. They may have not been under any illusion that Pompeius wished to dominate the Republic, but felt at least that would have been within the confines of the old Republican system, as *primus inter pa*res (first amongst equals), rather than an obvious Dictator such as Caesar. These men were best exemplified by Cato and Labienus.

In both cases, the majority saw that nothing had changed after Pharsalus. The Pompeian faction would continue to support their patron and had faith in his ability to turn this defeat around, whilst the diehard enemies of Caesar found nothing to change their fear that Caesar wished to overwhelm the Republic. If anything, their defeat at Pharsalus merely separated the diehard anti-Caesarians (Cato, Labienus) from the lukewarm ones (Brutus, Cicero).

The Two-Pronged Pompeian Retreat – The Army

The attitude of the Pompeian army, or the solders themselves, was in direct contrast to that of their leaders. They fell into two distinct elements: the Italian citizen legionaries and the non-Roman allies. As we have seen, at least two of the Pompeian legions fighting at Pharsalus had formerly been commanded by Caesar and had acquitted themselves well in the fight. Civil war had been a feature of Roman society for the last forty years and the standard Roman soldier did not seem to worry about the perceived rights and wrongs of the various sides; as there were no issues involved that affected them, they simply fought as ordered.

This lack of rancour meant that there would be few consequences for them once the battle had been decided. For all the Pompeian propaganda against Caesar, trying to mark him as a new Sulla, his track record of pardoning the soldiers he had defeated – as seen in Spain – would have preceded him at the rank and file level, especially amongst the legionaries who had fought at his side in Gaul. Consequently, unlike the Pompeian elite, who fought through either personal ties to Pompeius or belief in the defence of the Republic, they had no issue with accepting the result and changing commanders. Thus Caesar boasted:

> 'Of the Pompeian army about fifteen thousand appeared to have fallen, but more than twenty-four thousand surrendered, for even

the cohorts which had been on garrison duty in the forts surrendered to Sulla; many besides fled to the neighbouring communities.'[13]

Dio seems to confirm this situation:

'Those of them who were soldiers of the line Caesar enrolled in his own legions, exhibiting no resentment.'[14]

We can therefore assume that the bulk of the Italian legionaries, seemingly assured of their safety, chose not to flee but to surrender to Caesar, thereby boosting his army. So although the Pompeian army was not destroyed at the Battle of Pharsalus, it did disappear.

The other half of Pompeius' 'grand army', the non-citizen auxiliaries, the bulk of which came from the Eastern Republic, seem by contrast to have been particularly targeted during the battle itself (see Chapter Five).

Aside from the eastern element, we are told that there were a number of locally recruited Greeks, and these would simply have melted away back to their hometowns. For the greater part of the auxiliaries, those from the eastern provinces and its allied kingdoms, there was no such easy escape. Having come all that distance to support their patron, Pompeius, they now found themselves abandoned and on the wrong side of the Bosphorus. They would either have to flee eastwards and seek passage over the Bosphorus or the Ionian Sea, or come to an accommodation with Caesar to buy safe passage home. Dio provides a passage on Caesar's attitudes to Pompeius' eastern allies, but it is far from clear whether this accommodation was in force when Caesar reached the Near East or in Greece:

'This same attitude he adopted toward the princes and the peoples who had assisted Pompeius. He pardoned them all, bearing in mind that he himself was acquainted with none or almost none of them, whereas from his rival they had previously obtained many favours.'[15]

'A proof of his feeling is that he spared Sadalus the Thracian and Deiotarus the Galatian, who had been in the battle, and Tarcondimotus, who was ruler of a portion of Cilicia and had been of the greatest assistance to Pompeius in the matter of ships. But what need is there to enumerate the rest who had sent auxiliaries, to whom also he granted pardon, merely exacting money from them? He did nothing else to them and took from them nothing else.'[16]

Dio's account leaves us wondering whether these princes came to an accommodation in the immediate aftermath of the battle or later, when Caesar and his army were in Asia Minor. The only hard evidence we have is for the fate of Deiotarus, who appears in Plutarch's account of Pompeius' retreat (see below)[17] when he flees Greece by sea, seemingly without his army. Whatever the case, the effect was the same: the 'grand army' of Pompeius was no more. The eastern princes and provinces now found themselves on the losing side of a war with Rome, a position none of them wanted to be in and one which few of them had expected. This was a region that was still coming to terms with the Roman conquest of some twenty years earlier, a position that clearly did not bode well for Pompeius and his mission in the East.

Caesar's Dilemma – Pursue the Man or his Army?

Caesar had changed his destiny at Pharsalus, from the underdog to the favourite in this latest Roman civil war. Yet though he was victorious on the day, the war itself was far from over. He was now faced with the ultimate dilemma that generals face at such a time: how to convert success in battle into overall victory in the campaign. Furthermore, though he had scored a clear military victory, the aftermath seemed to be something of a let-down and the Pompeian retreat presented him with a tricky problem. Caesar himself doesn't say how long he stayed at Pharsalus after the battle, but Appian states:

> 'Caesar remained two days at Pharsalus after the victory, offering sacrifice and giving his army a respite from fighting.'[18]

Given Caesar's record for constantly taking the initiative, this inaction seems both uncharacteristic and costly. Whilst his army certainly needed to rest after the heavy physical toll the battle had taken, it also gave the retreating Pompeians vital recovery time. The cavalry pursuit after the battle only netted one minor Pompeian commander (Domitius

Responding to Victory, Recovering from Defeat 121

Ahenobarbus), with the others, and most importantly Pompeius himself, evading pursuit and reaching safe territory.

Aside from Caesar letting his army recover, there could have been two other factors at work. The first may have been the hope that the defeated Pompeian leaders would sue for peace, as their soldiers and allies had done. Yet the sole Pompeian supporter who came to Caesar's camp was M. Iunius Brutus, another comparative small fry. The second factor is illuminated in Plutarch's life of Brutus:

> 'Now, since no one could tell whither Pompeius was fleeing, and all were in great perplexity, Caesar took a long walk with Brutus alone, and sounded him on the subject.'[19]

Thus we can see Caesar's dilemma and the reason for his delay: he did not know whether Pompeius had fled eastwards or westwards, and until that could be determined he had to remain static, otherwise he would have to gamble and potentially lose his quarry by making the wrong choice. We must assume, therefore, that Caesar sent scouts in both directions to pick up Pompeius' trail and learn his whereabouts. In the meantime, these two days were used to allow the army to rest and recover, integrate the Pompeian legionaries who had surrendered, reward his allies and pardon any opponents who sought it. Again Appian sums up this period:

> 'Then he set free his Thessalian allies and granted pardon to the suppliant Athenians, and said to them, "How often will the glory of your ancestors save you from self-destruction?"'[20]

Appian also provides a final passage on the deceased Roman centurion Crastinus, the man who led the Caesarian charge and paid for it with his life:

> 'When sought for he was found among the dead, and Caesar bestowed military honours on his body and buried it and erected a special tomb for him near the common burial-place of the others.'[21]

Finally, at some point, most likely towards the end of the second day, Caesar's scouts were able to pick up the trail of Pompeius, who, we must be frank, had not kept a low profile at Amphipolis (see below). Appian writes: 'On the third day he marched eastward, having learned that Pompeius had fled thither.'[22]

Although this solved one dilemma, it left Caesar with another major problem: should he chase the man or the army? Pompeius had fled to his eastern powerbase, clearly looking to recruit fresh funds and a new army from his allies there. This may have spurred Caesar to adopt a softer policy to the Eastern kings fleeing Greece. However, the bulk of the remaining Pompeian forces lay to the west, between Caesar and Italy.

If Caesar marched eastwards after Pompeius, he would lose his chance of crushing the Pompeian forces in the west, who would use that time to recover their strength, still having naval dominance and control of North Africa and thus leaving Spain, Italy and more importantly Rome itself open to attack. Equally, if he chose to move westwards and not follow Pompeius, instead attempting to crush the remaining Pompeian forces, he would leave Pompeius a free hand in the East. Caesar could dispatch commanders to chase Pompeius, but he may have judged that they would not match Pompeius' status in the eyes of the Eastern Republic and its allies. Furthermore, Pompeius was the figurehead of the opposing faction, and if he could be captured and an accommodation reached, then the conflict would be ended with a settlement rather than there being a continuation of the civil war.

It was these calculations that Caesar faced in the hours that followed his gaining knowledge of Pompeius' retreat. Given that none of the Pompeian leaders had sought terms in the immediate aftermath of the battle, it must have been clear to Caesar that they intended to fight on, so any illusions he may have harboured about ending the war at Pharsalus had disappeared. With armies in Spain and Italy and a loyal commander to manage affairs there (see below), Caesar now chose to gamble on chasing down Pompeius in the East and risking the recovery of the Pompeian faction in the West. It would not have escaped him that the East was the richest part of the Mediterranean world and could be used to finance his campaigns via a series of forced donations, having already emptied Rome's treasuries.

Thus Caesar turned east and marched his army for Asia Minor, dispatching M. Antonius, his deputy, back to Rome to manage affairs in Italy and P. Cornelius Sulla to mop up the Pompeian garrisons in Greece. Nevertheless, we must be clear that this was a gamble, chasing the figurehead rather than the bulk of the Pompeian forces, and risked being seen as abandoning the Western Republic and potentially allowing the civil war to flourish there. Furthermore, not only did Pompeius have a two day start, but he was travelling light and could travel overseas, whereas Caesar had to march his army by land.

The Contest for Greece (Macedon, Illyria and Epirus)

The majority of the surviving sources (including Caesar himself) now move their narrative from the battle to the chase between Pompeius and Caesar, and thus overlook events in Greece. We must not forget that prior to the battle, Caesar was operating in what was mostly Pompeian-held land, having only carved out pockets of territory on the Illyrian coast and in central Greece (see Chapters Two and Three). Yet even with his victory, Caesar found himself surrounded by Pompeian-controlled territory to the north-east (Macedon), to the west (Illyria and Epirus) and to the south (the Peloponnese).

Despite the dissipation of the Pompeian 'grand army' after Pharsalus, we still know of Pompeian forces in Illyria (under Cato) and the Peloponnese (under P. Rutilius Lupus), the assumption being that the Macedonian legions came westwards with Metellus Scipio, leaving garrisons behind. These forces cannot have represented more than a handful of legions, and Caesar clearly now held the numerical advantage. In practice, this meant that offensive field operations could be ruled out for the Pompeians, but the cities and territories they held could, in theory, be defended, especially with naval superiority. The obvious counter to this proposal was that the locals of the cities of the region had shown marked indifference to supporting either side when it came to actual military involvement.

With the main Pompeian leaders having regrouped at Corcyra and recalled a number of their colleagues from naval operations (see Chapter Five), the collective leadership of the Pompeians in the West (Metellus and Cato) appear to have wanted to ensure that Greece did not fall uncontested and so moved south from Corcyra to take up an advanced position nearer to Caesar. They chose the Peloponnese, occupying the port city of Patrae (Patras) on the north-western Peloponnese coast, separated from Caesar's army by the Corinthian Gulf and the defendable Isthmus of Corinth. As attested by Dio, it was here that other Pompeian leaders joined them, notably M. Petreius and F. Cornelius Sulla. Thus, it seemed the Pompeians intended to hold at least part of mainland Greece whilst they rebuilt their strength.

Immediately after Pharsalus there were two Caesarian armies in Greece: the main one which had fought at Pharsalus and a smaller one under the command of Q. Fufius Calenus (see Chapters Two and Three). There are no clear details for the disposition of the main Caesarian army after Caesar had moved eastwards chasing Pompeius and Antonius had been dispatched to Rome, but command seems to have fallen to P. Cornelius Sulla, as can be seen from a passing reference by Caesar:

> '... for even the cohorts which had been on garrison duty in the forts surrendered to Sulla; many besides fled to the neighbouring communities.'[23]

With Caesar heading eastwards and Calenus already pushing southwards, the most logical orders Sulla would have been given would have been to push westward and secure the key cities on the Illyrian and Epirote coast, which still cut off Caesar's army from Italy. Though supported by the Pompeian navy, as events had shown in the previous months, these cities would prove difficult to defend in the face of a hostile population who had no wish to be involved in a Roman civil war. Furthermore, the ploy Labienus had used, to downplay the result of the battle, would soon have worn off in the face of the reality of a large Caesarian army in the field and no sign of a Pompeian one. Thus it seems that Macedon, having been abandoned, fell to Caesar and the Illyrian/Epirote coast began to fall too. As Cicero notes, a number of the Pompeian leaders evacuated Dyrrhachium, which was then looted:

> 'For the granaries were pillaged and their contents scattered and strewn all about the streets and alleys. You and your companions, in great alarm, suddenly embarked, and as you looked back at night towards town you saw the flames of the merchant ships, which the soldiers (not wishing to follow) had set on fire.'[24]

This just left Corcyra, the Adriatic and the Peloponnese. Annoyingly, we are told nothing of Corcyra and the Pompeian control of the Adriatic, other than the aborted attack on Brundisium. What we can determine comes from the silence of our surviving sources in terms of any more impediments being faced by the Caesarians in crossing back to Italy; certainly, Antonius' crossing seems to have been uncontested. We certainly hear nothing of the fate of Corcyra, but with the Pompeian fleet being based there it is unlikely to have fallen to a Caesarian assault. It either remained a Pompeian naval base or was abandoned by them. The fate of the Pompeian stand in the Peloponnese is briefly documented by Dio:

'Subsequently Quintus Fufius Calenus marched against them, whereupon they set sail, and coming to Cyrene …'[25]

Thus, in just a few weeks, the Pompeians chose not to defend the Peloponnese, despite their naval strength, and abandoned mainland Greece to the Caesarians. Furthermore, as Dio states in various passages, Calenus was initially campaigning against Athens and Megara before he marched into the Peloponnese:

'Calenus had been sent by Caesar into Greece before the battle, and he captured among other places the Piraeus, owing to its being unwalled. Athens, he had been unable to take, in spite of a great deal of damage he did to its territory, until the defeat of Pompeius.'[26]

'Accordingly Athens and most of the rest of Greece then at once made terms with him; but the Megarians in spite of this resisted and were captured only at a considerably later date, partly by force and partly by treachery. Therefore many of the inhabitants were slain and the survivors sold.'[27]

'After these achievements he marched upon Patrae and occupied it easily, as he had already frightened Cato and his followers away.'[28]

So both Athens and Megara held out against Caesar, until one came to terms and the other was taken by force. However, despite this uncharacteristic resistance from the locals, the Pompeians in the Peloponnese chose not to fight. Their choice of destination is interesting – the Roman province of Cyrene, between North Africa and Egypt. This perhaps provides us with the answer, namely that fresh orders had arrived from Pompeius to rendezvous with him in Egypt, using Cyrene as a convenient and

Pompeius' Retreat – Discerning the Plan

safe staging post. Thus, Greece, Macedon, Illyria and Epirus fell to the Caesarians.

Pompeius' Retreat – Discerning the Plan

The surviving sources are full of details of Pompeius' retreat from Greece, which allow them to utilize their full dramatic flourishes, akin to the earlier example of C. Marius. Plutarch offers the most detailed (and dramatic) account of Pompeius' withdrawal after Pharsalus, but it is only Caesar who presents an account that is free from melodrama and holds a key detail. This contrast allows us to see our biggest problem; namely, that every source who wrote an account of Pompeius' retreat did so knowing how it ended, meaning we face issues determining Pompeius' actual plan, separating the details from the drama. When trying to reconstruct this retreat and Pompeius' aims, we need to jettison the dramatic narrative of Pompeius being a broken figure wandering aimlessly through the Aegean (in the manner of Odysseus) and focus on Pompeius the general. Nevertheless, the dispassionate account of Caesar does allow us to recreate the outlines of his plan.

It is helpful if we break down the retreat into its distinct phases, the first of which was the immediate aftermath of the battle. With his army dissipated, Pompeius' immediate aim in the first few hours was to avoid capture and put distance between himself and Caesar's pursuit. As discussed above, the safest option would have been to go west towards the Pompeian strongholds of Dyrrhachium and Corcyra. Yet Pompeius and his companions chose to go eastwards. As discussed above, Caesar would have expected him to go west and by doing the opposite Pompeius created an immediate problem for Caesar; should he follow him eastwards and ignore Pompeius' forces in the Adriatic or concentrate on those and let his opponent slip free? Pompeius was clearly planning for the next phase of the war, and that would require men and money, both of which could be found in the Eastern Republic and its allied kingdoms.

In going east, Pompeius utilized the one remaining advantage he held over Caesar: his control of the seas. On land, even moving quickly as he was, there was a danger that he could be overtaken by Caesar's cavalry. Therefore, his immediate priority was to get to the Aegean and board a ship. Appian, Dio and Plutarch all agree that Pompeius' immediate destination after Pharsalus was the city of Larissa, which had been the staging post for the two Pompeian armies prior to the battle. Dio adds the following detail:

> 'He did not enter the city, because he feared that they might incur some blame in consequence; but bidding them go over to the victor, he himself took provisions, went down to the sea.'[29]

This was a sensible precaution, given that many Greek cities would be eager to ingratiate themselves with the victorious Caesar by handing Pompeius over to him. So the fleeing Pompeius collected essential supplies and made his way to the Aegean to find a boat. Of the surviving sources, only Plutarch provides details as to Pompeius taking to the seas, which involved spending a night in a fisherman's hut, persuading a local fisherman to take the party out to sea and then encountering a merchant ship, which they either commandeered or persuaded to allow them aboard. Whether or not there is any truth in this story is impossible to know. The important issue was that Pompeius had eluded Caesar's search parties, and by taking to the sea was now out of their reach.

Having achieved the first phase of his retreat, thoughts could now turn to the next step, his short-term destination. Here we have one of the most important divergences amongst the sources. Appian, Dio and Plutarch all have Pompeius sail directly across the Aegean to the island of Lesbos off the coast of Asia Minor and its capital Mitylene, a Pompeian stronghold, where his wife (Cornelia) and youngest son (Sextus) were, allowing for more dramatic flourishes (see Plutarch's account) between husband and wife. Caesar's account of this period maintains one important difference, which was actually alluded to in Plutarch,[30] that Pompeius put in at Amphipolis, a key Pompeian city in Greece:

> 'An edict had been issued at Amphipolis in the name of Pompeius that all the youths of that province, whether Greeks or Roman citizens, should assemble to take the oath. But no opinion could be formed whether Pompeius had proposed this to avert suspicion, in order that he might keep his purpose of a distant flight concealed as long as possible, or that with the new levies he might attempt to hold Macedonia if no one checked him. He himself stopped there

one night at anchor, and after inviting his friends at Amphipolis to a conference and collecting money for necessary expenses, on receiving news of Caesar's approach he quit that place and, in a few days, arrived at Mytilene.'[31]

Having outpaced his Caesarian pursuers, it made perfect sense for a number of reasons that Pompeius stop off there. Firstly, he would have been able to personally appraise the Pompeian commanders there of what actually had happened in the Pharsalus campaign and brief them on the next moves. Secondly, he could issue commands to the remaining Pompeian forces (on both and sea) and restore some co-ordination to the retreat. Thirdly, as the city was on the Via Egnatia, any retreating 'eastern' Pompeian forces would pass through there and he could appraise himself of how much of his army had survived the battle. Finally, as Caesar himself directly alludes to, he could take possession of what must have been a substantial treasury, ensuring that his eastwards journey was well provided for.

It is interesting that the other sources omit this crucial first port of call, and we can only speculate at their motives for doing so. The most obvious motive is that this rational and logical step was not the act of a man who had been broken by defeat and was fleeing aimlessly. This was instead the act of a man who was planning the next stages of the war.

Having assessed that there was little of his army left to regroup, Pompeius had no intention of defending Amphipolis and thus evacuated the city when Caesar's forces approached. He set sail for Mytilene, on the other side of the Aegean, which he could reach in matter of days, whereas Caesar's forces would take weeks, having to march through Greece and then Asia Minor. Caesar would also need to transport his army across the Bosphorus, where he could be blocked by a Pompeian fleet.

Having evacuated Amphipols and co-ordinated the Pompeian retreat from Eastern Greece, he could embark upon the third stage of his planned retreat, crossing the Aegean and then working his way along the coast of Asia Minor, hopefully picking up military and political support from the various cities and bases along the way. Lesbos and the city of Mitylene was just the first of several destinations in the eastern Mediterranean, and the current location of his wife and youngest son. This can be seen by the references in the surviving sources:

> 'There he joined his wife, Cornelia and they embarked with four triremes which had come to him from Rhodes and Tyre.'[32]
>
> 'The first city that he entered was Attaleia in Pamphylia; there some triremes from Cilicia met him, soldiers were assembled for him, and he was surrounded by Senators, sixty of them.'[33]
>
> '... he sent messengers round to the cities; to some also he sailed about in person, asking for money and manning ships.'[34]
>
> '... after adding to his fleet other small craft he came to Cilicia and thence to Cyprus.'[35]

Thanks to these efforts, Pompeius, who had started off as a refugee with just four companions on a fishing boat, now commanded a small army and fleet. The key to this retreat, however, lay in his ultimate destination. Whilst both Appian and Plutarch talk of a flight to the Parthian court being discussed (a totally unrealistic option), again it is Caesar who lays clear Pompeius' plan. His ultimate destination was the Roman province of Syria, the heartland of Rome's Eastern Republic and the very province which Pompeius had created some fifteen years earlier.

Whilst the bulk of Rome's Syrian legions would have been taken by Metellus Scipio the year before, the province would still provide an ample base to recruit men, from both the province itself and the allied kingdoms, and to secure funds to rebuild. Pompeius would have soon been informed that Caesar was marching his army overland, which meant that the next battle would be fought in the East, the site of Pompeius' greatest victories to date. It is Caesar who details the subsequent collapse of his opponent's plans:

> 'There [Cyprus] he [Pompeius] learns that, by the consent of all the people of Antioch and of the Roman citizens engaged in business there, arms had been taken up for the purpose of excluding him, and that messages had been sent to those who were said to have betaken themselves in flight to the neighbouring townships bidding them not to go to Antioch. If they did so, they were told, it would be at great peril of their lives. The same thing had happened at Rhodes to L. Lentulus, who had been Consul the previous year, to P. Lentulus, an ex-Consul, and to some others, who, when they were following Pompeius in flight and had come to the island, had not been allowed

admittance in the town and the harbour, and on messages being sent to them to quit these parts, had weighed anchor contrary to their intention. And already a report of Caesar's approach was being conveyed to the communities.'[36]

Here we see the unravelling of Pompeius' carefully orchestrated retreat and the true impact of the defeat at Pharsalus. Pompeius may well have been the patron of the provinces and kingdoms of the Eastern Republic, but now he was the loser in a civil war; past loyalties counted for nothing when faced with a Roman army and a commander that had already defeated the armies of the East. Pompeius was 'Magnus' no more, and no one wanted to support the loser or be the location for a second confrontation. The cities of Syria consequently opted for armed neutrality and opposed Pompeius.

This left Pompeius in a severe quandary. His limited military resources were not sufficient to launch an attack on a city such as Antioch. There would have been other cities on the Syrian coast where he might have been able to force an entry, but then he would be sited in a hostile province with a Caesarian army approaching. Thus, local resistance forced him to abandon his plans to use Syria as a base for the next phase of the civil war.

Moving to quarters in the relative – and temporary – safety of the island of Cyprus, Pompeius needed to rethink his plans. If the Caesarian army crossed the Bosphorus, then Asia Minor would be undefended, and whilst he could have held Cyprus, that would have done little to aid his overall campaign. He could also have set sail westward to link up with Metellus Scipio and Cato in the Adriatic or North Africa. The final option would have been to remain in the East and seek a new base of operations. Determined not to abandon his powerbase without a fight, Pompeius opted for the latter and chose to sail to the Roman – and theoretically Pompeian – client kingdom of Ptolemaic Egypt, having strengthened his forces further with the resources of Cyprus and Cilicia:

> 'Ascertaining these facts, Pompeius gave up his idea of visiting Syria, took the funds belonging to the association of tax-farmers, borrowed money from certain private persons, and deposited on shipboard a great weight of bronze coinage for the use of the soldiers; and having armed two thousand men, partly those whom he had selected

from the households of the tax-farmers, partly those whom he had requisitioned from the merchants and those of their own men whom each owner judged to be fit for the purpose, arrived at Pelusium.'[37]

The Turning Point – Caesar, Cassius and the Eastern Fleet

Once again, we can see that Caesar's decisive action had forced a change in Pompeius' plans. Before Pharsalus, Caesar's bold/reckless advances had made Pompeius give battle before he had time to properly integrate his two armies. Now, his eastward pursuit with his army, though slower, was clearly having an intimidatory effect on the local provinces and kingdoms, none of whom wanted to support Pompeius and raise the wrath of an advancing Roman army. Had Caesar not taken his army eastwards and exerted this pressure, then it is very likely that the cities of Syria would have welcomed Pompeius, albeit grudgingly.

Yet Caesar faced one key deficiency: his lack of naval power. For the most part this would not have been an issue, as he had the superior land force. Nevertheless, any march to the Near East faced the major obstacle of crossing the Bosphorus, and it was here that the course of the war nearly swung back in Pompeius' favour. If the Pompeian navy could blockade the Bosphorus, then Caesar would be trapped on the Greek side of the straits and unable to pursue his opponent.

We will never know if it was through luck or orders that there was a Pompeian fleet on hand to execute such a strategy. As we have described earlier (see Chapter Five), when news of the result of Pharsalus reached the various Pompeian battle fleets, most opted to return to Corcyra, whilst the Egyptian fleet deserted. However, the fleet composed of Syrian, Phoenician, and Cilician ships under C. Cassius Longinus, himself a commander with distinguished pedigree in the East – having served and commanded in the First Romano-Parthian War – did neither of these. Instead, the fleet broke off its attacks on Sicily and, still commanded by Cassius, sailed eastwards.

It is impossible to know just what Cassius had in his mind as he sailed to the Eastern Mediterranean. Appian claims that he had received new orders and his destination was the Bosphoran Kingdom of the Crimea, whose king, Pharnaces II (son of the legendary Mithridates VI of Pontus), owed his throne to Pompeius.[38] Given his fleet's eastern Mediterranean origin, the ships would have wanted to be nearer their homeland. Yet in none of the surviving sources is there any affirmation of the obvious military tactic that Pompeius needed to deploy to stop any Caesarian attack on the East; namely to block the Bosphorus. With enemy naval superiority and control of the straits, Caesar's newly won military superiority on land would count for nought if he was stuck on the Greek side of the channel. Cassius did not need his whole fleet to sail to the Crimea to seek aid from Pharnaces, and it would be logical that he had orders to block the straits as well. However, given the lack of source evidence, this can only be supposition.

Whatever the truth, Cassius did indeed reach the Bosphorus before Caesar's army, and so was well placed to stop the Caesarian advance in its tracks. Had he done so, then the subsequent history of the Third Civil War and the Republic itself may well have turned out very differently. Unsurprisingly, we find no account of this confrontation in Caesar's own narrative of the period, clearly not wishing to draw attention to how close to disaster the whole enterprise came. The only detailed account that survives is in Appian, though Dio mentions it in passing:

> 'On the third day he [Caesar] marched eastward, having learned that Pompeius had fled thither, and for want of triremes he essayed to cross the Hellespont in skiffs. Here Cassius came upon him in midstream, with a part of his fleet, as he was hastening to Pharnaces. Although he might have mastered these small boats with his numerous triremes, he was panic-stricken by Caesar's astounding success, which was then heralded with consternation everywhere, and he thought that Caesar had sailed purposely against him. So he extended his hands in entreaty from his trireme toward the skiff, begged for pardon, and surrendered his fleet.
>
> 'I can see no other reason myself, nor can I think of any other instance where fortune was more propitious in a trying emergency than when Cassius, a most valiant man, with seventy triremes, fell in with Caesar when he was unprepared, but did not venture to come to blows with him. And yet he who thus, through fear alone, disgracefully surrendered to Caesar when he was crossing the straits, afterward murdered him in Rome when he was at the height of his power.'[39]

'... while crossing the Hellespont in a kind of ferry-boat, he [Caesar] met Pompeius's fleet sailing with Lucius [Caius] Cassius in command, but so far from suffering any harm at their hands, he terrified them and won them over to his side.'[40]

It thus appears that Cassius caught Caesar crossing the Bosphorus, and despite having a fleet of seventy triremes, surrendered rather than attack and destroy him. It is clear that had Cassius not come to an arrangement with Caesar, then at best Caesar would have been trapped and unable to cross the Bosphorus with his army, whilst at worst he would have been killed, having been hopelessly outnumbered.

Yet if we lay aside the dramatic elements of Cassius, a battle-hardened commander who had survived the Battle of Carrhae and defended Syria from Parthian invasion, being overcome by the sight of Caesar, what are we to make of this extraordinary surrender? There are two obvious elements to consider: the fleet and Cassius himself. Having received the news of Pompeius' defeat, and bearing in mind the attitude of the defeated eastern armies, would Cassius' fleet have been in any mood to attack the victor? So was this a case of the fleet mutinying and refusing to attack Caesar, leaving Cassius with no choice but to negotiate terms?

Cassius had been a client of Crassus and seems to have transferred his allegiance to Pompeius, being elected a Tribune in the critical year of 49 BC. He then joined Pompeius in Greece, and enthusiastically and successfully commanded the naval assault on Sicily. Had he wanted to surrender, he could have easily done so after events in Sicily rather than continue to command the fleet. His subsequent career showed little enthusiasm for Caesar, remaining in Rome during the African campaign and then heading the conspiracy that resulted in Caesar's murder. Why, then, did he spurn this once–in–a–lifetime opportunity? Whilst it is impossible to be certain, the facts favour a mutiny amongst the eastern fleet, with it refusing to attack Caesar, thereby forcing Cassius' hand. Once more, we see Caesar's reckless policy come close to disaster, trying to cross the Bosphorus without naval support, but yet again him being saved by the actions of others, in this case a mutinous fleet.

It must be pointed out that there is considerable modern debate over the identity of the Cassius who was in command of the fleet. Appian is clear that the commander was none other than C. Cassius Longinus, who later famously co-led the conspiracy that led to Caesar's assassination. This ties in with earlier evidence that Cassius was in command of a Pompeian fleet off Sicily, who then received orders after Pharsalus to go to the Black Sea and the court of the Pontic King of the Bosphoran Kingdom (Crimea – see Chapter Five). Modern academia however disagrees[41] and argues that it must have been another hitherto unknown Cassius with a hitherto unknown fleet rather than C. Cassius himself based on a handful of other surviving fragments that have Cassius in the east seeking Caesar's pardon.

Thus despite all sources pointing to Cassius being in the East after Pharsalus and thus perfectly capable of being the commander, many feel the need to deny him the role and subsequent understanding of his later actions. These other sources do not preclude Cassius being the commander, but can be understood if we argue that Cassius did not surrender to Caesar, but was mutinied on by his fleet who threw in their lot with Caesar, as happened to other Pompeian fleets after Pharsalus. If Cassius opposed this then he may well have been the one to flee rather than go over to Caesar himself, only to have to backtrack and eat his words when faced with the news of Pompeius' murder and then have seen the need to reconcile with Caesar.

Having made it across the Bosphorus, not only did Caesar have unfettered access to Asia Minor and the Near East, but he now had a fleet of ships and naval control of the Eastern Mediterranean. This changed the dynamic of the situation completely as he would be able to quicken his chase of Pompeius by sea, instead of just by land, although there were insufficient ships for his whole army. Caesar narrates what happened next:

> 'When Caesar, after lingering a few days in Asia, had heard that Pompeius had been seen in Cyprus, conjecturing that he was on his way to Egypt because of his ties with the kingdom and the further advantages of the place, he went to Alexandria with one legion which he had ordered to follow him from Thessaly and another which he had summoned out of Achaea from his legate Q. Fufius, and also with eight hundred horse and with ten warships from Rhodes and a few from Asia.'[42]

Not only had Caesar avoided disaster, but he was closing in on Pompeius with both military and now naval superiority.

Pompeius' Egyptian Gamble – Magnus no More

Pompeius must have known that going to Egypt was a gamble. On the one hand, the kingdom was the wealthiest in the Mediterranean, was further away from Caesar's army marching across Asia and was far more defensible by land. Furthermore, Pompeius and his Triumviral colleagues had used military force to restore the Pharaoh, Ptolemy XII, to his throne and left behind a Roman garrison.[43]

However, even without the issue of the loss of reputation caused by the defeat at Pharsalus, there were enough warning signs that he would not receive a warm welcome in Egypt. Firstly, his client Pharaoh had died in 51 BC and the country had collapsed into its own civil war between his two heirs – and supposed joint rulers – Ptolemy XIII and his sister, Cleopatra VII. Furthermore, the garrison of Roman soldiers that had been stationed in Egypt had become notoriously unruly and a law unto themselves, and had infamously murdered two sons of the Proconsul of Syria, M. Calpurnius Bibulus, in 50 BC, though for what reason has not survived.[44] Not only was Bibulus a Pompeian supporter, but the garrison had been left behind by Pompeius' former agent, A. Gabinius (Cos. 58 BC), who was now a Caesarian supporter. Finally, there was the matter of the Egyptian fleet commanded by Pompeius' eldest son, Cnaeus, which had abandoned the Pompeian cause and returned to Egypt when news of Pharsalus reached them (see Chapter Five).

Thus, there were a number of warning signs that should have alerted Pompeius to his not receiving a warm welcome. Perhaps it was with this in mind that the Pompeian army evacuated from Greece and sailed to Cyrene, neighbouring Egypt, under the command of Cato (see above). Pompeius was hoping that a reminder that he still had a military force at his behest would override any local danger.

Ultimately, this calculation proved to be a calamitous one. Ptolemy XIII received a request from Pompeius for an audience, which would have given the new Pharaoh a dilemma. In the midst of a civil war with his sister, he would not have had the time, resources, or inclination to become the new powerbase for one of the factions of a Roman internecine conflict, which would only invite another Roman invasion, one which might end Egypt's independence forever.

Therefore, he decided that not only would he not support Pompeius, but he would ingratiate himself with Caesar. To the mind of a young

Ptolemaic ruler, that meant disposing of the problem by disposing of the man himself, so he ordered that Pompeius be murdered, clearly not thinking how killing Rome's most famous general would look to the Romans, even those who fought against him. In Roman eyes, Romans murdering each other was acceptable; for a foreigner to do so was beyond the pale, as Ptolemy swiftly found out when Caesar arrived.

A small party was dispatched by Ptolemy to meet Pompeius on the beach near Pelusium, with Pompeius making his final – and fatal – mistake to land without an armed force.[45] He was met by the ruler's representative, Achillas, and a Roman Centurion, L. Septimius, who had served under him in the Pirate War during the 60s BC. Upon landing, it was Septimius who did the deed, murdering Pompeius on the beach in full sight of his fleet. The date of his death equates to 28 September 48 BC, slightly more than six week after the Battle of Pharsalus.

As had happened with Pompeius' colleague Crassus, his head was severed, being sent to the Pharaoh as proof of the deed, the two former Triumviral colleagues having parallel deaths as they had lives. Appian records the following:

> 'The remainder of the body was buried by somebody on the shore, and a small monument was erected over it, on which somebody else wrote this inscription: "How pitiful a tomb for one so rich in temples."
>
> 'In the course of time the monument was wholly covered with sand and the bronze images that had been erected to Pompeius by his kinsfolk at a later period near Mount Cassius had all been outraged and afterwards removed to the secret recess of the temple, but in my time, they were sought for and found by the Roman Emperor Hadrian, while making a journey thither, who cleared away the rubbish from the monument and made it again conspicuous, and placed Pompeius' images in their proper places.'[46]

It appears that Pompeius' death was not the only one at this time. Although the details are scant, Orosius records a massacre of other Pompeian supporters:

> 'The wife and children of Pompeius took flight and the rest of Pompeius' fleet was destroyed and all those on board were slaughtered

with the utmost cruelty. Pompeius Bithynicus also lost his life there, while Lentulus, a man of Consular rank, was killed at Pelusium.'[47]

Other sources add a few details:

'L. [Cornelius] Lentulus was also arrested by the king and slain in prison.'[48]

'Moreover, all the companions and intimates of Pompeius who had been captured by the king as they wandered over the country, he treated with kindness and attached them to himself.'[49]

With the few surviving sources, we have no way of knowing how many other Pompeians were killed. News of Pompeius' death seems to have been slow to reach many who had been heading to Egypt to rendezvous with him separately. Despite Orosius' talk of a massacre, it seems that the majority of those captured were put in prison and released by Caesar. The only notable other casualty was the consul of 49 BC, L. Cornelius Lentulus Crus, but despite his office, he was hardly a prominent figure in the Pompeian faction.

Nevertheless, the key death was that of Pompeius and the civil war between him and Caesar thereby ended, not on the battlefield, but on an Egyptian beach. The key question now would be whether the civil war, which Pompeius had engineered as part of his strategy to dominate the Republic, would continue in his absence, having taken on a life of its own, or would it peter out without its architect to sustain it?

Summary

Far from fleeing the battlefield in a panic and wandering aimlessly across the Mediterranean, Pompeius' retreat from Pharsalus evolved into a carefully managed strategy. Finding the fishing boat was certainly a stroke of luck, but once he had accomplished this then a new plan of retreat formed in his mind, allowing for the recovery of his position.

Yet despite the planning, there were two key turning points which unravelled the whole scheme, both of which had the same cause: the 'revolt' of Syria and the loss of the Eastern fleet. Both of these incidents led to the collapse of Pompeius' recovery plan and his subsequent death.

The first meant that rather than base himself in a Roman province and act from a secure position of power, he had to gamble on the support of a young and temperamentally uncertain Pharaoh in Egypt. The second meant that the time he thought he had now disappeared, with Caesar being able to launch an effective and far swifter chase.

We will never know if news of the disaster at the Bosphorus reached Pompeius. However, if it did, then it would go a great way to explaining why he suddenly became so reckless. Having decided on Egypt as a destination, Pompeius thought he had time on his side. Even if Cassius and the Eastern fleet failed to prevent Caesar from crossing the Bosphorus, he would still have to march his army through Asia Minor and the whole of the Near Eastern coastline (Syria and Judea), giving Pompeius months to prepare and to defend Egypt. However, the fleet's defection meant that Caesar could send a legion across the Mediterranean in a matter of days. For Pompeius, this meant that time was now fast running out, forcing him into a desperate act when a calmer decision would have been to travel along the coast to Cyrene and meet up with Metellus, Cato and the remnants of the Pompeian forces.

For Caesar, Pompeius' death was both a triumph and a tragedy. Within less than a month, he had overcome the odds and defeated his enemy on the battlefield, in sight of the Senatorial oligarchy and all the allied kings of the East, and had now seen the death of his rival and the end of any renewal of the threat from the man himself. Yet – and this is what Ptolemy XIII could not understand – Caesar needed Pompeius alive, to take him captive and strike a deal that would end any further resistance from the two factions arraigned against him. Not only did Pompeius' death rob him of this, but now both opposing factions had a martyr in whose memory they could continue to fight. Consequently, Ptolemy's murderous act – which could soon be warped by Pompeian propaganda into having been ordered by Caesar himself – meant that the Third Civil War was more likely to continue, a probability that was enforced by Caesar's own subsequent actions.

Chapter Seven

The Civil War Without its Architect

With Pompeius dead, one of the two key men involved in the Third Civil War had been removed. As has been argued, we could go even further and say that he was the architect of this conflict. The key question would be whether the removal of its instigator would lead to this civil war fizzling out or whether, like the First Civil War, it would develop a momentum of its own and outlast its progenitor?

Caesar the (Absent) Dictator

Caesar does not detail how he dealt with matters back in Rome, but accounts can be found across the other surviving sources, with Dio being the best. Caesar was already serving as one of the Consuls, and his colleague, P. Servilius Isauricus, was overseeing matters in Rome, having had to crush a Pompeian-inspired rebellion by M. Caelius Rufus and T. Annius Milo.[1] Dio provides a description of the tense situation in a Rome dominated by Servilius and his Caesarian legions:

> 'In Rome, as long as the issue between Caesar and Pompeius was doubtful and unsettled, the People all ostensibly favoured Caesar, because of his troops that were in their midst and because of his colleague Servilius. Whenever a victory of his was reported, they rejoiced, and whenever a reverse, they grieved, some sincerely and some feignedly in each case; for there were many spies and eavesdroppers prowling about, observing all that was said and done on such occasions. But privately the talk and actions of those who detested Caesar and preferred Pompeius' side were the very opposite of their public expressions.'[2]

As Consul, Servilius was the highest-ranking Caesarian commander in Rome, yet Caesar dispatched M. Antonius to rule in his place, presumably overriding Servilius as he wanted a military commander to guard against a Pompeian counterattack. As Servilius was Consul and Antonius had not even held a regular Praetorship – having previously held a constitutional oddity, a Pretorian Tribunate, in 49 BC[3] – Caesar needed to circumnavigate the usual constitutional procedures, which had become something of a habit with him.

Caesar's answer, as it invariably was, was to have himself declared Dictator – even though he was not in Italy – and consequently he could name Antonius as Master of the Horse (the Dictator's deputy). Furthermore, he ensured that this Dictatorship was not for the usual six-month duration but for a whole year. Appointing a Dictator also meant the suspension of the normal offices of state, with the exception of the Tribunate.[4] Thus, Antonius became the temporary ruler of Rome.

With the few surviving sources we have, the chronology of events is far from clear. Plutarch's life of Antonius has Caesar receiving the news of his elevation before he set off in pursuit of Pompeius two days after Pharsalus, which is clearly impossible in terms of informing Rome of his victory and them then replying:

'And after the victory, when he had been proclaimed Dictator, he himself pursued Pompeius, but he chose Antonius as his Master of Horse and sent him to Rome. This office is second in rank when the Dictator is in the city; but when he is absent, it is the first and almost the only one. For only the Tribunate continues when a Dictator has been chosen; all the other offices are abolished.'[5]

What is more likely is that Caesar dispatched Antonius to Rome to inform the Caesarian faction of his decision for them to appoint him Dictator and Antonius as de-facto ruler of Rome. Dio seems to support this, with Caesar sending no official word, but clearly dispatching Antonius with his orders:

'When the Battle of Pharsalus was announced, the People were long incredulous. For Caesar sent no despatch to the government, hesitating to appear to rejoice publicly over such a victory, for which reason also he celebrated no Triumph; and furthermore the event was clearly very improbable in view of the relative equipment of the two forces and the hopes entertained.'[6]

The Civil War Without its Architect   141

Despite the constitutional irregularities of this appointment – Caesar being overseas and the position being held for a year – the Senate, composed of Caesarian supporters and neutrals, and the People raised no issues with this and duly voted it through:

> 'They appointed him [Caesar] arbiter of war and peace with all mankind [Dictator], using the conspirators in Africa as a pretext, without the obligation even of making any communication on the subject to the People or the Senate. This, of course, also lay in his power before, inasmuch as he had so large an armed force; at any rate the wars he had fought he had undertaken on his own authority in nearly every case. Nevertheless, because they wished still to appear to be free and independent citizens, they voted him these rights and everything else which it was in his power to have even against their will.'[7]

However, the same was not the case when it came to Antonius:

> '… and the Consul proposed the latter's name also, although the Augurs very strongly opposed him, declaring that no one might be Master of the Horse for more than six months. But for this course they brought upon themselves a great deal of ridicule, because, after having decided that the Dictator himself should be chosen for a year, contrary to all precedent, they were now splitting hairs about the Master of the Horse.'[8]

Nevertheless, despite the constitutional and religious objections raised, Servilius' control of the Senate and People ensured that Caesar's wishes were carried out and Antonius was voted in to rule Rome as the Master of the Horse. It is clear that Caesar's chosen political settlement bore the two hallmarks of all of his political decisions, being both practical and politically tone-deaf.

When Caesar was elected Dictator the previous year, there were at least some solid grounds for this action, with both Consuls having fled Italy and fighting raging (albeit briefly) across the peninsula. Being the first man since Sulla to hold the post simply played into the hands of the Pompeian propaganda. Yet by 48 BC, Italy was at peace, albeit with the threat of the Pompeians in Africa, and Rome was presided over by a duly elected Consul.

However, this second occasion raised dangerous constitutional issues. This was now his second Dictatorship in two years, and he had extended the role in two unprecedented ways. Firstly, he had turned it into another annual office – extended from an emergency six months – and was now utilizing it not for an emergency in Italy, but a Republic-wide one. It also allowed his underqualified deputy to rule Rome in his name, with only a purged Tribunate as a potential check.

Furthermore, Caesar was now an absent Dictator, not ruling from Rome but from overseas, and for many months ruling from Alexandria in the manner of absentee monarch. Though Antonius seems to have been a competent political deputy, there was no hiding the fact that this was unprecedented in Republican terms. Matters were not helped by the renewal of his Dictatorship for the following year (47 BC) and failure to return to Rome until September that year, over eighteen months since he had left Italy. Though many of the neutrals in the Senate would not have minded the absence of Caesar from Rome, it did mean that he continued to rule from overseas.

Caesar clearly favoured the simplicity of the office of Dictator, seemingly blind to the consequences of how his sole rule overturned the precedents of the Republic and to how it looked to both his allies and enemies alike. He was doing nothing to reassure any wavering opponents that the Republic would be safe in his hands; rather the reverse. As became all too clear, continued reliance on such apparently anti-Republican measures would bother even his allies.

Dio goes on to list a number of other privileges that were granted him, through some seem to relate to later years.[9] Whatever the case, they demonstrate that Caesar was not only ruling Rome, but looking like he was ruling Rome. This was a course that no other Roman aside from Sulla had taken and one which, though expedient, was politically tone-deaf amongst the Republican oligarchy, no matter on which side of the current divide they fell.

The Caesarian Crackdown – The Hirtian Law

Throughout the civil war to date, Caesar's attitude had been one of reconciliation, as could be seen by the (sometimes multiple) pardons he issued to captured Pompeian commanders. This was a calculated act of political showmanship to counter the Pompeian propaganda that was trying to paint him as a 'new Sulla', a bloodthirsty tyrant. We have also seen that this policy continued in the aftermath of Pharsalus, with Pompeian legionaries and Eastern kings receiving pardons. Yet there were also saw the first signs of a more expedient policy, as seen by the murder of L. Domitius Ahenobarbus.

Further signs of this change in policy can be seen in a law passed by one of the Tribunes,[10] the lex Hirtia. We know little detail of the law itself, merely that it was aimed at the supporters of Pompeius. Only Cicero makes direct reference to it in a later attack on M. Antonius, whom he hints was the true author of the law. There is also a passing reference to such a law (though unnamed) in Dio:

'[Do you not know] that no one of the party of Pompeius, who is still alive, can, by the Hirtian law, possess any rank?'[11]

'They [the People] granted him [Caesar] then, permission to do whatever he wished to those who had favoured Pompeius's cause, not that he had not already received this right from himself, but in order that he might seem to be acting with some show of legal authority.'[12]

'What, I should like to know, is the object of now making mention of the Hirtian law? – a law of which I believe the framer himself repents no less than those against whom it was passed. According to my opinion, it is utterly wrong to call it a law at all; and, even if it be a law, we ought not to think it a law of Hirtius.'[13]

All we know is that the law brought in restrictions against the supporters of Pompeius; those who had not yet sought a Caesarian pardon. We can see Caesar – or rather his Master of the Horse, Antonius – ratcheting up the campaign against the large numbers of the Senatorial oligarchy who still opposed him. On the one hand, adding legal pressure, on top of the military defeat, can be seen as a sound move to separate his moderate opponents from the diehards. However, it would have drawn uncomfortable parallels to the Sullan legislation which not only prescribed his enemies, but stripped citizen rights from their heirs; legislation which Caesar himself had fought to overturn.

Avoiding Victory: Caesar and the 'Wrong' Civil War

If we are to believe Appian's account, Caesar arrived in Egypt just three days after leaving Rhodes, showing how much time he had made up on Pompeius. Upon arriving at Alexandria, he was met with the news of Pompeius' murder and presented with his head and signet ring. As stated earlier, the Egyptians totally misread the reaction that Pompeius' killing was likely to engender in Caesar for two reasons. Firstly, there was the natural offence that any Roman commander would take at the murder of a fellow oligarch at the hands of 'perfidious foreigners', the second in a decade (after Crassus). That aside, as detailed earlier, in the context of the civil war, Caesar needed Pompeius alive – at least in the short term – to try to bring the civil war to a negotiated end. Pompeius' death removed that possibility and presented his opponents with a martyr.

It was at this point that the civil war reached a turning point. Until his arrival in Egypt, Caesar's campaign had been noted for its swiftness and at times reckless decision-making, always taking the initiative and disrupting Pompeius' plans. After this point, however, this swiftness deserted Caesar and contributed greatly to the continuation of the civil war. Victory seemed to be within his grasp; Pompeius was dead, and the Pompeian forces had been driven out of the Peloponnese. It is only Dio who notes that the Pompeian forces, commanded temporarily by M. Porcius Cato, had withdrawn to the Roman province of Cyrene (neighbouring Egypt, see Map 5), presumably as a base of operations before meeting up with Pompeius in Egypt.

Thus, the remnants of the Pompeian land forces and the majority of their key commanders lay within Caesar's reach. By the time Caesar landed in Egypt, he had just one legion with him, with reinforcements coming by land through the Near East. Based on his strategies to date in the Third Civil War, we would have expected Caesar to again seize the initiative and attack the Pompeian army in Cyrene before they had a chance to properly organize or retreat. Yet Caesar did no such thing and became entangled in the Ptolemaic Civil War between the heirs of Ptolemy XII (Ptolemy XIII and Cleopatra VII). It is Appian who sums the issue up here:

> 'He consumed nine months in this strife, at the end of which he established Cleopatra on the throne of Egypt in place of her brother.'[14]

Caesar argued that it was his duty as the duly appointed representative of Rome to take up the role as executor of Ptolemy XII's will and bring peace to the country. Yet this was hardly the time to do so. If he had hoped that Pompeius' death would end the civil war, then he would have been sorely disappointed. The full details of Caesar's campaigns in Egypt fall outside of the remit of this work and are covered in detail elsewhere, especially by Caesar himself, and take on something of a Shakespearean tinge when the figure of Cleopatra VII is involved.

Nevertheless, Caesar's involvement in the latest (and what was to be the last) Ptolemaic Civil War, though ultimately victorious, nearly saw him killed during the siege of Alexandria when outnumbered by Ptolemy's Egyptian army and Romano-Egyptian legions, formerly commanded by Gabinius. At one point, if we are to believe Appian, Caesar only avoided capture – and subsequent execution – by jumping off his ship into the sea and swimming to safety.

However, the key point remains that, based in Egypt and with Pompeius dead, Caesar's enthusiasm for the Third Civil War seemed to wane and handed the initiative to his enemies. We will never know for certain what caused this seeming inaction, though there are three possibilities. The first is that it was genuine overconfidence, brought about by his victory at Pharsalus and fate's intervention in the murder of Pompeius, with a belief that his enemies would dissipate without a key figurehead to rally behind. This would have combined with the seemingly irresistible lure of Egypt, with its wealth, connections to Alexander the Great and of course Cleopatra.

The second possibility is that, with Pompeius dead and his supremacy in the Republic seemingly assured, Caesar was laying the foundations for his next great project: picking up where Pompeius (and Crassus) had left off and finishing the Roman conquest of the East. For all his exploits in Gaul, the true test of a Roman commander – at least in their minds – came in following in the footsteps of Alexander the Great and fighting the new Persian/Parthian Empire. For that he needed a solid base of operations, and Egypt with its wealth and connections to the Alexander cult would have been a perfect choice. Thus it can be argued that Caesar's campaigns in Egypt, and later in Asia Minor, were establishing his dominance of the East in readiness for a greater campaign of conquest.

The third possibility is a more Machiavellian alternative, namely that Caesar did not want the civil war to end anytime soon, and that he was exploiting the continued crisis in the Western and Eastern halves of the Republic to continue his sole rule through the Dictatorship. If he had destroyed the remnants of the Pompeian forces in North Africa, then the civil war and the crisis would be over, as would his Dictatorship. Civil wars in Egypt and foreign wars in Asia Minor would not warrant its renewal. As long as the Republic was in crisis, then it needed – at least in Caesar's mind – his strong rule; peace would bring its own problems. It is perhaps no coincidence that the temporary ending of this stage of the civil war in 45 BC saw Caesar struggle with how to retain supreme power in peacetime; a situation which led to his assassination shortly afterwards. Nevertheless, whatever the motive, it would not be until 46 BC that he took to the field against the Pompeians, time his opponents used to regroup and renew their campaigns.[15]

The Pompeian Coalition without Pompeius

For the Pompeian faction, the death of their leader was the second blow they had suffered within a month. First had come the defeat at Pharsalus, when they had been so confident of victory, swiftly followed by Pompeius' treacherous murder on an Egyptian beach. Without their leader and talisman, the Pompeian faction was faced with the question of whether to continue the fight or fold?

As we have seen throughout this work, the Pompeian faction was actually a coalition between two different groupings within the Roman oligarchy: the supporters of Pompeius and the opponents of Caesar. This alliance was forged by Pompeius in the late 50s BC and reached its height with his engineering of the outbreak of a new civil war and the threat to the Republic posed by what he framed as the 'would-be tyrant' Caesar.

In effect, this meant that there would have been two different reactions to the setbacks from the two different groupings. The initial reaction amongst the Pompeian elite would have been one of shock and disgust at such an ignominious end and such an act of perfidy on the part of Ptolemy. This would have soon been followed by a desire for revenge and a determination to keep their leader's legacy intact. The Pompeian faction had two natural successors: one bound to Pompeius by blood and one by marriage.

Pompeius had two sons, Cnaeus and Sextus, both old enough to take part in the civil war campaigns, and it would have been to the eldest – (Cnaeus) – that the Pompeian supporters would have looked. Little definite is known about Cnaeus, other than that his mother was Pompeius' third wife, Mucia, to whom he was married between 79 and 62 BC. We have no firm date for his birth, but the mid-70s BC seems a logical guess, making him now aged in his late 20s. Although he seems to have inherited his father's title of Magnus, his youth would have precluded him from formally taking command in the civil war, being too young for the *cursus honorum*; not that this ever stopped his father.

Given Cnaeus' youth, the next natural leader of the faction – at least until Cnaeus became older – was Pompeius' father-in-law, Q. Caecilius Metellus Pius Scipio Nasica. Boasting an impeccable Republican heritage – a Scipio by birth and a Metellan by adoption – he had been Pompeius' closest adherent since 52 BC, the year of his Consulship, and thus was a natural choice to lead the Pompeian faction until Pompeius' sons became older.

That the Pompeian faction itself would fight on was taken for granted, as they would need to avenge the defeat at Pharsalus and their leader's untimely death. The key factor was what the attitude would be of the other half of this alliance, the Senators opposed to Caesar. As we had seen, some of the lesser members of the Senate – such as Brutus and Cicero – had already given up their opposition to Caesar when the prospect of an easy victory disappeared at Pharsalus. The majority, however, continued their opposition and were regrouping under Cato, determined to fight on. This determination would surely have been shaken by news of Pompeius' murder. Dio and Plutarch seem to provide the best summary of their reaction:

> '… and coming to Cyrene, learned there of the death of Pompeius. Their views were now no longer harmonious: Cato, through hatred of Caesar's domination, and some others in despair of receiving pardon from him, sailed to Africa with the army, added Scipio to their number, and were as active as possible against Caesar; but the majority scattered, some of them retiring and escaping wherever they could, while the rest, went to Caesar at once and received pardon.'[16]

> 'After reaching Libya, and while sailing along its coast, he [Cato] fell in with Sextus, the younger son of Pompey, who told him of his father's death in Egypt. All, of course, were deeply distressed, but no one, now that Pompeius was gone, would even listen to any other commander while Cato was at hand. For this reason also Cato, who had compassion on men who were brave and had given proof of fidelity, and was ashamed to leave them helpless and destitute in a foreign land, undertook the command, and went along the coast to Cyrene.'[17]

Dio's report seems to strike true, suggesting that many of the lesser figures of the anti-Caesarian faction would have taken news of Pompeius' murder as the final straw, coming so soon after the defeat at Pharsalus, and withdrawn to seek Caesar's pardon. However, no names are given, and the subsequent conflict finds all the key figures still fighting on the Pompeian side.

There may have been some relief amongst this grouping at the news of Pompeius' death. Many, such as Cato, were only ever reluctant Pompeian supporters, being of the 'better the devil you know' school of thought. Most would have been under no illusion that a Pompeian victory would have led to his attempted domination of the Republic. In many respects, a dead Pompeius was of more use to them, a martyred Republican figurehead rather than a live threat to the Republic. Metellus Scipio was certainly no threat, and nor (yet) were the Pompeian sons.

It seems that the majority of this faction chose to fight on, determined not to see Caesar seize control of the Republic, a cause that can only have been enhanced by the unsubtle political practices in which they saw Caesar indulging, namely remote rule through the Dictatorship. The key questions faced by both wings of the Pompeian alliance were whether Caesar would allow them the time to regroup, whether the two factions could co-operate without Pompeius to hold them together and whether they could reorganize themselves into a credible threat?

Africa and the Recovery of the Pompeian Faction

It was here that one of the Caesarian failures in 49 BC – the other being in Illyria – came back to hurt him. As we have seen (Chapter One), throughout 49 BC, Caesar's forces swept the Pompeians from the provinces of the Western Republic (Italy, Gaul, Spain, Sicily and Sardinia), yet they suffered a major reversal in Roman North Africa, where they were defeated at the Battle of Bagradas River thanks to the assistance the Pompeians received from the native kingdom of Numidia and King Juba I. Having been driven from Greece and with Caesarian armies marching through the Near East, Roman North Africa – safely in Pompeian control and supported by a friendly native kingdom – became the obvious choice for the Pompeians to regroup, even more so considering that they had already sailed to the neighbouring province of Cyrene. Plutarch provides the following description:

> 'There [in Cyrene] he [Cato] learned that Scipio, the father-in-law of Pompeius, had been well received by Juba the king, and that Attius Varus, who had been appointed governor of Libya by Pompeius, was with them at the head of an army. Cato therefore set out thither by land in the winter season, having got together a great number of asses to carry water, and driving along with him many cattle.
>
> 'Though the march lasted for seven days consecutively, Cato led at the head of his force, without using either horse or beast of burden. Moreover, he used to sup in a sitting posture from the day when he learned of the defeat at Pharsalus; yes, this token of sorrow he added to others, and would not lie down except when sleeping. After finishing the winter in Libya, he led forth his army; and it numbered nearly ten thousand.'[18]

Roman North Africa now became the new base of operations for the Pompeian faction, and the remnants of the Pompeian grand army in Greece – (some 10,000 men – was combined with the Pompeian garrison from 49 BC and the Royal Numidian army. Given that the Pompeian navy was still the largest in the Roman world (Appian says they had 300 triremes)[19], they were safe from the Caesarian armies in Spain, Greece and the East, and it would need a major Caesarian expedition to attack them. This naval-guaranteed safety and the inattention of Caesar – otherwise engaged in Egypt and Asia Minor – gave the Pompeian faction a safe base to rebuild and regroup, acting as a focal point for opposition to Caesar from across Rome's empire.

This naval superiority could also be used in an offensive capacity, with Spain, Sicily and even Italy itself open to attack from the sea. The Caesarian failure in 49 BC thus allowed the Pompeians the space and time to recover in 48 BC. The only remaining question was whether the two factions could co-operate without Pompeius at their head. From the sources, it appears this issue was one that caused no little contention, with four prominent leaders emerging: Cato, Metellus Scipio, P. Attius Varus (the Pompeian Governor of Roman Africa) and King Juba of Numidia. There are various accounts – of differing levels of drama – of the compromise that was achieved, including the following from Appian and Plutarch:

> 'Cato had been chosen commander of the forces in Africa, but he declined the appointment since there were consulars present who outranked him, he having held only the Praetorship in Rome. So Lucius Scipio was made the commander and he collected and drilled a large army there.'[20]
>
> 'Cato actually put a check upon Juba, who had all but made Scipio and Varus his satraps and reconciled the two Romans. And though all thought it meet that he should have the command, especially Scipio and Varus, who resigned and tendered to him the leadership, he refused to break the laws to support which they were waging war with one who broke them, nor, when a Proconsul was present, would he put himself, who was only a Propraetor, above him. For Scipio had been made Proconsul, and the greater part of the army were emboldened by his name; they thought that they would be successful if a Scipio had command in Africa.'[21]

Given his posthumous reputation, Cato is given a central role in the peace-making between the factions, which now numbered three with the Pompeian-Numidian faction of King Juba and Attius Varus. In the end, Roman seniority was restored and the most senior Roman commander, Metellus Scipio, was chosen in overall command. By the end of 48 BC, the Pompeian faction now had a secure base of operations, maintained naval superiority in the Mediterranean and could use the absence of Caesar – first in Egypt and later in Asia Minor – to rebuild their forces, supported by the largest native kingdom in North Africa.[22]

The Aborted Caesarian Thrust into Africa (48 BC)

Though the Pompeian position in North Africa was a strong one – protected to the north by their naval control, to the east by deserts (where anyway Caesar was tied up in the Egyptian Civil War) and to the west by Numidia – there was one avenue of attack left open to the Caesarian faction. Whilst Numidia was the largest kingdom in North Africa, it was not the only one; the other of note being the Mauri to the west (modern Morocco and elements of Algeria). The Mauri had grown at the expense of their larger neighbour Numidia, when their King Bocchus I, supported the Roman general Marius (Caesar's uncle) in the Romano-Numidian War (112–105 BC), capturing the Numidian King Jugurtha. In 49 BC, the two grandsons of Bocchus – Bocchus II and Bogud – succeeded their father, Mastanesosus, as joint kings. With Juba of Numidia clearly supporting the Pompeians in 49 BC, the two brothers threw in their lot on the opposing side and sent word to the Caesarian Senate of their support.

Thus, Caesar had a potential base of operations in far north-western Africa, which helpfully for him lay just across the Mediterranean from Caesarian-controlled Spain. Caesar sent word to the Governor of Southern Spain, Q. Cassius Longinus, to gather his existing forces and enrol fresh legions and cross the Strait of Gades to create a Caesarian base of operation in the Maurian kingdom, putting pressure on the Pompeian-Numidian western flank.

Rebellion in Caesarian Spain

Unfortunately for the Caesarians, this plan fell apart when the Spanish provinces rebelled against Roman/Caesarian rule, showing how weak a hold of the provinces Caesar actually had. Although Spain had been the Republic's oldest overseas province (excluding the islands) and there had been a large Roman military presence there since the 210s BC, the depth of Rome's control had always been questionable. The First Civil War had seen the province virtually independent of control by Rome, under various warlords, from C. Valerius Flaccus to Q. Sertorius and Pompeius himself. Although Caesar had defeated the Pompeian forces there, mostly due to the ineptitude of their commanders, this did not mean that he controlled the two Spanish provinces.

Matters were brought to a head by the Caesarian Governor of Farther Spain, Q. Cassius Longinus (Tr. 49 BC). Cassius had been a supporter of Pompeius and served under him in Spain in 52 BC, but by 49 BC had sided with Caesar and was one of the two Tribunes forced to flee Rome to join Caesar in Gaul (Caesar's *causus belli*). Following Caesar's defeat of the Pompeians in 49 BC, he remained as one of the governors and had to campaign in Lusitania later in the year, showing the thin Caesarian/Roman control of Spain. As governor, Cassius exacerbated this delicate situation by bribery and corruption, with heavy taxation and financial exactions, as Caesar himself somewhat disingenuously admits, having himself laid down the need for large amounts of money.[23]

As happened during the First Civil War, this led to an alliance between disgruntled natives and the survivors of the losing side (this time the Pompeians), of which there were a large number still in Spain. This resulted in an assassination attempt on Cassius in his headquarters at Corduba, which left him injured but still alive. Recently levied troops, including it seems many former Pompeians, then mutinied and a Caesarian Quaestor, M. Claudius Marcellus Aeserninus (Cos. 22 BC), declared for the Pompeians and took charge of the mutinous troops. Caesar and Dio, the two sources that cover the rebellion in detail, both question the sincerity of the rebel leaders' declaration for Pompeius, but agree that it was a useful banner for them to raise:

> '[The mutineers' leader] kept openly asserting that it was for Cn. Pompeius that he wished to recover the province. And it may even be that he did so wish, owing to his hatred for Caesar and affection for Pompeius, the latter's name carrying great weight with those legions which M. Varro had held.'[24]

This episode highlighted the danger of Caesar integrating Pompeian legionaries into his own armies and the wafer-thin loyalty of the majority of the Roman and native populace during a civil war. What started as a rebellion against a provincial governor soon took on a far more important civil war element. The seriousness of the rebellion can be seen by the amount of time that is devoted to it in the commentary on Caesars' Egyptian Civil War campaigns (*Bellum Alexandrinum*).[25] This rebellion not only disrupted Caesar's plan to invade North Africa via the Maurian kingdom, but also offered an opportunity to the Pompeians for a potential bridgehead into Spain. As Caesar was tied down in the Eastern Republic, trying to bring it under his control, his control of the Western Republic was loosening.

With the rebels holding Corduba, Cassius gathered his remaining loyal forces and moved on the city, also requesting help from the Governor of Nearer Spain (M. Aemilius Lepidus, Cos. 46 and 42 BC) and King Bogud of the Mauri. Thus, Bogud crossed the straits and entered Roman Spain with his Maurian forces, rather than the Romans going the other way.

The Battle of Corduba (48 BC)

The *de bellum alexandrinum* provides an excellent account of subsequent events:

> '[Marcellus] took his legions across the Baetis and drew up his line. On seeing that Cassius had drawn up his line facing him on higher ground in front of his own camp, Marcellus prevailed upon his troops to withdraw to their camp, putting them off with the excuse that the enemy refused to come down into the plain. And so he proceeded to withdraw his forces. Cassius employed his excellent cavalry, in which arm he was strong and knew Marcellus to be weak, to attack the retreating legionaries, and killed quite a number of their rearguard on the banks of the river. Made aware by this loss of the drawback and difficulty involved in crossing the river, Marcellus transferred his camp to the other side of the Baetis. Now both commanders frequently led out their legions to battle; there was, however, no engagement owing to the difficult nature of the ground.'[26]

Thus the battle, or rather a mere skirmish, was a Caesarian victory, but not one that ended the rebellion. Cassius seemingly contrived to throw this success away by allowing himself to be outmanoeuvred by Marcellus, forcing him to retreat to the city of Ulia (modern Montemayor):

> 'Marcellus was much stronger in infantry forces; for the legions he had were veteran ones, tested in many campaigns. Cassius relied on the loyalty rather than the valour of his legions. Consequently

when the two camps had been pitched over against one another and Marcellus had selected a position suitable for a stronghold which might enable him to prevent the enemy troops from getting water, [Cassius] Longinus was afraid of being shut up by a virtual blockade in territory controlled by others and hostile to himself; and so he silently set out from his camp by night and marched swiftly to Ulia, a town which he believed to be loyal to himself.'[27]

Marcellus followed Cassius and trapped him in the city, and set about besieging him:

'By siting strongholds at suitable points and carrying his field-works in a continuous ring round the town, he hemmed in Ulia and Cassius with entrenchments. But before these could be completed, [Cassius] Longinus sent out his entire cavalry force, in the belief that it would stand him in very good stead if it stopped Marcellus from collecting fodder and corn, whereas it would prove a great handicap if, shut up by blockade and rendered useless, it used up precious corn.'[28]

Battle of Ulia (48 BC)

The first attempt to end the siege was actually made by the arriving King Bogud:

'Bogud and his forces came up to the outer entrenchments of Marcellus: sharp fighting broke out between the two sides, and this recurred at frequent intervals, with the tide of fortune often turning from one side to the other. Marcellus, however, was never dislodged from his field-works.'[29]

The deadlock continued until the arrival of Lepidus with an additional 17,000 men (thirty-five cohorts), plus an unknown number of cavalry. Sensing the change in momentum, Marcellus opened negotiations with Lepidus and an accord was soon struck. Marcellus received a pardon and the rebellion was ended, though the now-leaderless natives would still bear a grudge.

To further defuse the situation, as the year was ending, Cassius' replacement, C. Trebonius (Cos. 45 BC), was sent out to Spain early, allowing the Caesarians to remove the obvious cause of the rebellion – Q. Cassius. Of the protagonists, Dio reports that Marcellus was banished but later restored to favour,[30] and even held the Consulship in 22 BC. Cassius, by contrast, died almost immediately when, suspiciously, his ship sank at the mouth of the Iberus whilst returning home.

Though the rebellion had been limited and ended without any major Caesarian losses, precious time had been lost in terms of the North African campaign, providing additional opportunity to the Pompeians there. Furthermore, Caesarian control of Spain had been shown to be weak with the underlying native resentment at Roman rule still simmering away beneath the surface, encouraged – and then enflamed – by Roman leadership and its subsequent betrayal. It also showed that the tactic of declaring for the Pompeian faction could be used as a useful banner under which to hide local grievances.

The Civil War Reignites in Illyria (48 BC)

As we have seen, Illyria had seen civil war campaigns in 49 BC (see Chapter One), with Pompeius determined to eliminate the Caesarian bridgehead in his sphere of influence. With the defeat of the Caesarian forces on land and at sea, Pompeian commander M. Octavius had continued with the siege of the city of Salonae, apparently the only native city holding out against the Pompeians, operating with a portion of the Pompeian fleet (see Chapter Five). As with the other naval campaigns, this siege was abandoned when news of Pharsalus reached Octavius, who nevertheless remained in the region. To re-secure Illyria, Caesar sent a Proquaestor, Q. Cornificius,[31] who utilized the remaining pro-Caesarian native forces and defeated Octavius, as the *de bellum alexandrinum* recorded:

> 'Again, when in the course of his flight from the Battle of Pharsalia Octavius took refuge with a large fleet upon that coast, Cornificius, with the aid of a few ships of the men of Iadera, those devoted supporters of the Republic, who were unsurpassed in their constant loyalty, made himself master of Octavius' scattered ships, and was accordingly enabled by the addition of these vessels to those of his allies to go into action with something like a fleet.'[32]

With Octavius defeated and his ships captured by Cornificius, the Caesarian naval forces were bolstered. Octavius was able to flee and returned to Dyrrhachium along with the other Pompeian commanders. Nevertheless, with the Pompeians still holding Dyrrhachium, Corcyra and other strongholds in the region, Caesar felt it necessary to reinforce Cornificius to prevent a Pompeian counterattack, and thus dispatched A. Gabinius – the former Pompeian commander, who had been at Brundisium in early 48 BC – to the region with additional legions, as recorded in the *de bello alexandrinum*:

> '[Caesar] sent despatches to Gabinius, bidding him set out for Illyricum with the legions of recruits which had recently been raised: there he was to join forces with Q. Cornificius and repulse any dangerous move that might be made against the province: if on the other hand no large forces were needed to ensure the safety of the province, he was to lead his legions into Macedonia. It was in fact his belief that the whole of that neighbourhood and area would revive the war, so long as Cn. Pompeius was alive.'[33]

We also have a brief mention in Appian which provides the size of the forces: 'Gabinius led fifteen cohorts of foot and 3,000 horse for him by way of Illyria.'[34]

As has previously been noted, Appian preserves a variant tradition that has Gabinius marching to Illyria by land, prior to Pharsalus, and being defeated by the native tribes en-route.[35] Nevertheless, the *de bello alexandrinum* records Gabinius arriving in the province in the winter of 48 BC. Again, however, though the Pompeian fleet had been defeated, many of the natives took the opportunity of the civil war to throw off Roman control and fight for their independence. In consequence, when Gabinius arrived he faced hostile native tribes who resented any Roman army, and was attacked and defeated:

> 'And so, as lack of supplies forced him to storm towns or strongholds in very adverse weather, he frequently sustained reverses, and was held by the natives in such contempt that, while retreating on Salona, a coastal town occupied by very gallant and loyal Roman citizens, he was forced to fight an action on the march. In this battle he lost

more than two thousand soldiers, thirty-eight centurions and four tribunes: with what was left of his forces he retired to Salona, where, under the stress of overwhelming difficulties of every kind, he fell sick and died within a few months.'[36]

Caesar's grip on the province was thereby further weakened with the loss of a seasoned commander and 2,000 of his 7,000 reinforcements. This weakness provided an opportunity and Octavius chose to stay in the region (having only been in Dyrrhachium) and challenge the Caesarian control rather than retreat to mainland Greece with the other Pompeian faction leaders. As happened in Spain, rebellious natives merged with the defeated Pompeians, Caesar recording that:

> '... he heard that M. Octavius had concluded treaties with the natives and in several places was attacking the garrisons of our troops, in some cases in person with his fleet, in others with land forces, employing native troops.'[37]

Therefore, by the end of 48 BC Octavius had reignited the civil war in Illyria, having taken a portion of the Pompeian fleet, and determined to provide a thorn in the side of the Caesarian faction. Again, as we have seen (Chapter Six), whilst the Pompeian faction chose not to contest mainland Greece – now having far fewer land forces than Caesar – Illyria comprised a perfect theatre of operations for them. Given the mountainous terrain of the province's coastline, higher troop numbers counted far less than naval power. Octavius could employ hit-and-run tactics, aided by the Caesarians being hampered by a native rebellion inland. Moreover, contesting control of Illyria would ensure disruption to the Caesarian lines of supply and communication between Italy and Greece, thus making it a vital strategic position.

As the year 48 BC ended, the civil war campaigns continued with active fighting between Pompeian and Caesarian forces in Illyria, further demonstrating both the longevity of the Pompeian faction without Pompeius and the thin veneer of control that the Caesar and his faction had over the Roman world.

The Outbreak of the Fourth Romano-Pontic War (48 BC)

Given the ongoing civil war across the Roman world and another one in Egypt, the last thing that Caesar needed was the outbreak of another war in the East, with a foreign power invading Rome's Eastern Republic with a view to conquest. Whilst many would have expected the Parthian Empire to take this opportunity to invade the under-defended provinces of the Roman East, one should consider Parthia's own weakened state and the mindset of its ruler, Orodes II, whose natural caution prevailed for now. Yet there was one eastern power that did chose to utilize the opportunity that the civil war presented, and it was a throwback to an earlier generation: Pharnaces II, a staunch Roman ally but son of the long-term Roman opponent Mithridates VI of Pontus, chose to invade Roman territory in pursuit of the recovery of his ancestral empire.

Pharnaces II ruled the Bosphoran Kingdom of the Crimea, which had been his reward for betraying his father in 63 BC to gain favour with Rome.[38] The Bosphoran Kingdom comprised one half of the Pontic Empire, which dominated the Black Sea region, and at its height in 88 BC stretched to the Adriatic. We will never know for certain what spurred Pharnaces to invade Roman territory to recover his people's former homeland, now the Roman province of Pontus. Pompeius' death would have ended any allegiance he had to his Roman patron, coinciding with the removal of the bulk of Roman and allied native forces from the region. The sources also speak of the Pompeian faction encouraging him to invade, to distract Caesar, and it is not beyond the realm of possibility that the Parthians were also encouraging him.

Whatever the motivation, Pharnaces timed his attack to perfection, sweeping down the eastern Black Sea coast and into Armenia and then Asia Minor, starting the Fourth Romano-Pontic War, commonly misnamed the Pharnacean War. Not only had the bulk of the Roman forces been withdrawn from the region by Metellus Scipio and transported to Greece, but most of Rome's allies were depleted too in the same manner:

> '[Pharnaces] got possession of Colchis without any difficulty, and in the absence of Deiotarus subjugated all Armenia, and part of Cappadocia, and some cities of Pontus that had been assigned to the district of Bithynia.'[39]

With the bulk of the allied kingdoms' rulers and forces in Greece, retreating after Pharsalus, the region was severely weakened and Pharnaces was able to swiftly recreate the greater Pontic Empire (see Map 5). It seems that he initially overran Colchis and then Lesser Armenia – which had been part of Pontus – and Cappadocia, but not Pontus proper. Though the sources talk of Armenia being overrun, it is not clear whether this was the Kingdom of Armenia or the province of Lesser Armenia, though it is likely to have been the latter, with the Parthians too invested in the Kingdom of Armenia to allow it to be overrun.

Not only was this a blow to Roman – and Caesarian – control of the Eastern Republic and its resources, but equally as important it was a potential major setback to Caesar's planning for the civil war campaigns. Although his entanglement in the Egyptian Civil War would keep him in Egypt until the spring of 47 BC, he would have ideally wanted to move on Pompeian Africa soon afterwards. If this war in Asia Minor could not be resolved, then he would have to abandon that campaign in favour of moving in the opposite direction. It fell to Caesar's few forces in the region to spare him this delay.

Though the bulk of Rome's troops in Asia Minor had been withdrawn by Pompeius, Caesar had marched his army through the region chasing Pompeius and had appointed Cn. Domitius Calvinus as governor, granting him three legions. Unfortunately for him, two of these legions had been dispatched to Caesar in Egypt, leaving him with just one, the Thirty-Sixth. To bolster his forces, Domitius used two native legions provided by King Deiotarus – of Galatia, including Lesser Armenia – who had made his peace with Caesar, and another raised from garrisons in Pontus, and then moved on Pharnaces whilst opening diplomatic negotiations.

In response, Pharnaces withdrew from Cappadocia but held onto Lesser Armenia as ancestral Pontic territory. Domitius' position was further weakened by Caesar's orders to bring the matter to a swift conclusion and reinforce him in Egypt, instructions which Pharnaces learned of. Consequently, Domitius committed to battle with Pharnaces at Nicopolis in Lesser Armenia.

Battle of Nicopolis (48 BC)

The *de bello alexandrinum* provides a quite detailed account of the battle, presumably based on Domitius' own reports:

'The signal to attack was given almost simultaneously on both sides then came the charge, with hotly contested and fluctuating fighting. Thus the Thirty-Sixth legion launched an attack on the king's cavalry outside the trench and fought so successful an action that it advanced up to the walls of the town, crossed the trench, and attacked the enemy in rear. The Pontic legion, however, on the other flank, drew back a little from the enemy, and attempted, moreover, to go round or cross the trench, so as to attack the enemy's exposed flank; but in the actual crossing of the trench it was pinned down and overwhelmed. The legions of Deiotarus, indeed, offered scarcely any resistance to the attack. Consequently the king's forces, victorious on their own right wing and in the centre of the line, now turned upon the Thirty-Sixth legion. The latter, nevertheless, bore up bravely under the victors' attack and, though surrounded by large enemy forces, yet with consummate presence of mind formed a circle and so made a fighting withdrawal to the foothills, where Pharnaces was loth to pursue it owing to the hilly nature of the ground. And so, with the Pontic legion an almost total loss and a large proportion of the troops of Deiotarus killed, the Thirty-Sixth legion retired to higher ground with losses not exceeding 250 men. There fell in that battle not a few Roman knights – brilliant and distinguished men. After sustaining this defeat Domitius none the less collected the remnants of his scattered army and withdrew by safe routes through Cappadocia into Asia.'[40]

Regardless of the fact that the single Roman legion had held firm, Pharnaces had secured a clear victory over the Roman forces of the region, which not only gave him a path to complete his conquest of central Asia Minor but made him the new figurehead for all anti-Roman sentiment in the region. Cappadocia was reoccupied, presumably along with Galatia, and then the Roman province of Pontus-Bithynia, confirming the re-emergence after twenty years of the Pontic Empire. As 48 BC ended, Caesar thus found himself controlling less of the Roman world than he had after Pharsalus, having now lost a large part of the Eastern Republic.

However, Caesar's more immediate problems were that there would be no further reinforcements from Asia to assist him in the Egyptian entanglement and that the land route from Rome's empire to Egypt was now threatened. In terms of the civil war, it was clear that if he was able to disentangle himself from the mess in Egypt, he would first have to move on the newly formed Pontic Empire and Pharnaces, abandoning his plans for an African campaign to confront the Pompeian faction, not only giving them time to regroup but to take the offensive.[41]

Summary – Winning the Battle but Losing the Peace

It would be fair to say that for Caesar, 48 BC had been a roller-coaster of a year. He started as the challenger in the Third Civil War, disrupting Pompeius' masterplan with a characteristically bold thrust over the Adriatic. His own campaign was then disrupted in the trench warfare at Dyrrhachium and nearly ended by his loss in the final battle there. Ironically, this defeat allowed him to regain his mobility and forced Pompeius to advance his timescales for integrating his two armies and giving battle.

The victory at Pharsalus was clearly the turning point in Caesar's career, though as it was against fellow Romans, we must doubt that he saw it that way. Within a morning, he went from rebel to Princeps of the Roman world, a supremacy that was enhanced by Pompeius' subsequent murder on an Egyptian beach. Yet with Caesar ending the year besieged in Alexandria, with the Pompeians regrouped in Africa, civil war in Illyria, revolts in Spain and having lost much of Asia Minor, we cannot help but ask what went wrong? Cicero, in one of his many letters, sums up how it looked in Rome, at least to a lapsed Pompeian:

> '… especially in the present circumstances, when such disasters have been sustained in Asia, in Illyricum, in the Cassius affair, in Alexandria itself, in the city, in Italy.'[42]

Though he was the temporary master of the Roman world, Caesar seemed to flounder when he was not campaigning. He had convincingly won the battle but had equally convincingly failed to win the wider war. Though his victory in the field at Pharsalus was a comprehensive one, he failed to extinguish his opposition in the Pompeian faction. This seems to have been due to a mixture of two factors: his being unable and unwilling to do so. In the immediate aftermath of the battle, we only hear of one

Pompeian commander – Domitius Ahenobarbus – being hunted down by Caesar's cavalry, with the rest, especially Pompeius himself, evading pursuit.

Thus, the entire leadership of the opposing faction was able to escape his grasp and be in a position to regroup. This recovery was aided by their naval mastery and use of Corcyra as a base of operations, a place which they could reach without Caesarian interference. The key turning point in the aftermath of Pharsalus came at the Bosphorus, when Cassius' fleet defected to Caesar rather than destroying him. After this near-defeat, Caesar had a fleet which again disrupted Pompeius' plans, forcing his ill-judged Egyptian adventure.

Yet no sooner had Caesar been presented with his own fleet and the head of Pompeius, thanks to the actions of others, then he nearly threw it all away in his own ill-considered Egyptian episode, becoming entangled in the Ptolemaic Civil War and ending up besieged in Alexandria. Whether this was a Machiavellian move to ensure he held onto the Dictatorship as the civil war continued, or was an amorous entanglement with Cleopatra VII or his being enamoured with the dreams of eastern conquest, we will never know.

What is clear is that in the months that followed Pharsalus, Caesar allowed his victory to become watered down and he lost the momentum which had been so characteristic of his strategy. The man who had started the year bolting across a Pompeian-held Adriatic in winter ended it in a siege in Alexandria. It was almost as if the energy he had been known for slipped away when Pompeius was killed as he had accomplished all he needed to.

As we have seen, whilst the victory at Pharsalus and Pompeius' subsequent death may have convinced Caesar that he had won, not everyone else was persuaded. The two sides of the Pompeian faction were not hounded after Pharsalus, being able to evacuate Greece for the relative safety of Pompeian-controlled North Africa and its ally Numidia, where they could rebuild and renew their campaign against Caesar, with what they must have judged would be a realistic chance of winning.

Today's image of Caesar would not have been one that those opposed to Caesar would have recognized. They would not have considered him unbeatable, as Dyrrhachium had shown. Certainly, he was talented and lucky, but his list of blunders that nearly cost him everything was growing:

trapped at Ilerda in Spain, trapped in Illyria before Dyrrhachium, the setback at Dyrrhachium itself, being cornered in Greece before Pharsalus, the Bosphoran encounter and now being trapped in Alexandria.

Moreover, his control of the Roman world was only paper-thin. Most Romans and most natives didn't care who wanted to be in charge, so long as they left them alone. Caesar's victory didn't impress the legions in Spain who revolted, nor the Egyptians, Pharnaces, Juba or of course his opponents in the Senatorial oligarchy, only some of whom were in Africa, the rest being in the Senate and officially tolerant of his heavy-handed constitutional rule – an overseas Dictatorship.

The Third Roman Civil War did not end with Caesar's victory at Pharsalus, nor with the murder of Pompeius. All that had changed was the dynamic of the conflict, with Caesar transformed from rebel to ruler, which as we have seen brought him a whole new range of problems to overcome. Conversely, the Pompeians had now become the rebels and gained the freedom of movement which that brought.

It would take much more military, and most importantly political, effort on Caesar's part to convert battlefield victory into a lasting dominance of the Roman world. Pompeius had ultimately failed in this endeavour and was murdered for that failure. The question now was whether Caesar could avoid this fate?

The answer to this will be covered in the third and fourth volumes of this series: *The Battle of Thapsus (46 BC): Caesar, Metellus Scipio, and the Renewal of the Third Roman Civil War* and *The Battle of Munda (45 BC): Caesar, Pompey, Labienus, and the Continuation of the Third Roman Civil War*.[43]

Appendix I

Who's Who in the Third Roman Civil War (48 BC)

Given the continuous narrative of Caesar and the number of other surviving sources that comment on this period, we know the identities of a large number of Roman politicians and officers who were took part in the conflict, in both major and minor roles. That being the case, the following is a brief 'Who's Who' of those involved in the various campaigns of 48 BC, along with their subsequent fates.

The Main Protagonists

Cn. Pompeius 'Magnus' (Cos 70, 55 & 52 BC), killed 48 BC
Son of a First Civil War general. Rose to prominence during the First Civil War as a supporter, and then son-in-law, of Sulla. Based his earlier career on the threat of force rather than the reality. Brought the First Civil War to an end in 70 BC in partnership with M. Licinius Crassus, and the two men's reforms ushered in a new period for the Republic (the Pompeian-Crassan). Carved out a large empire for Rome in the Great Eastern War (74–62 BC) and returned to Rome to convert his military prestige into lasting dominance. Reforged his alliance with Crassus in 60–59 BC and the two men then effectively seized control of the Republic in 55 BC (along with Caesar). Crassus' absence and eventual death helped to ferment the bloody chaos that engulfed the Republic in the late 50s BC and became sole consul (or Princeps) in 52 BC. With only one rival left, manipulated events to force Caesar to attack his own country and become an enemy of the state, with the rest of the oligarchy having no choice but to turn to him to defend the state.

Victorious at Dyrrhachium, but defeated heavily at the subsequent Battle of Pharsalus, he nevertheless determined to regroup and fight on. Murdered on an Egyptian beach on the orders of Pharaoh Ptolemy XIII to curry favour with Caesar, a ploy which failed spectacularly.

Appendix I 165

C. Iulius Caesar (Cos. 59, 48, 46 & 45 BC), killed 44 BC
Nephew of the great C. Marius, who was a leading general in the First Civil War, and son-in-law of L. Cornelius Cinna, who ruled Rome from 87–84 BC. Came to notice in Roman politics in the 60s BC, championing the Marian cause against the ruling Sullan faction, but was still only a minor figure. Won the consulship for 59 BC as an agent of Pompeius (and latterly Crassus) and was rewarded with a command in Gaul. Defied expectations by launching a war of conquest, backed by Pompeius and Crassus. Formed a fresh alliance with Pompeius and Crassus, whilst still being the junior member, and remained in Gaul throughout the 50s BC. Identified by Pompeius as the last obstacle to his dominance in Rome and manipulated into invading Italy as an 'enemy of the state'.

Defeated at Dyrrhachium, he regrouped and won a major victory at the subsequent Battle of Pharsalus. Neither this victory nor the subsequent murder of Pompeius brought the war to a conclusion and he fought further battles of Thapsus in 46 BC and Munda in 45 BC. Having finally defeated all his civil war opponents, he was preparing a major war of conquest against the Parthian Empire when he was murdered in the Senate by a large group of senators, composed of former enemies and many of his own officers, to prevent him becoming sole ruler of Rome.

Notable Leading Figures

M. Aemilius Lepidus (Cos. 46 & 42 BC)
Son of a First Civil War general. One of the Caesarian faction. Left by Caesar in charge of Rome in 49 BC. Proposed Caesar as Dictator. Became one of the main leaders of the faction after Caesar's death but politically outmanoeuvred by M. Antonius and Caesar Octavianus after the Battles of Philippi in 42 BC. Left alive by Octavianus (Augustus) as Princeps Maximus (Chief Priest). Died of natural causes in 13/12 BC.

L. Afranius (Cos. 60 BC), killed 46 BC
Long-serving Pompeian commander, having fought under Pompeius during the First Civil War and then in the Eastern Wars. Elected as Consul under Pompeius' patronage (the year before Caesar). Commanded Pompeius' legions in Spain but was defeated by Caesar. Captured and pardoned, he immediately returned to fighting for Pompeius, being at

both Dyrrhachium and Pharsalus. Murdered in the aftermath of the Battle of Thapsus.

C. Antonius (Pr. 44 BC), killed 42 BC
Younger brother of M. Antonius and Caesarian officer. In command of Caesar's province of Illyria but defeated and captured by Pompeius' forces in 49 BC. Caesarian Governor of Macedonia following Caesar's murder but overthrown and murdered by Brutus.

M. Antonius (Tr. 49, Cos. 44, 34 & 31 BC), suicide 30 BC
One of the two Tribunes who fled to Caesar at the beginning of 49 BC. Received an extraordinarily Propraetorian command (which technically he could not hold as a serving Tribune). Held command in Italy during 49 BC and led the defence of Brundisium in early 48 BC. Took command of the Caesarian relief army which crossed into Illyria in early 48 BC. Present at the Battles of Dyrrhachium and Pharsalus. Was Caesars's deputy during his Dictatorship and became one of the leaders of the Caesarian faction following Caesar's murder in 44 BC. Seized control of the Republic as one of the Second Triumvirate and took control of the Eastern Republic. Took command of the Second Romano-Parthian War and attempted to carve out his own familial empire in the East. Defeated by Caesar Octavianus at the Battel of Actium in 31 BC. Committed suicide following Octavianus' invasion of Egypt.

P. Attius Varus (Pr. *c*.53 BC), killed 45 BC
Pompeian commander. Briefly fought Caesar's men in Italy before withdrawing. Seized command of Roman Africa and defeated the Caesarian invasion (with Numidian help). Created a Pompeian stronghold and quasi-independent fiefdom in North Africa. Became one of the Pompeian faction leaders in the aftermath of Pharsalus. Fled from Africa to Spain after the defeat at Thapsus. Killed during the final Battle of Munda.

Q. Caecilius Metellus Pius Scipio Nasica (Cos. 52 BC), suicide 46 BC
Scion of two of Rome's leading families. Became Pompeius' father-in-law and then fellow Consul in 52 BC and de-facto deputy. Sent to the Eastern Republic in 49 BC to raise an army, he returned to Greece in

early 48 BC to fight Caesar's officers but too late to take part in the Battle of Dyrrhachium. He fought a significant part in the subsequent Battle of Pharsalus and retreated to North Africa in its aftermath, becoming commander of the Pompeian forces following Pompeius' murder in Egypt. Rebuilding these forces, he faced Caesar at the Battle of Thapsus (46 BC) but was defeated and committed suicide in the aftermath.

M. Caelius Rufus (Tr. 52, Pr. 48 BC), killed 48 BC
Former supporter of Milo, who backed Caesar in 49 BC. Elected as Peregrine Praetor for 48 BC, and caused a political disturbance by proposing popular legislation on the issue of debt. Attempted to raise a revolt with former colleague Milo but was killed.

M. Calpurnius Bibulus (Cos. 59 BC), died 48 BC
Caesar's colleague in the Consulship of 59 BC and long-time opponent. Commanded in Syria following Rome's defeat in the First Parthian War. Took command of Pompeius' fleet in the Adriatic and attacked Caesar's fleet trying to reinforce him in Epirus. Died of an illness in the Adriatic in early 48 BC.

C. Calvisius Sabinus (Cos. 39 BC)
Caesarian commander dispatched to secure Aetolia in 48 BC. Backed the Triumvirate after the murder of Caesar and supported Octavianus in the war against Sex. Pompeius. Supported Octavianus against Antonius and became part of the Augustan elite. Date of death remains unknown.

C. Cassius Longinus (Pr. 44 BC), killed 42 BC
Former supporter of Crassus who took over the defence of the Roman East in the aftermath of the Battle of Carrhae. Pompeian naval commander in 48 BC and led an abortive attack on Sicily. Took his navy to the East in the aftermath of Pharsalus, but rather than defeat Caesar as he crossed the Bosphorus he defected, providing Caesar with an effective navy and quickening his pursuit of Pompeius. One of the co-leaders of the conspiracy that murdered Caesar in 44 BC and co-leader of the 'Republican' faction in the subsequent civil war. Killed in 42 BC after the Battles of Philippi.

L. Cassius Longinus (Tr. 44 BC)

Caesarian commander dispatched to secure Thessaly in 48 BC but heavily defeated by Metellus Scipio. Became a Tribune in 44 BC. His subsequent career is not known.

Q. Cassius Longinus (Tr. 49 BC), died 47 BC

One of the two Tribunes who fled to Caesar at the beginning of 49 BC. Became Caesarian Governor of Further Spain but ruled tyrannically, sparking a rebellion and his replacement. Died in 47 BC in a shipwreck.

C. Claudius Marcellus (Cos. 49 BC)

Pompeian Consul in 49 BC. Helped precipitate the final breach with Caesar. Withdrew to Epirus along with Pompeius. Recorded as being commander of Pompeius' Rhodian fleet, but then disappears from the surviving sources. Date and cause of death unknown.

Claudius Marcellus Aeserninus, M. (Cos. 22 BC)

Caesarian quaestor in Spain who led the rebellion against Q. Cassius. Surrendered his force to the Caesarian governor, Lepidus, and was pardoned.

P. Cornelius Dolabella (Cos. 44 BC), suicide 43 BC

Caesarian legate in charge of the Adriatic fleet in 49 BC, but defeated by the Pompeians and withdrew. Clashed with M. Antonius as Tribune in 47 BC but took Caesar's place in the Consulship of 44 BC and command of the proposed Parthian War. Clashed with C. Trebonius and C. Cassius in the East, then committed suicide in Syria in 43 BC.

L. Cornelius Lentulus Crus (Cos. 49 BC), killed 48 BC

Pompeian Consul of 49 BC. Fled to Egypt after the Battle of Pharsalus but was murdered on the orders of Ptolemy XIII.

P. Cornelius Lentulus Spinther (Cos. 57 BC), killed 48 BC (?)

Pompeian commander in Italy in 49 BC. Captured by Caesar and pardoned, he rejoined Pompeius. Fled to Rhodes after the Battle of Pharsalus but is believed to have been murdered on the orders of Caesar.

F. Cornelius Sulla, killed 46 BC
Son and heir of the late Dictator, and son-in-law of Pompeius. Held command of Pompeian forces in Macedonia and fought Domitius Calvinus. Withdrew to Africa after the defeat at Pharsalus. Murdered in the aftermath of the Battle of Thapsus.

P. Cornelius Sulla (Cos. 65 BC), died 45 BC
Nephew of the late Dictator and brother-in-law of Pompeius, but a Caesarian commander. Fought in the Battles of Dyrrhachium and Pharsalus. Died, presumably of natural causes, in 45 BC.

Q. Cornificius (Pr. 45 BC), killed 42 BC
Caesarian Governor of Illyria who resecured the province for the Caesarian faction, defeating Pompeian commander M. Octavius. Later became Caesarian Governor of Africa but was proscribed by the Triumvirate. Killed in battle with his Triumviral successor.

L. Domitius Ahenobarbus (Cos. 54 BC), killed 48 BC
Senate-appointed successor to Caesar in Gaul. Defeated by Caesar at Corfinium. Commanded Massilia against a Caesarian siege. Rejoined Pompeius in Greece. Killed in the aftermath of the Battle of Pharsalus.

Cn. Domitius Calvinus (Cos. 53 & 40 BC)
Caesarian commander dispatched to face Metellus Scipio in 48 BC and later took part in the Battle of Pharsalus. Became Governor of Asia but was defeated by Pharnaces II later in 48 BC. Became an ally of Octavianus following Caesar's murder and remained a key member of Octavianus' circle of supporters. His date of death is unknown.

Q. Fufius Calenus (Cos. 47 BC), died 40 BC
Caesarian commander in Spain and Greece. Commanded Caesarian forces which recovered Greece in the aftermath of Pharsalus. Became Consul in 47 BC and joined M. Antonius in the aftermath of Caesar's murder. Died of (presumed) natural causes in 40 BC whilst commanding forces in Transalpine Gaul against Caesar Octavianus.

A. Gabinius (Cos. 58 BC), died 48/47 BC
Former Pompeian commander who sided with Caesar after being discarded by Pompeius. Possible commander at Brundisium who marched a portion of the Caesarian army into Illyria by land but was defeated by the local tribes. Fought in Illyricum in 48 BC, dying of (presumed) natural causes in late 48 or early 47 BC.

Sex. Iulius Caesar, killed 46 BC
Kinsman of Caesar and one of his junior officers in Spain. Appointed Governor of Syria in 47 BC, he was murdered in a Pompeian-sponsored revolt.

D. Iunius Brutus Albinus (Pr. 45 BC), killed 43 BC
Caesarian commander placed in charge of the naval siege of Massilia. Went on to hold a Praetorship in 45 BC. Was one of the leading conspirators who murdered Caesar in 44 BC. Took up command in Cisalpine Gaul, where he fought against M. Antonius in 43 BC, but was forced to flee when his army mutinied. Captured and murdered by a Gallic chief.

M. Iunius Brutus (Pr. 44 BC), suicide 42 BC
Scion from a family that claimed to be descended from the Bruttii who helped (perhaps inadvertently) found the Republic. Rumoured to be the bastard son of Caesar himself. Supported Pompeius in 48 BC and was present at the Battle of Pharsalus, and reconciled with Caesar after the battle. One of the co-leaders of the conspiracy that murdered Caesar in 44 BC and co-leader of the 'Republican' faction in the subsequent civil war. Committed suicide in 42 BC after the Battles of Philippi.

T. Labienus (Pr. *c.*59 BC), killed 45 BC
Senior Caesarian commander in Gaul but defected to join Pompeius when Caesar invaded Italy. Became a senior Pompeian commander, fighting at both Pharsalus and Thapsus. Fled to Spain after Thapsus and (by default) found himself as joint-leader of the Pompeian faction (along with Pompeius' sons). Killed at the Battle of Munda. His son became a Parthian client who conquered Asia Minor in 40 BC.

L. Manlius Torquatus (Pr. 49 BC), killed 46 BC
Pompeian commander who led the Pompeian forces who were attacked by Caesar during the final battle at Dyrrhachium. Seems to have played a key role in the victory. Retreated to North Africa after the Battle of Pharsalus but died in the aftermath of the Battle of Thapsus after being captured; either executed or by his own hand.

L. Munatius Plancus (Cos. 42 BC), died c.15 BC
Caesarian commander in Spain in 49 BC. Supported the Triumvirate in the aftermath of Caesar's assassination and became Consul in 42 BC, along with Lepidus. Proconsul of Syria during the Second Romano-Parthian War, he defected to Caesar Octavianus before his war with M. Antonius. Appointed one of the last two ever Censors in 22 BC before the position became part of imperial power. Died of natural causes in c.15 BC.

M. Octavius
Pompeian naval commander in Illyria, who helped to defeat the Caesarian forces there in 49 BC. Defeated by Cornificius in 48 BC in the aftermath of Pharsalus. Continued his naval command in Africa in 47–46 BC. Subsequent career and fate unknown.

Q. Pedius (Cos. 43 BC), died 43 BC
Caesarian commander, who served in Gaul and was a nephew of Caesar. Crushed Milo's rebellion in 48 BC. Fought in Spain in 45 BC. Named an heir in Caesar's will, along with his cousin Caesar Octavianus. Supported the Triumvirate and made consul in 43 BC along with Octavianus, but died in office.

M. Petreius, suicide 46 BC
Fought in both the First and Second Civil Wars. Pompeian commander in Spain. Defeated by Caesar, he rejoined Pompeius in Greece. Retreated to North Africa after the Battle of Pharsalus, where he served as a commander. Committed suicide after defeat at the Battle of Thapsus.

Cn. Pompeius 'Magnus', killed 45 BC
Eldest of the two sons of Pompeius Magnus and his political inheritor. Commanded a Pompeian fleet in 48 BC. Relocated to North Africa in

the aftermath of both Pharsalus and his father's murder. Excluded from command due to his youth, he launched a failed attack on the Caesarian-supporting Maurian Kingdom in 46 BC. With the deaths of the majority of the Pompeian faction leaders after Thapsus, along with T. Labienus, he became head of the Pompeian faction and commanded the Pompeian forces at the Battle of Munda in 45 BC, during which he was killed.

Sex. Pompeius, killed 35 BC
Younger of the two sons of Pompeius Magnus and an accomplished naval commander. Became joint leader of the Pompeian faction after the Battle of Thapsus and faced Caesar in Spain at the Battle of Munda in 45 BC. Becoming sole leader after the murder of his elder brother, he again took to the sea and opposed first Caesar and then the Caesarian Triumvirate, seizing control of Sicily. Fought civil war campaigns against Caesar Octavianus and was ultimately defeated, before fleeing east to fight civil war campaigns against Antonius' forces. Captured and murdered in 35 BC by the Antonine general M. Titius.

M. Porcius Cato (Pr. 54 BC), suicide 46 BC
More commonly known today as Cato the Younger. Contemporary of Caesar who opposed the various Triumvirs during the 60s and 50s BC. Pompeian supporter in the civil war. Commander in Sicily in 49 BC but withdrew rather than defend the island. Kept away from further military commands, and withdrew to Africa after the defeat at Pharsalus. Committed suicide after the defeat at Thapsus rather than compromise with Caesar.

C. Scribonius Curio, killed 49 BC
Caesarian commander. Led the campaign to seize control of Roman North Africa. Defeated his Roman opponent but was killed in a battle with Numidian army of King Juba, who had declared his support for Pompeius and the exiled Roman government.

L. Scribonius Libo (Cos. 34 BC)
Pompeian commander who took charge of the Adriatic campaign in 48 BC. After the murder of Caesar, sided with Sex. Pompeius (his son-in-law), but after his defeat made peace with Caesar Octavianus (his brother-in-

law). Became consul in 34 BC and remained a part of the Senatorial elite who supported Caesar Octavianus. Date of death is unknown.

P. Servilius Isauricus (Cos. 48 & 41 BC)
Son of a First Civil War general (Sullan faction). Caesar's fellow Consul in 48 BC. Defended Rome against Caelius and Milo. Named Caesar as Dictator after the Battle of Pharsalus. Sided with Caesar Octavianus after Caesar's murder and remained loyal throughout the subsequent civil war, earning another Consulship in 41 BC. Date and cause of death unknown.

C. Trebonius (Cos. 45 BC), killed 43 BC
Caesarian commander who had served with Caesar in Gaul and was placed in charge of siege of Massilia. As Praetor in 48 BC, opposed Caelus' measure on debt alleviation. Served in Spain as a Provincial Governor and went on to hold a Consulship in 45 BC. Became one of the conspirators in the murder of Caesar in 44 BC. Took up command in Asia, where he fought against P. Cornelius Dolabella in 43 BC but was captured and murdered.

M. Tullius Cicero (Cos. 63 BC), killed 43 BC
Famous political commentator and lawyer who held the Consulship in 63 BC and was central in the events of the Second Civil War. Remained in Italy during Caesar's invasion and only latterly joined Pompeius in Greece. Returned to Italy after the Battle of Pharsalus and was pardoned by Caesar. Murdered in 43 BC on the orders of M. Antonius.

P. Vatinius (Cos. 47 BC)
Caesarian commander in charge of the defence of Brundisium in 49 and 48 BC. Campaigned in Illyria during 47 BC and defeated Pompeian commander M. Octavius, recovering the province. Was rewarded with a Consulship in late 47 BC.

Non Romans

Bocchus II (King of the Mauri 49–33 BC), died 33 BC

Bogud (King of the Mauri 49–31 BC), killed 31 BC
Joint kings of the Maurian Kingdom in North Africa. Supported Caesar in opposition to their rivals in Numidia. Were preparing to act as a Caesarian

base for attack on Numidia and Pompeian Africa from the west when a revolt broke out in Caesarian Spain. Bogud led Maurian forces into Spain to assist the Caesarians against the rebels. In the subsequent civil war between Antonius and Octavianus the two brothers took opposing sides, with Bogud being deposed and dying during the prelude to the Battle of Actium.

Deiotarus (King of Galatia c.105–40s BC)
King of Galatia who supported Rome during the Third Romano-Pontic War. Supported Pompeius and was present at the Battel of Pharsalus. Sought and received Caesar's pardon and supported Caesarian governor Domitius Calvinus in his war against Pharnaces II. Supported Brutus and Cassius in their war against the Caesarian faction and again sought pardon when they were defeated. Died of old age.

Juba I (King of Numidia c. 85–46 BC), suicide 46 BC
King of Numida who threw his whole support behind Pompeius. Defeated Caesarian invasion of North Africa in 49 BC and butchered the survivors. Continued to support Pompeian faction in the aftermath of Pharsalus and helped them to rebuild. Was unable to take part in the Battle of Thapsus in 46 BC and fled in the aftermath, dying in a suicide pact with Roman commander M. Petreius.

Roucillus and Egus, killed 48 BC
Sons of an Allobrogian chieftain and part of Caesar's Gallic allied contingent. Betrayed Caesar and defected to Pompeius before the final clash of the Battle of Dyrrhachium. At least one was killed in the early skirmishes of Pharsalus.

Pharnaces II (Bosphoran King c.97–47 BC), killed 47 BC
Son of the legendary Mithridates VI of Pontus, nevertheless betrayed his father during the Third Romano-Pontic War, leading to his father's suicide, and received the northern part of the Pontic Empire (the Crimean Kingdom of the Bosphorus) in return. A client of Pompeius, used the chaos of the civil war to invade Rome's Eastern Republic in 47 BC (perhaps with Pompeian encouragement). Defeated by Caesar in 47 BC, fled back to his kingdom but was betrayed and killed by a subordinate.

Ptolemy XIII (Ptolemaic Pharaoh), killed 47 BC
One of the heirs of Ptolemy XII, who engaged in a civil war with his sister (Cleopatra VII). Ordered murder of Pompeius and his supporters in ill-thought-out bid to ingratiate himself with Caesar, a ploy which backfired spectacularly. When Caesar ruled in favour of his sister, he took up arms and was defeated by Caesar in early 47 BC, dying in the aftermath.

Lesser Figures

L. Aelius Tubero (Pr. ?)
Senatorially appointed Governor of Roman Africa in 49 BC. Deposed by the Pompeian commander P. Attius Varus. Withdrew to rejoin Pompeius in Greece.

C. Asinius Pollio
Caesarian commander in Sicily and Africa. Became noted historian.

M. Aurelius Cotta
Pompeian commander, driven out of Sardinia by revolt in 49 BC.

L. Caecilius Metellus (Tr. 49 BC)
Tribune who stayed in Rome in 49 BC. Attempted to prevent Caesar from seizing the state treasury but backed down when his life was threatened by Caesar. Nothing further is recorded about him.

P. Cornelius Lentulus Marcellinus
Caesarian commander at Battle of Dyrrhachium.

D. Laelius
Pompeian naval commander. Attacked Brundisium at same time as Battle of Pharsalus.

C. Lucilius Hirrus
Pompeian commander in Italy, later sent as Pompeius' envoy to the Parthian court.

Pompeius Bithynicus
Pompeian commander, murdered in Egypt on orders of Ptolemy XIII in 48 BC

M. Pomponius
Caesarian naval commander in Sicily in 48 BC.

P. Rutilius Lupus (Pr. 49 BC)
Pompeian commander who defended Achaea from Caesarian forces in 48 BC and retreated to the Peloponnese.

C. Sallustius Crispus (Pr. 46 BC)
Caesarian commander who held junior command in Illyria but was defeated by Pompeian forces. Became a famous historian.

L. Septimius
Roman centurion who murdered Pompeius on an Egyptian beach in 48 BC.

Sulpicius Rufus, P. (Pr. 48 BC)
Caesarian naval commander in Sicily in 48 BC.

M. Terentius Varro
Pompeian commander in Spain. Rejoined Pompeius after being defeated by Caesar. Pardoned after the Battle of Pharsalus, he retired and became one of Rome's' greatest academics, producing over seventy works. Died in 27 BC, in his late 80s.

Valerius Flaccus, killed 48 BC
Grandson of the civil war general (Cinnan Faction) and a Pompeian commander. Killed during a Pompeian attack on Caesarian defences at Dyrrhachium.

L. Vibullius Rufus
Pompeian legate who conveyed Pompeius' orders to his commanders in Spain in 49 BC.

Appendix II

How Many Civil Wars?[1]

As readers will note, I have deliberately chosen to include the provocative subtitle of the Third Roman Civil War for this series of books. This challenges the cosy status quo that has emerged in modern historiography of the Roman civil war period, which ignores a fundamental question for anyone studying this period of Roman history: when is a civil war not a civil war? The short answer seems to be when it is a rebellion, a revolt or even a conspiracy. There appears to have developed a very narrow and illogical definition of when a Roman army fighting a Roman army constitutes a civil war and when one does not. In consequence, we have the absurdity of a consul marching his army on Rome itself in 88 and 87 BC constituting a civil war, whilst a proconsul doing so just ten years later (in 77 BC) does not.

Throughout my various works, I have sought to challenge this cosy and somewhat lazy consensus that has emerged, first by lengthening the duration of the First Civil War from its traditional 88–82 BC to 91–70 BC, which allows us to include the Lepidian, Sertorian and Marian campaigns, where again Roman fought Roman, as sequels to the events of the 80s BC.[2] Under this schema, the war only ended in 70 BC – the last military campaign being fought in 71 BC – with the consulships of Pompeius and Crassus and their political reform and general amnesty. This approach owes more to Appian, with his work on the civil wars covering 133–31 BC, than to the writing of Florus, which has each campaign being a separate war.

All too often, modern historiography ignores this question and seems to follow the Florine route, wanting to separate these various conflicts into nice self-contained wars. This is not just a problem with Roman history. Modern historiography seems to demand that civil wars be clearly defined between two opposing sides, each with a different ideological standpoint.

178 The Battle of Pharsalus (48 BC)

Thus, English history only has one Civil War (1642–51), with two clearly defined sides, each with separate ideological standpoints (monarchy vs parliament) and even clearly defined costumes. Yet this war was at least the seventh fought between English factions in the last thousand years. We have the civil war between Stephen and Matilda for the crowns of England and Normandy (1135–53), the two civil wars fought between Kings John and Henry III and their rebellious barons (1215–17 and 1264–67), another in the reign of Edward II (1321–1322), and the two wars fought for the English crown between the various branches of the Plantagenet dynasty from 1399–1403 and then 1455–87 (the latter being dubbed the Wars of the Roses).

Therefore, English history has at least six civil wars in the last thousand years, yet only one makes the cut as an 'official' Civil War. This begs the question of why the others are ignored and downgraded into non-civil wars, each with a meaningless title (Barons' Wars, Wars of the Roses)? Is it because they do not fit into a nice ideological framework, or an unwillingness to admit that societies collapse more often that we would like to admit?

Throughout history, we can discern two broad types of civil war. One is the 'modern' version, where we have a clash between two clearly defined sides, each with its own ideological standpoint, usually centred on a question of governance. Thus, we have the classic English, American, Spanish and Chinese Civil Wars. A second type is where there is a complete breakdown of government and society collapses into anarchy, with various competing warlords emerging and fighting for supremacy. This second type can most commonly be seen in modern Africa.

Returning to Rome, which type of civil wars can we see? All too often, modern historians want them to be the clear-cut ideological civil wars between optimates and *populares* (terms which have been grossly distorted). Our two 'official' civil wars of the period – Sulla vs Marius and Caesar vs Pompeius – are often painted in these terms. Yet having reviewed these events, such terms are meaningless. The various protagonists did not go to war over differing views of how to govern, but turned to their armies to defend their own positions from the attacks of their enemies. The events of the 80s and 40s BC both snowballed out of everyone's control, with the Republican system collapsing, leading to periods of anarchy where various Roman generals fought for supremacy amongst themselves until a victorious individual emerged who could rebuild central authority and calm the bloodshed, that is, dominate without looking like they were doing do; Pompeius and Crassus in 71–70 BC and Octavianus in 30–27 BC.

Consequently, modern Roman historiography leaves us with a Florine-like patchwork of different wars:

Social War	(91–88 BC)
First Civil War	(88–81 BC)
Sertorian Rebellion	(81–72 BC)
Lepidian Revolt	(78–77 BC)
Catiline Conspiracy	(63–62 BC)
Second Civil War	(49–31 BC)

The clear danger of following such an approach is that it shifts focus away from the underlying causes of these conflicts and onto the individuals, thereby blurring the line between symptom and cause. Should we be focusing on Sulla, Lepidus, Catilina and Caesar, or the underlying issues that were at work behind them? Having examined this volume, the reader will understand that focussing on the individuals at the expense of the wider picture is not a method I choose to pursue. Not one of these men woke up one morning and thought that they would like to march their army against their own state simply to gain power for themselves; rather, Republican politics had forced them to believe that they had no alternative and that what they were doing was for the benefit of the Republic.

Ultimately, as these events proved, the Republican system did not provide a robust-enough framework to keep the various tensions between the Senatorial oligarchy from spilling over into violence and civil war. Various attempts were made to modify the Republic; be it a Triumvirate (official or unofficial) or sole rule (subtle or obvious). The one version that emerged victorious from this period was sole rule, with a single figure guiding and overseeing the smooth running of the Republic and acting as arbiter to keep the others in check. Yet this system too was flawed and laid the foundations for the role of Emperor, first on a hereditary basis and then through merit or armed force.

But if we are to reject the Florine version of the wars in this period, what are we to replace it with? Do we simply follow the Appianic version and state that all this period was one giant civil war, or do we reject altogether the notion of a civil war in a society such as Rome? I have argued, and will continue to do so, that within this period of Roman history there were distinct periods of civil wars, when the clashes and tensions within the Republican system boiled over into full-blown military conflict, and in two out of the three cases, total systemwide (and empire-wide) collapse.

Civil war within a country was one thing, but civil war in a society that had a wide-ranging empire was another matter altogether, magnifying the chaos and fighting on a Mediterranean-wide level. As we have seen in two out of three cases, Rome's empire became a battleground for the various parties of the civil war and led to the extinction of independent kingdoms which became too closely associated with a losing side (namely Numidia and Egypt).

Having rejected the modern Florine notion of multiple separate wars, I would like to offer a fresh scheme for the civil wars within this period, if only to stimulate further debate on a subject that can never have a 'right' answer.

The First Civil War, 91–70 BC

All too often, discussions of the First Civil War ignore the fact that Italy had been riven by civil warfare for three years, with two rebel factions fighting the Republican government. This is the very reason that Sulla had an army of battle-hardened veterans in Italy within marching distance of Rome, and citizen distribution was at the heart of the political manoeuvring which led to Sulla's loss of command. Thus, the war that broke out in 91 BC between the various societies that made up the Roman system must be classed as a civil war, with neighbour fighting neighbour and – if we are to believe the more dramatic sources – brother fighting brother.

The First Civil War period had a number of different phases, which were not neatly separate conflicts but were all intertwined. The war in Italy led to the consular attack on Rome in 88 BC, both of which mixed together to spark off the war of 87 BC. There then followed a lull whilst at least two different Roman armies separately fought off a foreign invasion. When that invasion had been dealt with, all sides then engaged in a fight for supremacy which brought about another lull as Sulla consolidated his control of Italy and the Western empire. Some regions were forcibly reunited (Sicily and Africa), whilst others (Spain and Gaul) were brought together through negotiation between warlords. The faction that lost Italy soon stoked a rebellion in Spain, where the civil war continued – mixed in with a native rebellion, as it had done in Italy – for another nine years. Whilst the civil war continued in the Western Republic (in Spain), other elements of the faction that lost Italy spearheaded another foreign invasion of Rome's empire, again blurring the lines between civil war and foreign war.

During this period there were no neat delineations between civil war, native rebellion and foreign wars, all becoming inexorably interlinked in one great collapse of the Republican system. It is also no coincidence that the largest slave rebellion in Roman history happened during this period of chaos, when a slave named Spartacus took advantage of the devastation in Italy, disaffection with Rome and overseas wars to launch his revolt.

By 71 BC there emerged another lull, with the fighting ended in Spain, Italy and Asia, yet it took the actions of Pompeius and Crassus, who chose to unite Rome rather than continue the division and personally benefit from it. Their consulship set an example that two oligarchs could work in a peaceful manner, as they cooperated through a constitutional settlement they introduced which removed a number of tension points – though some would say reintroduced them – and saw a very public recall of all Romans exiled during the previous twenty years of tumult. It can thus be argued that a lull became a definite end.

The Second Civil War, 63–62 BC

That the events of 63/62 BC constitute a civil war should not be difficult to argue. Although the ancient sources and modern histography chooses to focus on events in Rome, the key facts are that there were widescale rebellions against Rome throughout Italy and native rebellions in Gaul (again mixing the two), and two Romano-Italian armies fought one another in a set-piece battle. That there was only one pitched battle, and that that it was over relatively quickly should not disqualify this from being classed as a civil war. Indeed, the surviving sources paint a picture of wider military action across Italy, but we only have the barest of detail for it. Had we fuller sources for this fighting, we would be able to see the true scale of the civil war in Italy.

The other point is that if this was a civil war, was it a continuation of the first war and can we thus extend the First Civil War down to 62 BC? As we have reviewed, the causes of this conflict did have their roots in the first war, be they disgruntled Sullan politicians and veterans or displaced Italian communities. Yet I would argue that it was a separate conflict from that of 91–70 BC and that the years 69–64 BC were not merely a lull in the first war, but that the Pompeian-Crassan consulships ended the First Civil War. That a war can be finished but still leave matters unsettled can be seen frequently throughout history; most recently in the First and Second World Wars, particularly in Europe. So although the Second Civil War had its roots in the First, they were, I believe, separate conflicts. This can also be seen by the fact that the New Republic reconstituted out of the ashes of the First Civil War did not collapse as it had done in 91–70 or 49–30 BC.

The Third Civil War, 49–27 BC

This is perhaps the most uncontentious of the three conflicts, with it being widely accepted that the events between the crossing of the Rubicon in 49 BC and the victory of Octavianus constitute another period of one civil war, which again saw a total collapse of the Republican system and the emergence of various factions and warlords. It too saw the blurring between civil war and foreign war, again most easily seen in the East with the attack of the Parthian Empire being spearheaded by Roman generals. This period also saw lulls in the fighting between the various overlapping conflicts. There was no certainty that Octavianus' victory at Actium in 31 BC would be the final major battle of the war, any more than had the Battle of Pharsalus in 48 BC or Philippi in 42 BC

If there is one contentious issue, then it must be the end date of this civil war. It clearly did not finish in 31 BC with the Battle of Actium, as Antonius fought on with his defence of Egypt, which only fell in 30 BC. Yet as we have explored above, winning a campaign did not bring about victory, especially in a civil war; it was winning the peace that mattered. This is where both Sulla and Caesar failed when they had military control of the Republic. Roman civil wars did not seem to end when one side was victorious in battle, as new opponents soon emerged. They only ended when everyone agreed that there was no more need to fight and that the supposed imbalances in the Republican system had been righted. For that reason, I would argue that the Third Civil War did not end until the First Constitutional Settlement of the newly renamed Augustus in 27 BC, the intervening years from 30–27 BC being merely a lull in the fighting. Thus, Republican politics was both the cause of the civil wars and the solution, however temporary.

Notes

Chapter One
1. See G. Sampson, *Rome's Great Eastern War: Lucullus, Pompey, and the Conquest of the East, 74–62 BC* (Barnsley: 2021).
2. See G. Sampson, *The Defeat of Rome: Crassus, Carrhae and the Invasion of the East* (Barnsley: 2008).
3. See J. Lazenby, 'The Conference of Luca and the Gallic War; A Study in Roman Politics 57–55 BC', *Latomus* 18 (1959), pp.63–76.
4. See G. Sampson, *The Collapse of Rome: Marius, Sulla, and The First Civil War 91–70 BC* (Barnsley: 2013).
5. See T. Frank, 'Caesar at the Rubicon', *Classical Quarterly* 1 (1907), pp.223–25; F. Sirianni, 'Caesar's Decision to Cross the Rubicon', *L'Antiquité Classique* 48 (1979), pp.636–38; R. Tucker, 'What Actually Happened at the Rubicon ?', *Historia* 37 (1988), pp.245–48; C. Ehrhardt, 'Crossing the Rubicon', *Antichthon* 29 (1995), pp.37–41; G. Stanton, 'Why Did Caesar Cross the Rubicon?', *Historia* 52 (2003), pp.67–94; A. Rondholz, 'Crossing the Rubicon: A Historiographical Study', *Mnemosyne* 62 (2009), pp.432–50; J. Beneker, 'The Crossing of the Rubicon and the Outbreak of Civil War in Cicero, Lucan, Plutarch and Suetonius', *Phoenix* 65 (2011), pp.74–99; L. Fezzi, *Crossing the Rubicon: Caesar's Decision and the Fate of Rome* (London: 2019).
6. Cic., *Att.* 8.11.2, though other letters contradict the pre-planned nature of this withdrawal. See K. von Fritz, 'Pompey's Policy before and after the Outbreak of the Civil War of 49 BC', *Transactions and Proceedings of the American Philological Association* 73 (1942), pp.145–80; and D. Shackleton Bailey, 'Expectatio Corfiniensis', *Journal of Roman Studies* 46 (1956), pp.57–64.
7. Cic., *Att.* 9.10.6.
8. R. Syme, 'The Allegiance of Labienus', *Journal of Roman Studies* 28 (1938), p.114. Also see K. von Fritz, 'Pompey's Policy before and after the Outbreak of the Civil War of 49 BC', *Transactions and Proceedings of the American Philological Association* 73 (1942), pp.145–80.
9. See G. Sampson, *The Battle of Dyrrhachium (48 BC): Caesar, Pompey, and the Early Campaigns of the Third Roman Civil War* (Barnsley: 2022).
10. See K. von Fritz, 'The Mission of L. Caesar and L. Roscius in January 49 BC', *Transactions and Proceedings of the American Philological Association* 72 (1941), pp.125–56; F. Sirianni, 'Caesar's Peace Overtures to Pompey', *L'Antiquité Classique* 62 (1993), pp.219–37.
11. See L. Grillo, *The Art of Caesar's Bellum Civile: Literature, Ideology, and Community* (Cambridge: 2012); A. Peer, *Julius Caesar's Bellum Civile and the Composition of a New Reality* (London: 2015); R. Westall, *Caesar's Civil War: Historical Reality and Fabrication* (Leiden: 2017).

12. Oros. 6.15.8.
13. Flor. 2.13.31–33.
14. Dio., 41.40.1–2.
15. Oros. 6.15.8–9.
16. App., *BC* 49.1.
17. Caes., *BC* 1.7.
18. *Ibid.*, 1.33.
19. Cic., *Att.* 10.4.
20. See G. Sampson (2022).
21. Caes., *BC* 1.53.
22. Dio., 41.21.1.
23. *Ibid.*, 41.21.2.
24. Dio., 41.21.4.
25. Caes., *BC* 1.60.

Chapter Two
1. Caes., *BC* 3.19; App., *BC* 2.56–58; Dio., 41.47.2.
2. See G. Sampson (2022).
3. Caes., *BC* 3.34.
4. App., *BC* 2.60.
5. Dio., 41.51.2–3
6. *Ibid.*
7. Caes. *BC.* 3.47
8. See G. Veith. (1920). *Der Feldzug von Dyrrhachium zwischen Caesar und Pompeius* (Wien), pp.5–12.
9. Caes., *BC* 3.63.
10. *Ibid.* 3.45–46
11. See A. Anders, 'The Face of Roman Skirmishing', *Historia* 64 (2015), pp.263–300.
12. See L. Grillo (2012), A. Peer (2015) & R. Westall (2017).
13. Dio., 41.50.
14. App., *BC* 2.60.
15. Caes., *BC* 3.51.
16. *Ibid.*, 3.52.
17. Caes., *BC* 3.53.
18. Dio., 41.50.4.
19. See B. Kavanagh, 'The citizenship and nomen of Roucillus and Egus', *Ancient History Bulletin* 15 (2001), pp.163–71.
20. Caes., *BC* 3.61.
21. *Ibid.*
22. Caes., *BC* 3.64.
23. *Ibid.*, 3.65.
24. Caes., *BC* 3.71.
25. See R. Westall, 'The Sources for the Civil Wars of Appian of Alexandria', in K. Welch (ed.), *Appian's Roman History: Empire and Civil War* (Swansea: 2015), pp.125–67.
26. App., *BC* 2.61–62.
27. Such as C. Asinius Pollio, see L. Morgan (2000), pp.51–69, & R. Westall, 'The Relationship of Appian to Pollio', *Analecta Romana Instituti Danici* 38 (2013), pp.7–34.

28. App., *BC* 2.63.
29. App., *BC* 2.64.
30. Dio. 41.51.1.
31. Plut., *Pomp* 65.4–5. See App. 2.62.
32. Plut., *Caes* 39.4–6.
33. *Ibid.*, 39.6–7.
34. Plut., *Caes* 39.8.
35. *Ibid.*, 39.9.
36. Oros. 6.15.18.
37. Caes., *BC* 3.71.
38. Plut., *Pomp* 66.4.

Chapter Three
1. Caes., *BC* 3.73.
2. App., *BC* 2.65; Plut., *Pomp* 66.
3. Caes., *BC* 3.79.
4. *Ibid.*
5. Caes., *BC* 3.75–78.
6. *Ibid.*, 3.75.
7. Caes., *BC* 3.76–77.
8. *Ibid.*
9. Caes., *BC* 3.77.
10. As he himself admits (Caes., *BC* 3.79).
11. Caes., *BC* 3.78.
12. *Ibid.*, 3.79.
13. See G. Sampson (2022).
14. Caes., *BC* 3.79.
15. Though sent with two legions, he had been defeated by Metellus in battle with an unknown number of losses.
16. App., *BC* 2.64; Plut., *Caes* 41.
17. This has been the subject of much scholarship and no agreed opinion has been reached. See B. Perrin, 'Pharsalia, Pharsalus, Palaepharsalus', *American Journal of Philology* 6 (1885), pp.170–89; T. Rice Holmes, 'The Battle-Field of Old Pharsalus', *Classical Quarterly* 2 (1908), pp.271–92; F. Lucas, 'The Battlefield of Pharsalos', *Annual of the British School at Athens* 24 (1921), pp.34–53; W. Gwatkin, 'Some Reflections on the Battle of Pharsalus', *Transactions and Proceedings of the American Philological Association* 87 (1956), pp.109–24; M. Rambaud, 'Le Soleil de Pharsale', *Historia* 3 (1955), pp.346–78; C. Pelling, 'Pharsalus', *Historia* 22 (1973), pp.249–59. The best single discussion is J. Morgan, 'Palaepharsalus – The Battle and the Town', *American Journal of Archaeology* 87 (1983), pp.23–54.
18. App., *BC* 2.75.
19. See Strabo 9.5.6.
20. Such as Eutrop. 6.20.
21. J. Morgan, 'Palaepharsalus – The Battle and the Town', *American Journal of Archaeology* 87 (1983), pp.23–54.
22. App., *BC* 2.64.
23. See G. Sampson (2021).
24. App., *BC* 2.65.
25. Plut., *Pomp* 67.

26. Plut., *Caes* 40.
27. Again, the exact site of the battle has never been identified and ancient accounts differ as to the exact topography. See Note 79.
28. Caes., *BC* 3.84–85.
29. *Ibid.*, 3.84.
30. *Ibid.*
31. *Ibid.*
32. App., *BC* 2.66.
33. *Ibid.*, 2.68.
34. Caes., *BC* 3.84.
35. *Ibid.*
36. Caes., *BC* 3.85.
37. Plut., *Pomp* 68.
38. Plut., *Caes* 43.
39. Plut., *Pomp* 68.
40. Plut., *Caes* 44.

Chapter Four
1. Caes., *BC* 3.88.
2. *Ibid.*, 3.89.
3. Plut., *Caes* 42.
4. App., *BC* 2.70.
5. Oros. 6.15.22.
6. Flor. 2.13.44.
7. See T. Stevenson, 'Appian on the Pharsalus Campaign: Civil Wars 2.48–91', in K. Welch (ed.), *Appian's Roman History: Empire and Civil War* (Swansea: 2015), pp.257–75.
8. App., *BC* 2.70.
9. *Ibid.*, 2.71.
10. Caes., *BC* 5.88.
11. *Ibid.*, 5.89.
12. A Caesarian commander present at the Battle of Pharsalus, who later wrote a contemporary (now lost and much lamented) history of the civil wars. For Pollio's judgements on Caesar's history, see Suet., *Iul.* 56.4. Also see C. Coulter, 'Pollio's History of the Civil War', *Classical Weekly* 46 (1952), pp.33–36; A. Rossi, 'The Camp of Pompey: Strategy of Representation in Caesar's Bellum Civile', *Classical Journal* 95 (2000), pp.239–56; L. Morgan, 'The Autopsy of C. Asinius Pollio', *Journal of Roman Studies* 90 (2000), pp.51–69; R. Westall, 'The Relationship of Appian to Pollio', *Analecta Romana Instituti Danici* 38 (2013), pp.7–34, & 'The Sources for the Civil Wars of Appian of Alexandria', in K. Welch (ed.), *Appian's Roman History. Empire and Civil War* (Swansea: 2015), pp.125–67.
13. App., *BC* 2.75.
14. See Caes., *BC* 3.101.
15. *BA* 48.1.
16. Frontin., *Str* 2.3.22.
17. Cic., *Phil* 2.71.
18. Cic., *Phil* 14.23.
19. Cic., *Lig* 9.

20. See Chapter Three, note 17.
21. See J. Morgan (1983).
22. App., *BC* 2.76.
23. See J. Morgan (1983).
24. Caes., *BC* 5.89.
25. App., *BC* 2.76.
26. Plut., *Caes* 44.3.
27. Frontin., *Str* 2.3.22.
28. See G. Sampson (2008).
29. Caes., *BC* 3.92.
30. *Ibid.*, 3.91.
31. Caes., *BC* 3.99.
32. Plut., *Caes* 44.12.
33. Flor. 2.13.46.
34. Caes., *BC* 5.93.
35. Dio., 41.60.2. See R. Westall, 'The Sources of Cassius Dio for the Roman Civil Wars of 49–30 BC', in C. Lange and J. Madsen (eds), *Cassius Dio: Greek Intellectual and Roman Politician* (Leiden: 2016), pp.51–75.
36. Plut., *Pomp* 71.
37. Caes., *BC* 5.93.
38. App., *BC* 2.78.
39. Plut., *Pomp* 71.
40. Caes., *BC* 5.93.
41. App., *BC* 2.78.
42. Plut., *Pomp* 71.
43. Caes., *BC* 3.93–94.
44. Plut., *Caes* 45.
45. App., *BC* 2.79.
46. See J. Morgan (1983).
47. App., *BC* 2.80.
48. See G. Bucher, 'Fictive Elements in Appian's Pharsalus Narrative', *Phoenix* 59 (2005), pp.50–76.
49. App., *BC* 2.80.
50. Caes., *BC* 3.95.
51. *Ibid.*, 3.96.
52. Caes., *BC* 3.99.
53. App., *BC* 2.82.
54. Plut., *Caes* 46.4.
55. Plut., *Pomp* 72.3.
56. Vell. 2.52.3.
57. Dio., 41.62.
58. *Ibid.*
59. Cic., *Phil* 2.71.
60. Lucan, *Phar.* 7.622–631.
61. Caes., *BC* 3.101.

Chapter Five
1. Dio., 42.10.1–2.
2. See L. Grillo (2012), pp.168–69, for the argument that this is a deliberate Caesarian literary ploy to stress to his audience that the civil war had not ended.

3. Caes., *BC* 3.100.
4. How Caesar himself refers to the Battle of Pharsalus.
5. Caes., *BC* 3.101.
6. Dio., 42.13.1.
7. *Ibid.*, 42.12.
8. See G. Sampson (2022).
9. Dio., 42.11.

Chapter Six
1. App., *BC* 2.81.
2. Vell. 2.53.1.
3. Plut., *Pomp* 73.6.
4. App., *BC* 2.87.
5. Dio., 42.10.1–11–1.
6. Front., *Str* 2.7.13.
7. Cic., *Div* 1.68.
8. The link between the Iunii Bruti of the late Republic and the founding father of the Republic is far from clear.
9. Plut., *Brut* 6.
10. Liv., *Per* 111.
11. Plut., *Caes* 39.
12. Cic., *Deiot* 29.
13. Caes., *BC* 3.99.
14. Dio., 41.62.
15. *Ibid.*
16. Dio., 41.63.
17. Plut., *Pomp* 73.6.
18. App., *BC* 2.88.
19. Plut., *Brut* 6.3.
20. App., *BC* 2.88.
21. *Ibid.*, 2.82.
22. App., *BC* 2.88.
23. Caes., *BC* 3.99.
24. Cic., *Div* 1.68.
25. Dio., 42.13.3.
26. *Ibid.*, 42.14.1.
27. *Ibid.*, 42.14.3. Also see L. Amela (2008). 'The Campaign of Quintus Fufius Calenus in Greece During the Year 48 B.C. and the City of Megara. The Consequences of the War', *Athenaeum* 96, pp.279–291.
28. *Ibid.*, 42.14.5.
29. *Ibid.*, 42.2.2.
30. Plut., *Pomp* 74.1.
31. Caes., *BC* 3.102.
32. App., *BC* 2.83.1.
33. Plut., *Pomp* 76.1.
34. *Ibid.*, 76.3
35. Caes., *BC* 3.102.
36. *Ibid.*
37. Caes., *BC* 3.103.

38. App., *BC* 2.87. See G. Sampson (2021).
39. *Ibid.*, 2.88.
40. Dio., 42.6.
41. T. Broughton, *The Magistrates of the Roman Republic* 2 (1952), p. 283.
42. Caes., *BC* 3.106.
43. See I. Shatzman, 'The Egyptian Question in Roman Politics (59–54 BC)', *Latomus* 30 (1971), pp.363–69, & M. Siani-Davies, 'Ptolemy XII Auletes and the Romans', *Historia* 46 (1997), pp.306–40.
44. See R. Syme, 'M. Bibulus and Four Sons', *Harvard Studies in Classical Philology* 91 (1987), pp.185–98, & M. Gray-Fow, 'The Mental Breakdown of a Roman Senator: M. Calpurnius Bibulus', *Greece & Rome* 37 (1990), pp.179–90.
45. See R. Westall, 'Pompeius at Pelusium', *Hermathena* 196/197 (2014), pp.309–40.
46. App., *BC* 2.86.
47. Oros. 6.15.28.
48. Caes., *BC* 104.
49. Plut., *Caes* 48.3.

Chapter Seven
1. See G. Sampson (2022).
2. Dio., 42.17.
3. See G. Sampson (2022).
4. Though it is never explicitly stated that this happened, and new elections for the Curule offices of 47 BC took place and were occupied even through Caesar's Dictatorship continued.
5. Plut., *Ant* 8.
6. Dio., 42.18.1.
7. *Ibid.*, 42.20.1–2.
8. *Ibid.*, 42.21.1–2.
9. *Ibid.*, 42.20.
10. The office is never explicitly stated, and the year is open to debate. See G. Niccolini, *I Fasti dei Tribuni della Plebe* (Milan: 1934), pp.335–38.
11. Dio., 42.20.1.
12. Dio., 42.20.1.
13. Cic., *Phil* 13.32.
14. App., *BC* 2.90.
15. See. G. Sampson, *The Battle of Thapsus (46 BC): Caesar, Metellus Scipio, Cato and the Roman Civil War in Africa* (Barnsley: 2024).
16. Dio., 42.13.3–4.
17. Plut., *Cat Min* 56.
18. *Ibid.*, 57.
19. App., *BC* 2.87.
20. *Ibid.*
21. Plut. *Cat. Min.* 57.2–3.
22. We shall see what happened in the next book in the series; see G. Sampson (2024).
23. *BA* 49.
24. *Ibid.*, 58. See also Dio., 42.15–16.
25. *Ibid.*, 48–64.
26. *BA* 60.

27. *Ibid.*, 61.
28. *Ibid.*
29. *BA* 62.
30. Dio., 42.16.2.
31. See E. Rawson, 'The Identity Problems of Q. Cornificius', *Classical Quarterly* 28 (1978), pp.188–201.
32. *BA* 42.
33. *Ibid.*
34. App., *Ill* 12.
35. See G. Sampson (2022).
36. *BA* 43.
37. *Ibid.*, 44.
38. See G. Sampson (2021).
39. Dio., 42.45.3.
40. *BA* 40.
41. See G. Sampson (2023).
42. Cic., *Att* 11.16.
43. Forthcoming in 2024 & 2025.

Appendix Two
1. This is a variation of the appendix found in G. Sampson (2019), pp.307–13.
2. See G. Sampson (2013).

Bibliography

Abbott, F., 'Titus Labienus', *Classical Journal* 13 (1917), pp.4–13.
Amela, Luis, 'The Campaign of Quintus Fufius Calenus in Greece During the Year 48 B.C. and the City of Megara. The Consequences of the War', *Athenaeum* 96 (2008), pp.279–291.
Amela Valverde, L., *Cneo Pompeyo Magno. El defensor de la República Romana* (Madrid: 2003).
Anders, A., 'The Face of Roman Skirmishing', *Historia* 64 (2015), pp.263–300.
Appel, H., 'Pompeius Magnus: his Third Consulate and the senatus consultum ultimum', *Biuletyn Polskiej Misji Historycznej* 7 (2012), pp.341–60.
Badian, E., 'The Early Career of A. Gabinius (Cos. 58 B.C.)', *Philologus* 103 (1959), pp.87–99.
Badian, E., 'The Attempt to Try Caesar', in J. Evans (ed.), *Polis and Imperium: Studies in Honour of Edward Togo Salmon* (Toronto: 1974), pp.145–66.
Badian, E., 'Tribuni Plebis and Res Publica', in J. Linderski (ed.), *Imperium Sine Fine* (Stuttgart: 1996), pp.187–214.
Balsdon, J., 'The Veracity of Caesar', *Greece & Rome* 4 (1957), pp.19–28.
Bartsch, S., *Ideology in Cold Blood. A Reading of Lucan's Civil War* (Cambridge: 1997).
Batstone, W. & Damon, C., *Caesar's Civil War* (Oxford: 2006).
Bexley, E., 'Replacing Rome: Geographic and Political Centrality in Lucan's Pharsalia', *Classical Philology* 104 (2009), pp.459–75.
Bell, A., 'Fact and "Exemplum" in Accounts of the Deaths of Pompey and Caesar', *Latomus* 53 (1994), pp.824–36.
Beneker, J., 'The Crossing of the Rubicon and the Outbreak of Civil War in Cicero, Lucan, Plutarch and Suetonius', *Phoenix* 65 (2011), pp.74–99.
Berdowski, P., 'Cn. Pompeius, the son of Pompey the Great: an embarrassing ally in the African War? (48–46 BC)', *Palamedes* 7 (2012), pp.117–42.
Billows, R., *Julius Caesar: The Colossus of Rome* (London: 2008).
Boak, A., 'The Extraordinary Commands from 80 to 48 BC: A Study in the Origins of the Principate', *American Historical Review* 24 (1918), pp.1–25.
Brown, R., 'Two Caesarian Battle-Descriptions: A Study in Contrast', *Classical Journal* 94 (1999), pp.329–57.
Broughton, T., *The Magistrates of the Roman Republic Volume 1 & 2* (New York: 1951/52).
Broughton, T., *Supplement to the Magistrates of the Roman Republic* (New York: 1960).
Broughton, T., *Supplement to the Magistrates of the Roman Republic* (New York: 1986).
Broughton, T., 'M. Aemilius Lepidus: His Youthful Career', in R. Curtis (ed.), *Studio Pompeiana & Classica in Honour of Wilhelmina F. Jashemski, vol. II* (New York: 1989), pp.13–23.
Brunt, P., *Social Conflicts in the Roman Republic* (London: 1971).
Brunt, P., *The Fall of the Roman Republic* (Oxford: 1988).
Bucher, G., 'Fictive Elements in Appian's Pharsalus Narrative', *Phoenix* 59 (2005), pp.50–76.

Bibliography 193

Canfora, L., *Julius Caesar: The Life and Times of the People's Dictator* (Edinburgh: 2007).
Chrystal, P., *Rome: Republic into Empire: The Civil Wars of the First Century BC* (Barnsley: 2019).
Collins, H., 'The Decline and Fall of Pompey the Great', *Greece & Rome* 22 (1953), pp.98–106.
Cornwell, H., 'The Construction of One's Enemies in Civil War (49–30 BC)', *Hermathena* 196/197 (2014), pp.41–68.
Coulter, C., 'Pollio's History of the Civil War', *Classical Weekly* 46 (1952), pp.33–36.
Damon, C., 'Caesar's Practical Prose', *Classical Journal* 89 (1994), pp.183–95.
De Ruggiero, P., *Mark Antony: A Plain Blunt Man* (Barnsley: 2013).
Drogula, F., *Cato the Younger: Life and Death at the End of the Roman Republic* (Oxford: 2019).
Duncan, M., *The Storm Before the Storm: The Beginning of the End of the Roman Republic* (London: 2017).
Eden, P., 'Caesar's Style: Inheritance versus Intelligence', *Glotta* 40 (1962), pp.74–117.
Ehrhardt, C., 'Crossing the Rubicon', *Antichthon* 29 (1995), pp.37–41.
Epstein, D., *Personal Enmity in Roman Politics 218–43 BC* (London: 1987).
Evans, R., 'Caesar's use of the tribuni plebis', *Questioning Reputations* (Pretoria: 2004), pp.65–92.
Evans, R., 'Pompey's Three Consulships: The End of Electoral Competition in the Late Roman Republic', *Acta Classica* 59 (2016), pp.80–100.
Ezov, A., 'The "Missing Dimension" of C. Julius Caesar', *Historia* 45 (1996), pp.64–94.
Frank, T., 'Caesar at the Rubicon', *Classical Quarterly* 1 (1907), pp.223–25.
Fezzi, L., *Crossing the Rubicon: Caesar's Decision and the Fate of Rome* (London: 2019).
Field, N., *Warlords of Republican Rome: Caesar Versus Pompey* (Barnsley: 2009).
Flower, H., *Roman Republics* (Princeton: 2010).
Fuller, J., *Julius Caesar: Man, Soldier, and Tyrant* (London: 1965).
Gelzer, M., *Caesar: Politician and Statesman* (London: 1980).
Gerrish, J., *Sallust's Histories and Triumviral Historiography: Confronting the End of History* (London: 2019).
Golden, G., *Crisis Management during the Roman Republic: The Role of Political Institutions in Emergencies* (Cambridge: 2013).
Goldsworthy, A., *Caesar: Life of a Colossus* (Yale: 2006).
Goodman, R. & Soni, J., *Rome's Last Citizen. The Life and Legacy of Cato, Mortal Enemy of Caesar* (New York: 2012).
Greenhalgh, P., *Pompey: The Roman Alexander* (London: 1980).
Greenhagh, P., *Pompey: The Republican Prince* (London: 1981).
Girardet, K., 'Caesars Konsulatsplan fur das Jahr 49: Griinde und Scheitern', *Chiron* 30 (2000), pp.679–710.
Gray, E., 'The Consular Elections held in 65 BC', *Antichthon* 13 (1979), pp.56–65.
Grillo, L., *The Art of Caesar's Bellum Civile: Literature, Ideology, and Community* (Cambridge: 2012).
Gruen, E., *The Last Generation of the Roman Republic* (Berkeley: 1974).
Gwatkin, W., 'Some Reflections on the Battle of Pharsalus', *Transactions and Proceedings of the American Philological Association* 87 (1956), pp.109–24.
Haley, S., 'The Five Wives of Pompey the Great', *Greece & Rome* 32 (1985), pp.49–59.
Hayne, L., 'L. Paullus and his Attitude to Pompey', *L'Antiquité Classique* 41 (1972), pp.148–55.
Hayne, L., 'Caesar and Lentulus Crus', *Acta Classica* 39 (1996), pp.72–76.
Hillman, T., 'Pompeius ad Parthos?', *Klio* 78 (1996), pp.380–99.

Holland, T., *Rubicon: The Triumph and Tragedy of the Roman Republic* (London: 2003).
Holliday, V., *Pompey in Cicero's Correspondence and Lucan's Civil War* (Hague: 1969).
Holzapfel, L., 'Die Anfänge des Bürgerkrieges zwischen Cäsar und Pompejus', *Klio* 4 (1904), pp.327–82.
Huzar, E., *Mark Antony: A Biography* (Minneapolis: 1978).
Isayev, E., 'Unruly Youth? The Myth of Generation Conflict in Late Republican Rome', *Historia* 56 (2007), pp.1–13.
Jal, P., 'Le rôle des Barbares dans les guerres civiles de Rome, de Sylla à Vespasien', *Latomus* 21 (1962), pp.8–48.
Jal, P., *La guerre civile à Rome* (Paris: 1963).
Jameson, S., 'The Intended Date of Caesar's Return from Gaul', *Latomus* 29 (1970), pp.638–60.
Jehne, M. & Pina Polo, F. (eds), *Foreign 'Clientelae' in the Roman Empire: A Reconsideration* (Stuttgart: 2015).
Kavanagh, B., 'The citizenship and nomen of Roucillus and Egus', *Ancient History Bulletin* 15 (2001), pp.163–71.
Keaveney, A., *The Army in the Roman Revolution* (London: 2007).
Knight, D., 'Pompey's Concern with Pre-eminence After 60 BC', *Latomus* 27 (1968), pp.878–83.
Kopij, K., 'Propaganda war over Sicily? Sicily in the Roman Coinage during the Civil War 49–45 BC', *Studies in Ancient Art and Civilization* 16 (2012), pp.167–82.
Lange, C., *Triumphs in the Age of Civil War: The Late Republic and the Adaptability of Triumphal Tradition* (London: 2018).
Lange, C. & Scott, A., *Cassius Dio: The Impact of Violence, War, and Civil War* (Leiden: 2020).
Lange, C. & Vervaet, F., *The Historiography of Late Republican Civil War* (Leiden: 2019).
Lazenby, J., 'The Conference of Luca and the Gallic War; A Study in Roman Politics 57–55 BC', *Latomus* 18 (1959), pp.63–76.
Leach, J., *Pompey the Great* (London: 1978).
Lintott, A., *Violence in Republican Rome* (Oxford: 1968).
Lintott, A., 'Lucan and the History of the Civil War', *Classical Quarterly* 21 (1971), pp.488–505.
Lintott, A., 'Cicero and Milo', *Journal of Roman Studies* 64 (1974), pp.62–78.
Lintott, A., *The Constitution of the Roman Republic* (Oxford: 1999).
Lounsbury, R., 'History and Motive in Book Seven of Lucan's Pharsalia', *Hermes* 104 (1976), pp.210–39.
Long, G., *The Decline of the Roman Republic Volumes 1–5* (London: 1864).
López Barja de Quiroga, P., 'The Bellum Civile Pompeianum: The War of Words', *Classical Quarterly* 69 (2019), pp.700–14.
Lucas, F., 'The Battlefield of Pharsalos', *Annual of the British School at Athens* 24 (1921), pp.34–53.
MacKay, L., 'Pharsalus and the Roman Fate', *Phoenix* 6 (1952), pp.147–50.
Marin, P., *Blood in the Forum: The Struggle for the Roman Republic* (London: 2009).
Masters, J., *Poetry and Civil War in Lucan's Bellum Civile* (Cambridge: 1992).
Meier, C., *Caesar: A Biography* (London: 1995).
Meyer, E., *Caesars Monarchie und das Prinzipat des Pompejus* (Stuttgart: 1919).
Millar, F., 'Popular Politics at Rome in the Late Republic', in I. Malkin & Z. Rubinsohn (eds), *Leaders and Masses in the Roman World: Studies in Honor of Zvi Yavetz* (Leiden: 1994), pp.91–113.
Morgan, J., 'Palaepharsalus – The Battle and the Town', *American Journal of Archaeology* 87 (1983), pp.23–54.

Morgan, L., 'Levi Quidem de re…: Julius Caesar as Tyrant and Pedant', *Journal of Roman Studies* 87 (1997), pp.23–40.
Morgan, L., 'The Autopsy of C. Asinius Pollio', *Journal of Roman Studies* 90 (2000), pp.51–69.
Morrell, K., *Pompey, Cato, and the Governance of the Roman Empire* (Oxford: 2017).
Morstein-Marx, R., 'Caesar's Alleged Fear of Prosecution and His "*Ratio Absentis*" in the Approach to the Civil War', *Historia* 56 (2007), pp.159–78.
Nordling, J., 'Caesar's Pre-Battle Speech at Pharsalus (B.C. 3.85.4): *Ridiculum Acri Fortius … Secat Res*', *Classical Journal* 101 (2005), pp.183–89.
Osgood, J., 'Ending Civil War at Rome: Rhetoric and Reality, 88 BC–197 AD', *American Historical Review* 120 (2015), pp.1,683–95.
Peaks, M., 'Caesar's Movements, January 21 to February 14, 49 BC', *Classical Review* 18 (1903), pp.346–49.
Pelling, C., 'Pharsalus', *Historia* 22 (1973), pp.249–59.
Peer, A., *Julius Caesar's Bellum Civile and the Composition of a New Reality* (London: 2015).
Perrin, B., 'Pharsalia, Pharsalus, Palaepharsalus', *American Journal of Philology* 6 (1885), pp.170–89.
Pina Polo, F., 'Hispania of Caesar and Pompey. A Conflict of Clientelae?', in M. Garcia-Bellido, A. Mostalac & A. Jimenez (eds), *Del Imperium de Pompeyo a la Auctoritas de Augusto* (Madrid: 2008), pp.41–48.
Pina Polo, F., 'Pompey's Clientelae in Hispania: A Reappraisal', in M. Haake & A. Harders (eds), *Politische Kultur und soziale Struktur der Römischen Republik* (Stuttgart: 2017), pp.269–86.
Pina Polo, F., 'Losers in the Civil War between Caesarians and Pompeians. Punishment and Survival', in K. Hölkeskamp & H. Beck (eds), *Verlierer und Aussteiger in der Konkurrenz unter Anwesenden. Agonalität in der politischen Kultur des antiken Rom* (Stuttgart: 2019), pp.147–67.
Pocock, L., 'What Made Pompeius Fight in 49 BC?', *Greece & Rome* 6 (1959), pp.68–81.
Postgate, J., 'Pharsalia Nostra', *Classical Review* 19 (1905), pp.257–60.
Powell, A. & Welch, K., *Sextus Pompeius* (London: 2002).
Raaflaub, K., 'Caesar the Liberator? Factional Politics, Civil War, and Ideology', in F. Cairns & E. Fantham (eds), *Caesar Against Liberty? Perspectives on his Autocracy* (Cambridge: 2003), pp.35–67.
Rambaud, M., 'Le Soleil de Pharsale', *Historia* 3, pp.346–78.
Rawson, E., 'The Identity Problems of Q. Cornificius', *Classical Quarterly* 28 (1978), pp.188–201.
Rice Holmes, T., 'The Battle-Field of Old Pharsalus', *Classical Quarterly* 2 (1908), pp.271–92.
Ridley, R., 'The Extraordinary Commands of the Late Republic: A Matter of Definition', *Historia* 30 (1981), pp.280–97.
Ridley, R., 'Pompey's Commands in the 50s: How Cumulative?', *Rheinisches Museum für Philologie* 126 (1983), pp.136–48.
Ridley, R., 'The Dictator's Mistake: Caesar's Escape from Sulla', *Historia* 49 (2000), pp.211–29.
Ridley, R., 'Attacking the World with Five Cohorts; Caesar in January 49', *Ancient Society* 34 (2004), pp.127–52.
Riggsby, A., *Caesar in Gaul and Rome: War in Words* (Austin: 2006).
Rossi, A., 'The Camp of Pompey: Strategy of Representation in Caesar's *Bellum Civile*', *Classical Journal* 95 (2000), pp.239–56.

Rondholz, A., 'Crossing the Rubicon: A Historiographical Study', *Mnemosyne* 62 (2009), pp.432–50.
Rowe, G., 'Dramatic Structures in Caesar's *Bellum Civile*', *Transactions of the American Philological Association* 98 (1967), pp.399–414.
Ryan, F., 'The Praetorship of L. Aelius Tubero', *L'Antiquité Classique* 65 (1996), pp.239–42.
Sabin, P., 'The Face of Roman Battle', *Journal of Roman Studies* 90 (2000), pp.1–17.
Sage, E., 'The Senatus Consultum Ultimum', *Classical Weekly* 13 (1920), pp.185–89.
Sampson, G., *A re-examination of the office of the Tribunate of the Plebs in the Roman Republic (494–23 BC)* (Unpublished Thesis, 2005).
Sampson, G., *The Defeat of Rome: Crassus, Carrhae and the Invasion of the East* (Barnsley: 2008).
Sampson, G., *The Crisis of Rome: The Jugurthine and Northern Wars and the Rise of Marius* (Barnsley: 2010).
Sampson, G., *The Collapse of Rome: Marius, Sulla, and The First Civil War 91–70 BC* (Barnsley: 2013).
Sampson, G., *Rome, Blood and Politics: Reform, Murder and Popular Politics in the Late Republic 146–70 BC* (Barnsley: 2017).
Sampson, G., *Rome, Blood and Power: Reform, Murder and Popular Politics in the Late Republic 70–27 BC* (Barnsley: 2019).
Sampson, G., *Rome and Parthia: Empires at War: Ventidius, Antony and the Second Romano-Parthian War, 40–20 BC* (Barnsley: 2020).
Sampson, G., *Rome's Great Eastern War: Lucullus, Pompey, and the Conquest of the East, 74–62 BC* (Barnsley: 2021).
Sampson, G., *The Battle of Dyrrhachium (48 BC): Caesar, Pompey, and the Early Campaigns of the Third Roman Civil War* (Barnsley: 2022).
Sanford, E., 'The Career of Aulus Gabinius', *Transactions and Proceedings of the American Philological Association* 70 (1939), pp.64–92.
Seager, R., *Pompey: A Political Biography* (Oxford: 1979).
Searle, A., 'Note on the Battle of Pharsalus', *Harvard Studies in Classical Philology* 18 (1907), pp.213–18.
Shatzman, I., 'The Egyptian Question in Roman Politics (59–54 BC)', *Latomus* 30 (1971), pp.363–69.
Siani-Davies, M., 'Ptolemy XII Auletes and the Romans', *Historia* 46 (1997), pp.306–40.
Sirianni, F., 'Caesar's Decision to Cross the Rubicon', *L'Antiquité Classique* 48 (1979), pp.636–38.
Sirianni, F., 'Caesar's Peace Overtures to Pompey', *L'Antiquité Classique* 62 (1993), pp.219–37.
Southern, P., *Pompey the Great* (Stroud: 2002).
Stanton, G., 'Why Did Caesar Cross the Rubicon?', *Historia* 52 (2003), pp.67–94.
Stevenson, T., 'Appian on the Pharsalus Campaign: Civil Wars 2.48–91', in K. Welch (ed.), *Appian's Roman History: Empire and Civil War* (Swansea: 2015), pp.257–75.
Syme, R., 'The Allegiance of Labienus', *Journal of Roman Studies* 28 (1938), pp.113–25.
Syme, R., *The Roman Revolution* (Oxford: 1939).
Syme, R., 'Ten Tribunes', *Journal of Roman Studies* 53 (1963), pp.55–60.
Syme, R., 'M. Bibulus and Four Sons', *Harvard Studies in Classical Philology* 91 (1987), pp.185–98.

Taylor, L., 'Caesar's Early Career', *Classical Philology* 36 (1941), pp.113–32.
Taylor, L., 'The Rise of Julius Caesar', *Greece & Rome* 4 (1957), pp.10–18.
Taylor, L., *Party Politics in the Age of Caesar* (Berkeley: 1949).
Treggiari, S., 'Pompeius' freedman biographer again', *Classical Review* 19 (1969), pp.264–66.
Tucker, R., 'What Actually Happened at the Rubicon?', *Historia* 37 (1988), pp.245–248.
Tyrrell, W., 'Labienus' Departure from Caesar in January 49 BC', *Historia* 21 (1972), pp.424–40.
van Ooteghem, J., *Pompee le Grand. Batisseur d'Empire* (Bruxelles: 1954).
Veith, G., *Der Feldzug von Dyrrhachium zwischen Caesar und Pompeius* (Wien: 1920).
Vervaet, F., 'The Official Position of Cn. Pompeius in 49 and 48 BC', *Latomus* 65 (2006), pp.928–53.
von Fritz, K., 'The Mission of L. Caesar and L. Roscius in January 49 BC', *Transactions and Proceedings of the American Philological Association* 72 (1941), pp.125–56.
Von Fritz, K., 'Pompey's Policy before and after the Outbreak of the Civil War of 49 BC', *Transactions and Proceedings of the American Philological Association* 73 (1942), pp.145–80.
von Ravensburg, A., *Burgerkrieg Zwischen Casar Und Pompejus, Im Jahre 50/49 V. Chr. Und Die Kampfe Dei Dyrrhachium Und Pharsalus* (1961).
Watts, E., *Mortal Republic: How Rome Fell into Tyranny* (London: 2019).
Welsh, K., *Julius Caesar as Artful Reporter: The War Commentaries as Political Instruments* (London: 1998).
Welsh, K., *Magnus Pius: Sextus Pompeius and the Transformation of the Roman Republic* (Swansea: 2012).
Westall, R., 'The Relationship of Appian to Pollio', *Analecta Romana Instituti Danici* 38 (2013), pp.7–34.
Westall, R., 'Pompeius at Pelusium', *Hermathena* 196/197 (2014), pp.309–40.
Westall, R., 'The Sources for the Civil Wars of Appian of Alexandria', in K. Welch (ed.), *Appian's Roman History: Empire and Civil War* (Swansea: 2015), pp.125–67.
Westall, R., 'The Sources of Cassius Dio for the Roman Civil Wars of 49–30 BC', in C. Lange and J. Madsen (eds), *Cassius Dio: Greek Intellectual and Roman Politician* (Leiden: 2016), pp.51–75.
Westall, R., *Caesar's Civil War: Historical Reality and Fabrication* (Leiden: 2017).
Wiseman, T., 'Crossing the Rubicon, and Other Dramas', *Scripta Classica Israelica* 15 (1996), pp.152–58.
Wiseman, T., 'The Two-Headed State: How Romans Explained Civil War', in B.W. Breed, C. Damon & A. Rossi (eds), *Citizens of Discord: Rome and its Civil Wars* (Oxford: 2010), pp.25–44.
Woodman, A.J. (ed.), *Velleius Paterculus: The Caesarian and Augustan Narrative* (Cambridge: 1977).
Wylie, G., 'Why Did Labienus Defect From Caesar in 49 BC?', *Ancient History Bulletin* 3 (1989), pp.123–27.
Wylie, G., 'The Road to Pharsalus', *Latomus* 51 (1992), pp.557–65.
Yarrow, L., *Historiography at the End of the Republic: Provincial Perspectives on Roman Rule* (Oxford: 2006).
Yates, D., 'The Role of Cato the Younger in Caesar's "*Bellum Civile*"', *Classical World* 104 (2011), pp.161–74.
Yavetz, Z., 'Caesar, Caesarism, and the Historians', *Journal of Contemporary History* 6 (1971), pp.184–201.

Index

Achillas, 136
Acilius Caninus, M (Pr. 47 BC?), 108
Actium, Battle of (31 BC), 97
Adriatic, 9, 12, 14–19, 25–9, 32–5, 49, 53–4, 56, 73, 99, 104–106, 108, 124, 126, 130, 158, 161–2
Aeginium, 61
Aelius Tubero, L. (Pr. ?), 13
Aemilius Lepidus, M. (Cos. 46 & 42 BC), 18, 153–4
Aetolia, 30, 75
Afranius, L. (Cos. 60 BC), 20–3, 49, 55–6, 76, 115
Africa, 6, 12–14, 16, 18, 23–4, 106, 112, 114, 122, 125, 130, 133, 141–2, 146–52, 155, 159, 161–3
Alesia, Battle of (52 BC), 33–4
Alexander III (Macedonian Emperor 336–323 BC), 6–7, 65, 99, 145
Allobroges, 39, 60
Amphipolis, 122, 127–8
Androsthenes, 61
Annius Milo, T. (Tr. 57 BC), 139
Antioch, 129–30
Antonius, C. (Pr. 44 BC), 10, 15–16, 109
Antonius, M. (Cos. 44, 34 & 31 BC), 15, 18, 28–31, 41, 77, 96, 122, 124–5, 139–43
Apollonia, 26, 28, 36, 57, 59
Apsus, River, 26, 28
Ariobarzanes III (King of Cappadocia 51–42 BC), 75
Armenia, 158–9
Asinius Pollio, C. (Cos 40 BC), 77, 81, 94–5
Asparagium, 31–2
Athens, 10, 125
Attius Varus, P. (Pr. c.53 BC), 13, 114, 149–50
Aurelius Cotta, M. (Pr. ?) 12

Bagradas River, Battle of (49 BC), 13, 149
Bithynia, 75, 158, 160
Bocchus I (Maurian King c.111–80 BC), 151
Bocchus II (Maurian King 49–33 BC), 151

Bogud (Maurian King 49–31 BC), 151
Bosphoran Kingdom, 131, 134, 158
Brundisium, 11–12, 26, 28, 106, 108–109, 117, 156
Brundisium, Battle of (49 BC), 12, 26
Brundisium, Battle of (48 BC), 104–105, 125

Caecilius Metellus, L. (Tr. 49 BC), 17–18
Caecilius Metellus Pius Scipio Nasica, Q. (Cos. 52 BC), 25, 27–33, 39–40, 48–50, 54–7, 59–65, 73, 75, 98, 112, 114, 117, 123, 129–30, 138, 147–8, 150, 158
Caelius Rufus, M. (Pr. 48 BC), 139
Calpurnius Bibulus, M. (Cos. 59 BC), 28, 135
Calvisius Sabinus, C. (Cos. 39 BC), 30–1
Cappadocia, 75, 158–60
Capua, 11
Carrhae, Battle of (53 BC), 3–5, 83, 97, 133
Cassius Longinus, C. (Pr. 44 BC), 106–107, 110, 114, 131–4, 138, 162
Cassius Longinus, L. (Tr. 44 BC), 30–1
Cassius Longinus, Q. (Tr. 49 BC), 24, 151–5, 161
Cilicia, 75, 119, 129–30
Civil War, First (91–70 BC), 3–4, 7–8, 19, 23–4, 139, 151–2
Claudius Marcellus Aeserninus, M. (Cos. 22 BC), 152–5
Cleopatra VII (Ptolemaic Pharaoh 51–30 BC), 135, 144–5, 162
Colchis, 158–9
Corcyra, 13, 26, 28, 104–105, 108–10, 113–15, 123–6, 131, 156, 162
Corduba, 24, 152–3
Corduba, Battle of (48 BC), 153–4
Corfinium, Battle of (49 BC), 11, 96
Cornelia, 127, 129
Cornelius Dolabella, P. (Cos. 44 BC), 15–16
Cornelius Lentulus Crus. L. (Cos. 49 BC), 114, 129, 137
Cornelius Lentulus Marcellinus, P. (Q. 48 BC), 41, 47, 129

Cornelius Lentulus Spinther, P. (Cos. 57 BC), 114
Cornelius Sulla, F., 31, 117, 124
Cornelius Sulla, L. (Cos. 88 & 80, Dict. 82–81 BC), 7–8, 10–11, 24, 55, 118, 141–3
Cornelius Sulla, P. (Cos. 65 BC), 37–9, 77, 119, 122, 124
Cornificius, Q. (Pr. 45 BC), 155–6
Crastinus, C., 83–4, 86
Cynoscephalae, Battle of (197 BC), 71
Cyprus, 129–30, 134
Cyrene, 125, 135, 138, 144, 147–9

Deiotarus (King of Galatia c.105–42 BC), 99, 119–20, 158–60
Domitius Ahenobarbus, L. (Cos. 54 BC), 11, 20, 94, 96, 98, 111, 121, 143, 162
Domitius Calvinus, Cn. (Cos. 53 & 40 BC), 30–1, 56, 77, 159
Duumvirate, 4, 6
Dyrrhachium, 13, 26–50
Dyrrhachium, Battle of (48 BC), 31, 33–50

Eastern War (74–62 BC), 5, 10
Egus, 39, 60
Enipeus River, 63, 77–81, 97
Epirus, 26, 28, 30, 35, 53–4, 57, 59, 104, 108–109, 115, 123, 126

Favonius, M. (Pr. 49 BC), 114
Fufius Calenus, Q. (Cos. 47 BC), 27, 124–125

Gabinius, A. (Cos. 58 BC), 109–10, 135, 145, 156
Gades, 23–4, 151
Galatia, 99, 159–60
Gaul, Cisalpine, 10, 75
Gaul, Transalpine, 20, 75
Genusus, River, 31, 58, 69, 83
Gomphi, 61–2, 67, 69

Hellespont, 132–13

Ilerda, Battle of (49 BC), 20–1, 23, 163
Illyria, 10, 12, 14–16, 18–19, 25, 30–3, 53, 57, 63, 104, 109, 123–4, 126, 148, 155–7, 161, 163
Italy, 5–13, 15, 18–21, 24–5, 30, 49, 54–5, 65, 99, 104–107, 113, 115–16, 122, 124–5, 140–2, 149–50, 157, 161
Iulius Caesar, I. (Cos 59, 48, 46–44 BC), 3–50, 53–100, 103–53, 155–63

Iulius Caesar, Sex., 24
Iunius Brutus, M. (Pr. 44 BC), 116, 118, 121, 147

Juba I (Numidian King c.85–46 BC), 13–14, 114, 149–51, 163
Judea, 138

Labienus, T. (Pr. ?), 110, 114–16, 118, 124
Laelius, D., 105–106, 109
Larissa, 62–4, 67, 116, 127
Lesbos, 127–8
lex Hirtia (48 BC), 143
lex Trebonia (55 BC), 6
Licinius Crassus, M. (Cos. 70 & 55 BC), 3–4, 6, 83, 133, 136, 144–5
Licinius Crassus, P., 4
Lissus, 59

Macedonia, 25–7, 29–34, 46, 56, 112, 123–4, 126–7, 156
Manlius Torquatus, L. (Pr. 49 BC), 47
Marius, C. (Cos. 107, 105–100, 87 BC), 10, 126, 151
Massilia, 17, 20, 24, 96
Mauri, 151–3
Megara, 125
Metropolis, 62–4, 69
Minucius Basilus, L. (Pr. 45 BC), 15–16
Mithridates VI (Pontic Emperor 120–63 BC), 131, 158
Mytilene, 128

Nicopolis, Battle of (48 BC), 159
Numidia, 13–14, 114, 149–51, 162

Octavius, M., 15–16, 109–10, 115, 155–7
Oricum, 26, 28, 36, 59, 107–108
Orodes II (Parthian Emperor 57–37 BC), 158

Parthian Empire, 3–6, 83, 129, 133, 145, 158–9, 165
Parthini, 103–104, 115
Peloponnese, 123–5, 144
Pelusium, 131, 136–7
Petra, 33
Petreius, M. (Pr. c.64 BC), 20–3, 124
Pharnaces II (Bosphoran King c.97–47 BC), 114, 131–2, 158–61, 163
Pharsalus/Palaepharsalus, 63, 65–8, 70–2

Pharsalus/Palaepharsalus, Battle of (48 BC), 53, 74–100, 103–104, 106–12, 114–20, 122–4, 126–8, 130–1, 134–7, 140, 143, 145–9, 155–6, 159–64
Pompeius Bithynicus, Q., 137
Pompeius 'Magnus', Cn., 108, 110, 114, 147
Pompeius 'Magnus', Cn. (Cos. 70, 55, 52 BC), 3–50, 53–100, 103–104, 108, 110–40, 143–52, 155–9, 161–3
Pompeius, Sex., 12, 114, 127, 147–8
Pomponius, M., 106
Pontic Empire, 5, 158–61
Porcius Cato, M. (Pr. 54 BC), 12–13, 103–104, 108, 114–15, 117–18, 123, 125, 130, 135, 138, 144, 147–50
Ptolemaic Empire, 130
Ptolemy XII (Ptolemaic Pharaoh c.80–58 BC), 135, 144–5
Ptolemy XIII (Ptolemaic Pharaoh 51–47 BC), 135–6, 138, 144, 146

Rhodes, 129, 134, 144
Romano-Parthian War, First (55–50 BC), 146, 131
Romano-Pontic War, Fourth (48–47 BC), 158–61
Rome, 3–10, 12, 17–19, 21–2, 24, 49, 55, 61, 66–7, 99, 115, 122, 124, 132–3, 139–42, 145, 150–2, 161
Roucillus, 39, 60
Rubicon, 8–9, 63
Rutilius Lupus, P. (Pr. 49 BC), 123

Saburra, 13
Sallustius Crispus, C. (Pr. 46 BC), 16
Salonae, 109, 155
Sardinia, 12, 14, 149
Scapula, 114
Scribonius Curio, C., 12–14
Scribonius Libo, L. (Cos. 34 BC), 15, 28, 105
Scotussa, 70–1
Seleucid Empire, 5

Septimius, L., 136
Sertorius, Q. (Pr. 83 BC), 19, 23, 151
Servilius Isauricus, P. (Cos. 48 & 41 BC), 139
Sicily, 12–14, 18, 103, 106–107, 131, 133–4, 149–50
Spain, 9–11, 14, 17, 19–20, 23–5, 49, 55–6, 65, 73, 99, 106, 115, 118, 122, 149–55, 157, 161, 163
Sulpicius Rufus, P. (Pr. 48 BC), 106
Syria, 31, 75–6, 106, 110, 129–31, 133, 135, 137–8

Tarcondimotus (Cilician King ?–31 BC), 119
Taxiles, 75
Terentius Varro, M. (Pr. ?), 20, 23–4, 152
Thessalonica, 26, 30, 113
Thessaly, 30–1, 46, 59, 61–5, 67, 78, 98, 105, 107, 134
Thrace, 25, 27
Trebonius, C. (Cos. 45 BC), 154
Tribunate of the Plebs, 13, 15, 17–18, 133, 140, 142–3, 152, 157
Triumvirate, 6, 135–6
Tullius Cicero, M. (Cos. 63 BC), 10, 17, 78, 96, 115–18, 124, 143, 147, 161
Tyre, 129

Ulia, Battle of (48 BC), 154–5
Utica, Battle of (49 BC), 13–14

Valerius Flaccus, 38
Valerius Flaccus, C. (Cos. 93 BC), 151
Valerius Flaccus, L. (Pr. 63 BC), 38
Valerius Orca, Q. (Pr. 57 BC), 12
Vatinius, P. (Cos 47 BC), 105–106
Via Egnatia, 26–7, 29–30, 60, 62, 64, 104, 128
Vibullius Rufus, L., 20
Vulteius Capito, C., 15

Xerxes I (Persian Emperor 486–465 BC), 10